Research Methods for Generalist Social Work

Other Titles of Related Interest in Social Welfare

Christine Marlow
New Mexico State University

Research *Methods*
FOR GENERALIST SOCIAL WORK

Brooks/Cole Publishing Company
Pacific Grove, California

Brooks/Cole Publishing Company
A Division of Wadsworth, Inc.

© 1993 by Wadsworth, Inc., Belmont, California 94002. All rights reserved. No part of this book may be reproduced, stored in a retrieval system, or transcribed, in any form or by any means, without the prior written permission of the publisher, Brooks/Cole Publishing Company, Pacific Grove, California 93950, a division of Wadsworth, Inc.

Printed in the United States of America

10   9   8   7   6   5   4   3   2

Library of Congress Cataloging-in-Publication Data
Marlow, Christine.
     Research methods for generalist social work / Christine Marlow.
          p.   cm.
     Includes bibliographical references and index.
     ISBN 0-534-14838-7
     1. Social service—Research—Methodology.   I. Title.
HV11.M3493   1992
361′.0072—dc20   92-25663

Sponsoring Editor: Peggy Adams
Editorial Assistant: Dorothy Zinky
Production Editor: Jerilyn Emori
Interior and Cover Designer: Cloyce Wall
Print Buyer: Randy Hurst
Art Editor: Donna Kalal
Permissions Editor: Robert Kauser
Copy Editor: Jennifer Gordon
Technical Illustrator: Alexander Teshin Associates
Signing Representative: Rusty Johnson
Interior Photographs: Leslie Parr
Cover Photograph: © 1972 Roger Lubin/Jeroboam
Compositor: G & S Typesetters, Inc.
Printer and Binder: Malloy Lithographing, Inc.

To my parents
James Marlow   Janet Marlow

Contents

CHAPTER 2
Deciding on the Question   23

CHAPTER 10
Analysis of Quantitative Data:
Inferential Statistics   213

CHAPTER 11
Analysis of Qualitative Data   231

CHAPTER 12
Research Writing   247

CHAPTER 13
Using Research Findings in Practice and Evaluating Research   277

Preface

My reason for writing this text is not unusual. After several years of seeking a social work research methods text and unsuccessfully trying a new text each year, I gave up and started to write. From teaching the same course repeatedly, I had developed a number of ideas of what a text needed. These ideas became crystallized through many discussions with students and colleagues and through my experiences with the Council on Social Work Education (CSWE) accreditation process. What emerged were the themes outlined below.

Themes and Organization

A Focus on Generalist Practice   Undergraduate and foundation graduate courses in social work programs usually are taught from a generalist perspective. Research methods must also be taught within this framework; consequently, the text includes examples from generalist practice. The relevance of research to the rest of the curriculum is thereby increased.

Practice–Research Link   By emphasizing the parallels between generalist practice and research, research becomes more accessible because practice is often perceived as being more intuitive and understandable. Consequently, the text illustrates these parallels.

Alternatives to the Scientific Method   Research texts often neglect to point out that the scientific method is only *one* way of understanding our world and that alternatives such as direct experience are equally important. Students need to know that alternatives do exist; these other approaches are discussed in the text.

Variations of the Scientific Method   Similarly, the scientific method can be conceptualized in different ways, conceptualizations that allow for the expression of many different voices of particular importance in social work research. Thus, the text includes a discussion of these variations, including feminist research methods and research methods developed by other groups.

Production and Consumption   The text presents research methods from the perspective that social workers can be both producers and consumers of research. This also ensures compliance with the CSWE accreditation requirements for the research curriculum.

Agency Focus   In line with ensuring the relevance of research methods, the text discusses the application of research methods in agency rather than academic settings because agencies are where the majority of the B.S.W. and M.S.W. graduates will be employed.

Ethics Content   Ethical issues are included for each stage of the research process; that is, they are integrated into each chapter and not viewed as separate, discrete topics.

Human Diversity Content   Similarly, issues concerning human diversity as they relate to research methods are included. Although partly addressed through discussions of alternatives within and to the scientific method, this content (as with the ethics content) is considered for each stage of the research process.

In addition to these themes, the *Example* boxes throughout the text emphasize the link between research and practice by presenting real-life social work studies.

The book is written so that each of the chapters can stand independently if necessary. The statistics chapters (Chapters 9 and 10) may be omitted if students have already completed statistics courses. Important terms appear in the text in **boldface** type and are defined there. These terms also are included in the *Glossary* at the back of the text. Each chapter includes a *References* section, as well as a *Summary, Further Reading,* and *Study/Exercise Questions.* If possible, students should complete the exercises as a group; this often offers a richer educational experience.

Acknowledgments

Completion of the book depended on many people (too many for me to name them all), but I would like to thank the following specific individuals and groups: Alvin Sallee, academic department head of the Department of Social Work at New Mexico State University, initially convinced me to write the text and then encouraged and supported me throughout the process; Pat Sandau, assistant professor at New Mexico State University, co-authored Chapter 13; Jane Sandburg helped write the computer content, assisted in the text's early stages, and provided ideas from the B.S.W. student perspective; Kim Collins offered invaluable feedback from a M.S.W. student's point of view and diligently sought articles to use as examples throughout the book; Donnelyn Curtis contributed the bulk of the literature review and library resource material; and Michael Ames provided feedback on the statistics chapters.

The reviewers of the manuscript contributed critical comments as the book progressed, and I would like to thank Faye Abram, Marygrove College; Frank Clark, University of Montana; Thomas Kruse, Millersville University; Steve Marson, Pembroke State University; Philip Popple, Auburn University; John Poulin, Widener University; Jim Rosenthal, University of Oklahoma; Tina Rzepnicki, University of Chicago; Jacqueline Smith, Howard University; and David Storm, Central Missouri University.

Other contributors include all the students who have enrolled in the research methods courses I have taught over the years. In many ways, they wrote the book by teaching me how the material could be presented so that it would make sense to them.

The Wadsworth staff, particularly Peggy Adams and Jerilyn Emori, made this book possible, and I thank them for their support and efficiency and for their responsiveness to a novice in the publishing world. Jennifer Gordon's edit of the manuscript is much appreciated, as is Cloyce Wall's work in designing the text. I would like to thank Leslie Parr, Loyola University, New Orleans, for the superb photographs. Leslie and I have been friends for many years; her photography continually reminds us that social work research has to do with people rather than numbers. I would also like to extend special thanks to Roberta Yarbrough for her clerical assistance with the drafts of the manuscript. I cannot thank her enough for her patience and thoroughness.

Finally, thank you to my six-year-old son Sam, who reminds me daily of what every researcher should know: Answers to questions always generate more questions.

Research Methods for Generalist Social Work

Research and Generalist Social Work Practice

"The social work research methods course was the course I was dreading the most. I didn't want to take it."
B.S.W. student

The attitude reflected in this student's statement is not unusual in social work classrooms. Social workers often express suspicion and even some phobia of research. Have you ever skipped over articles in social work journals, because you were intimidated by the language and the displays of results? Have you ever shuddered at the thought of undertaking a research project? If so, you are not alone. Because we typically associate research with mathematics, we may be unenthusiastic to apply what is perceived as a cold, impersonal technique to human needs and problem solving. After all, most of us in the field of social work want to work with people, not numbers. Research, however, is simply a means of gaining knowledge, and in social work practice we need all the knowledge we can muster if we are to be optimally responsible to ourselves, our clients, and our agencies.

Once you understand the research process, you will have access to a vast amount of information in the literature. Articles that had at one time eluded you with discussions of validity and correlation coefficients will become meaningful and will provide information that you can apply to your practice.

When you are equipped with the knowledge and skills to apply research methods, you will also know how to answer many of the questions that arise in your role as a generalist social worker, such as

- Are my visits to Mrs. Garcia and the provision of other support services really helping her recover from the death of her husband?

- Program X received additional funding for next year. How can we show that *our* program is effective and deserves more money?

- Bob is a teenage father in our community, and I don't know about any kinds of support programs for him. Is Bob unique in his need for services, or are there lots of Bobs in the community? And what kinds of services do they need?

This book emphasizes the strong links between the research and practice processes and helps you answer these types of questions and understand the research of others. The steps of generalist social work practice have their equivalents in social work research. Thus, in the following chapters we will take you through the steps of research in a process similar to the way you learn the steps of practice.

This chapter will discuss

▶ Common types of explanation
▶ The scientific approach and its variations
▶ The relationship between theory and research
▶ Generalist practice
▶ The purpose of research in generalist practice
▶ Research roles in generalist practice
▶ Research and generalist practice processes

Certain themes of this text will help explain research methodology and its relevance to your practice as a generalist social worker:

▶ The connection between the research process and generalist social work is stressed.
▶ You may be either a consumer of research or a producer of research.
▶ The text research examples are those you will encounter as a generalist researcher.
▶ Alternative research approaches—for example, feminist research—may be more compatible with generalist social work than the more traditional research methods.
▶ There are special issues involved when you conduct research in agency settings.
▶ Ethical issues are associated with each stage of the research process.
▶ Human diversity concerns are involved with each stage of the research process.

These overlapping themes support the mission of the book, which is to present research methods within a generalist social work framework.

Many new concepts are introduced in this book. These terms are boldfaced in the text where they are first defined; they also are listed in the Glossary at the end of the book. Each chapter includes a Summary, recommended Further Reading, and Study/Exercise Questions.

Common Types of Explanation

In our attempt to understand the world, we have developed many different ways of understanding and thinking about human behavior. Our efforts to bring or-

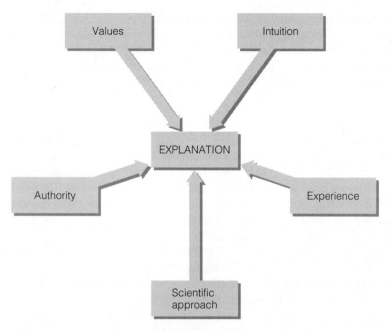

FIGURE 1.1 *Types of explanation*

der and meaning to existence have resulted in different types of explanations, including values, intuition, experience, the scientific approach, and authority (see Figure 1.1). Social work can involve any or all of these types of inquiry, and it is important to know about them and the role they play in generalist social work practice.

Values

Values refer to beliefs about what is right and wrong. They are closely tied to our respective cultures. For example, among many Hispanics, there is a strong value placed on children having respect for their parents. Education is highly valued by recent Asian immigrants to the United States. Values can be institutionalized by religion. For example, certain values characterize Christianity, such as the Protestant belief that work is the means of gaining societal and individual worth. Buddhists, on the other hand, value reincarnation, and their belief in reincarnation affects how people live their present lives.

Although values may be fundamental to a culture's tradition, these traditions can undergo change over time. For example, in the United States many people now recognize that women should have the same career opportunities as men. This was not the case a hundred years ago.

Social work as a profession is based on certain values. These include fundamental notions about the most desirable relationships between people and their environment. Some social work values include:

▶ Respect for the dignity and uniqueness of the individual
▶ Client's right to self-determination
▶ Confidentiality

Intuition

Intuition can be defined as a form of insight; when we intuitively know something, we understand it without recourse to specialized training or reasoning. Intuition may also be based on past experiences. In some cultures, intuition is a powerful tool for understanding and explaining the world. People with strong intuition may be viewed as having magical powers; if they also exhibit experience and skills, they may enjoy special status in the culture. An example is the *curandera,* a woman who is perceived to possess healing powers, in the Hispanic culture in the Southwest and Mexico.

Sometimes we call upon intuition in social work practice. Although we would be unlikely to act on intuition alone, we might use it to give ourselves leads for investigating further. For example, we might have an intuition that a child is being sexually abused. It may be hard for us to explain this feeling rationally, but the insight can provide a base or starting point for gathering information, which may or may not support the intuition.

Experience

Experience can be defined as firsthand, personal participation in events that provides a basis of knowledge. We often use this experience to guide our present and future actions, particularly when the experience had a successful outcome (even though we may not understand *why* it was successful). Clearly, these experiences will vary from individual to individual and according to the type of situation. In the practice of social work, we often refer to this experience as practice wisdom.

Authority

Sometimes we explain events and circumstances by referring to outside sources of knowledge or to authorities on specific topics. We credit the authority with knowledge we do not directly possess. Thus, in lieu of direct knowledge—whether obtained through values, intuition, or experience—we accept an explanation by virtue of our confidence in authorities. Who or what the authority is depends upon the nature and context of the problem.

In social work practice, we depend upon authority in a number of ways. We identify experts in different fields of practice and seek their opinions and knowledge, either by consulting with them personally or by reading their publications. We have vested authority in our professional organizations—such as the National Association of Social Workers (NASW)—and we use their authority to direct us in different areas. For instance, as members of NASW we believe we should adhere to the organization's Code of Ethics.

Scientific Approach

Specific characteristics of the scientific approach distinguish it from the other forms of explanation discussed in this section. It consists of rational, logical thinking combined with empiricism. **Empiricism** refers to observation through the use of our senses. In the next section, we will describe the characteristics of the scientific approach.

The Scientific Approach and Its Variations

Principles of the Scientific Approach

Because the scientific approach is the dominant method of inquiry today, we will use it as the focus of this text. Most individuals and organizations in the industrialized nations depend on science. For example, the medical profession relies on knowledge derived from the application of the scientific method. Business uses scientifically based theories and strategies (such as marketing surveys) that are developed from scientific principles. Social work is no exception; the profession has historically recognized the contributions of the scientific approach.

Before describing the scientific method, we need to note that the scientific approach has not always dominated the thinking in the United States. For example, Greek rationalism once ruled Western thought; it offered logic as the test of truth and did not rely on empirical evidence. Even in the United States today, scientific thinking does not prevail in all subcultures. In some Native American cultures, direct experience of an event is the primary means of explanation. Also, some argue that the scientific approach represents a male way of knowing, while intuition is more characteristically a female way of knowing. More importantly, the argument maintains that each are legitimate ways of viewing the world.

The scientific method is composed of theories and research methods (Rubin & Babbie, 1989). **Theories** provide the logical thinking part of science. Briefly, they describe and/or explain logical relationships among phenomena in our world. Logical thinking has two principal elements. First, there is the understanding that a given event cannot cause another event that occurred earlier in time. A child's birth defect cannot logically be caused by inadequate nutrition later in life. Second, there is the understanding that a given event cannot have mutually exclusive characteristics. For example, a child cannot be both undernourished and well nourished.

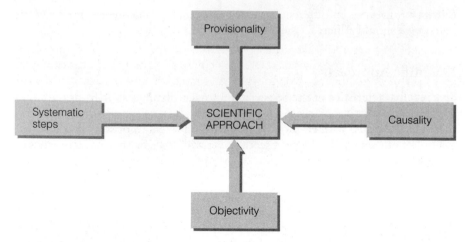

FIGURE 1.2 *Principles of the scientific approach*

However, theories cannot stand alone in science; they also need to be supported by empiricism, or observation using our senses. **Research methods,** the other component of the scientific method, provide ways of systematically organizing these observations.

Beyond this basic logical and empirical framework, this approach specifically involves several scientific principles, among which are systematic steps, causality, provisionality, and objectivity (see Figure 1.2).

Systematic Steps

Systematic steps must be followed. They include identifying the problem, collecting and analyzing the data, and drawing the conclusion. Do these sound familiar? These are similar steps to those we undergo in social work practice. We will continue to discuss these similarities later in this chapter.

Causality

Science is concerned with looking for causes. An assumption underlying the scientific approach is that there is a certain order in the world and that we can discover this order. We will come back to this topic of causality in later chapters.

Provisionality

An important characteristic of the scientific approach—and one that is often overlooked—is the realization that all findings are tentative or provisional and that there are no ultimate truths that can be established. We are constantly learning new perspectives and problems.

Objectivity

Objectivity refers to the condition in which, to the greatest extent possible, the researchers' values and biases do not interfere with their study of the problem. Different research techniques enable us to achieve this objectivity: for example, very careful development of data evaluation methods and refinement of such instruments as questionnaires. However, we will also see that pure objectivity is virtually impossible.

As we refer more often to these basic ideas of the scientific method, they will soon become a part of your thinking. Perhaps it will help you become more comfortable with these ideas if you realize that you began applying the principles of the scientific approach from a very early age. The young child who drops a toy behind a chair and then searches for it is using the scientific principles of causality and systematic steps, as is the older child who builds a structure out of blocks. As you will soon see, social workers use many scientific strategies in generalist practice. The key, however, is to make the scientific method a conscious part of our thoughts and actions.

Variations of the Scientific Approach

Before fully submerging ourselves in a description of this approach, we need to remember that not only is this approach just one way of explaining the world, but also that the scientific approach itself is periodically scrutinized. Although there is general agreement that the approach adheres to most of the principles outlined here, there is debate about how much each of the principles should and can be emphasized (see, for example, Guba, 1990). Two variations of the scientific approach will be discussed in this section: (1) the role that values play in employing the scientific approach, and (2) the impact that diverse populations have on our conceptualization of science.

The Role of Values in the Scientific Approach

Thomas Kuhn explores the values issue in *The Structure of Scientific Revolutions* (1970). From studying the history of science, Kuhn concluded that factors other than empirical evidence and theoretical necessity lead to the emergence and acceptance of the best theory. These other factors include values. Kuhn wrote about "paradigms," defining paradigm as "the entire constellation of beliefs, values, techniques and so on shared by members of a given [scientific] community" (Kuhn, 1970, p. 175). Paradigms function as maps—directing us to the problems that are important to address, the theories that are acceptable, and the procedures needed to solve these problems. Kuhn proposed that paradigms shift over time; they reflect changing values, which counters the idea of a fixed reality. Objective reality appears to change as paradigms change.

An example of a paradigm shift occurred in social work during the last 50 years. In the 1920s and 30s, the psychoanalytic framework was the prevailing paradigm for social work practice, and it was tied closely to a medical model. In the 1960s a more ecological/systems framework was adopted. This paradigm shift has important implications not only for how social workers conceptualize their practice but also for how research is conducted. Research questions deriving from a medical model differ substantially from those deriving from a systems perspective.

In part as a result of Kuhn's work, science is now increasingly recognized as being relative rather than absolute. Although scientists continue to use the scientific criteria outlined earlier (systematic steps, causality, provisionality, and objectivity), they also recognize that agreement rests on shared values.

The Impact of Diverse Populations on the Scientific Approach

The views of diverse groups, which had previously been virtually denied access to the traditional scientific paradigm, have had increasing impact on how science is perceived. These diverse groups began to cast doubt on traditional scientific methodology.

For example, there has been more attention to feminist research methods (Carlson, 1972; Davis, 1986) and to research methods that are sensitive to ethnic and racial diversity (Liu, 1982). The feminist and minority research approach stresses allowing the subjects of studies to be full participants in the research process. In addition, these studies take into consideration the whole complexity of the phenomenon, rather than isolating incidents and studying them out of context. This is facilitated by the type of data that are collected. We will discuss these approaches more extensively throughout this text.

Kuhn's writing and the contributions of alternative voices have resulted in some different perspectives on science—particularly in the social sciences.

Bearing this discussion in mind, we must be cautious in using the scientific approach. We must recognize that its use will not result in the absolute truth but instead, simply provide us with one way of understanding the world. Similarly, we need to creatively apply the approach. Rigidly adhering to a scientific method may not always be appropriate in our roles as generalist social workers. Instead, we need to selectively use the principles to optimally inform our practice.

The Relationship Between Theory and Research

We noted earlier how theory and research methods are the two basic components of the scientific approach. Here we explore the relationship between these two components: first, the ways in which they contribute to knowledge building, and second, the relative extent to which theories are supported by empirical evidence.

Strategies for Knowledge Building

Theory and research methods can work together in two different ways to build knowledge: deductively or inductively. **Deductive reasoning** involves drawing conclusions from the general to the particular. A theory may lead us to ask further questions. These questions are then compared with observations that are made while using research methods. For example, various researchers have attempted to investigate if Piaget's theory of child cognitive development is valid in different cultures (e.g., Mangan, 1978). Here the researcher takes Piaget's theory and tests its occurrence across different cultures. The results can then feed back into the theory.

Inductive reasoning employs an opposite strategy: using observation to examine the particular and then developing a generalization to explain the relationship among many of the particulars. Inductive reasoning involves finding patterns among separate phenomena. For example, we might notice certain characteristic similarities in children we have been seeing in our agency for behavioral problems in school. We then start systematically collecting these observations using the scientific approach. With these observations, we may develop a theory that states that the children have several characteristics in common besides the behavioral problems. The majority may be found to be new immigrants whose parents do not speak English, and their behavioral problems may be the result of teachers failing to appreciate the difficulty the children experience in the transition from home to school.

Extent of Empirical Evidence

Some theories in social work have a stronger empirical base than others. For example, psychoanalytical theory as propounded by Freud can very thoroughly explain certain aspects of behavior. However, it lacks a strong research or empirical base. In part this is the result of the difficulty of translating some psychoanalytic terms, such as *ego,* in a way that allows them to be measured and accurately observed.

Other complex theories have a strong empirical or research base. A good example is operant conditioning. Reinforcement produces an increase in behavior, and the rate of behavior increase is directly affected by when and how often the reinforcement occurs. The strong research base supporting operant conditioning was first developed by B. F. Skinner in his work with rats and then later with humans.

Many theories that we use in social work practice fall somewhere between these two extremes. For example, we have some theories about why child abuse occurs. Some suggest that children in single-parent families are at greater risk for child abuse. Research findings have provided some empirical evidence for this (Gelles, 1989). Gelles confirmed that children in single-parent homes are at increased risk for abuse. Poverty was also found to be associated with risk for abuse, but in mother-only homes, not father-only homes. Other factors associated with child abuse have also been identified, but we are still far from knowing all the elements involved.

In addition to theories drawn from the social and behavioral sciences, there are newer theories that relate to the effectiveness of specific interventions. An increasing number of these theories are developing strong empirical bases, such as the task-centered treatment model developed by Reid and Epstein (1972). This model requires the clear specification of tasks for the worker and client; whether or not and to what extent these tasks are accomplished then can be used to measure the success of the intervention.

In social work practice, we use a great number of theories from the social and behavioral sciences and from the field of social work itself. However, the research base of these theories constantly needs to be enhanced. The next section will explore why this is so critical.

Generalist Practice

Before discussing how research is linked to generalist practice, let's explain what we mean by **generalist social work practice.** Generalist social work has been practiced for over a hundred years. Today, it is the form of social work practice taught in undergraduate programs nationwide, and it provides the foundation curriculum in M.S.W. (Master of Social Work) programs for specialized social work practice. There is also a specialization known as advanced generalist.

Over the years, various views have developed as to what constitutes generalist practice. Several studies have been tried to clarify its components (Baer & Federico, 1978; Hoffman & Sallee, 1990; Schatz & Jenkins, 1987), and texts have been written proposing different conceptualizations (Anderson, 1981; Hoffman & Sallee, in press; Johnson, 1989; Pincus & Minahan, 1973). Schatz, Jenkins, and Sheafor (1990) drew from some of these studies and conceptualizations and suggest that generalist social work has the following perspective:

▶ Informed by socio-behavioral and ecosystems knowledge

▶ Reflects ideologies such as democracy, humanism, and empowerment

▶ Theoretically and methodologically open

▶ Involves direct and indirect intervention

▶ Client centered and problem focused

▶ Research based

Generalist social workers are expected to have the following competencies according to Schatz, Jenkins, and Sheafor (1990):

▶ Engage in interpersonal helping

▶ Manage change processes

▶ Use multilevel intervention modes

▶ Intervene in multisized systems

▶ Perform varied practice roles

▶ Able to assess/examine their own practice

▶ Function within a social agency

The Purpose of Research in Generalist Social Work Practice

As generalist social workers, why do we need to be concerned with building a strong, empirical base for theories? Because we are taught to view the world scientifically, we must understand and work from the scientific perspective as social workers to establish our discipline's legitimacy to others (although this does not mean dismissing other forms of explanation).

Given our acceptance of the importance of scientific thinking, there are two additional issues regarding incorporating research into our practice: ethical responsibility and fiscal accountability. Each of these will be discussed in turn.

Ethical Issues

Social workers need to be knowledgeable about research for ethical reasons: We must be accountable for our practice. Social workers are ethically responsible for providing the best possible services to their clients. The NASW Code of Ethics specifically addresses this issue.

> *Development of knowledge—The social worker should take responsibility for identifying, developing and fully utilizing knowledge for professional practice.*
>
> 1 *The social worker should base practice upon recognized knowledge relevant to social work.*
>
> 2 *The social worker should continually examine and keep current with emerging knowledge relevant to social work.*
>
> 3 *The social worker should contribute to the knowledge base of social work and share research knowledge and practice wisdom with colleagues. (NASW, 1980, Part V, Section O)*

To abide by the NASW Code of Ethics, the social worker needs to be proficient in social work research methods.

Fiscal Accountability

As long as social work practice is predominantly supported by public and voluntary funds, accountability will be a critical issue in the field. There are two aspects of financial accountability to consider. First, social programs must demonstrate that they are spending money responsibly, including ensuring that goals are being met and that funds are being efficiently distributed. This can occur at the agency or individual practitioner level. Second, as generalist social workers, we are often called upon to establish new services and programs, particularly in rural areas. To do this and to solicit funds for this purpose, we must substantiate our claim by providing solidly researched evidence of need.

Research Roles in Generalist Practice

One of the perspectives that characterizes generalist social work practice is that it is research based and that practitioners are able to assess their own practice. To accomplish these goals and to ensure fiscal and ethical responsibility, the generalist social worker needs to adopt two types of research roles: the consumer and the producer.

The Consumer

A knowledge of research methods allows the social work practitioner to draw on large amounts of information. Much of this information is derived from theory, but, as we discussed previously, the extent to which theories are research based varies. The social worker who has some knowledge of research methods can thus evaluate the extent of the research base of a theory. However, just because research has been conducted does not mean the research is of good quality. Thus, a social worker who is knowledgeable about research can also evaluate the quality of that research base. Katzer, Cook, and Crouch (1991), in their user's guide to social science research, point out that many errors occur even in published research.

This type of critical analysis is also useful in the social worker's assessment of specific practice techniques. For example, the generalist practitioner commonly provides home-based services, and a whole body of literature and research exists on these services. The research-informed practitioner can turn to this research for guidelines for practice. Using research in this way may help answer questions such as, "How do I know if home visits to 85-year-old Mrs. Garcia will help her avoid being placed in a nursing home?" We discuss how to consult research to enhance our practice in Chapter 13.

This ability to evaluate theories is known as the consumer function of research knowledge.

The Producer

The second reason why social workers need to know research methods is the most obvious one. Armed with this knowledge, social workers can then use the methods directly in their own practice to answer questions that arise. This is vital whenever answers cannot be found in the existing literature. Unfortunately, this is a frequent occurrence in social work, whether or not the social worker is engaged in generalist practice.

> *Relative to other professions, social workers appear to publish proportionately fewer empirically based reports. . . . When they do publish empirically based reports, the methods that social workers use reflect little mastery of basic scientific methods . . . (Fraser & Taylor, 1990)*

Because of the lack of studies in the literature, social workers often need to carry out their own research on the effectiveness of the interventions they use. In addition, generalist social workers are often required to demonstrate the need for new services or the improvement of existing services. Clearly, this type of inquiry also demands a knowledge and implementation of research methods.

In sum, generalist social workers, acting as producers of research, can build new knowledge for practice. No doubt this sounds overwhelming at this stage; however, in this book we will describe how to do this step by step. This text will provide you not only with the tools to become a producer of research, but also with the information to become a critical and intelligent consumer.

Research and Generalist Practice Processes

Social workers are often intimidated by research because they think it involves very different types of knowledge and skills from those of practice. In fact, the processes of practice and research are very similar; this is particularly the case for generalist social work practice. An overview of the relationship between research and practice is shown in Table 1.1.

Comparing Research and the Problem-Solving Process

Apart from the generalist social work perspectives and competencies discussed earlier in this chapter, you may know from your practice courses that there are specific steps involved in carrying out generalist social work. This is often referred to as the **problem-solving process.** There are close similarities between the steps of the generalist problem-solving process and the research process. For our purposes, we will draw on the problem-solving process as presented by Johnson (1989).

TABLE 1.1 *The relationship between research and practice*

Practice	Research
Preliminary statement of the problem	Deciding on the questions
Statement of preliminary assumptions	Developing questions
Selection and collection of information	Collecting the data, sampling, and design
Analysis of information available	Organizing the data, analyzing the data
Development of a plan	Research writing
Intervention / Implementation of a plan	Utilization of research findings
Evaluation of the plan	Evaluation of research

Preliminary Statement of the Problem

In formulating the preliminary statement of the problem in practice it is critical to be precise. As Johnson (1989) states, "The more precise the statement and the more individualized the situation, the more relevant and salient can be the goals and desired solutions" (p. 78). The first step in research is also to develop a preliminary statement of the problem or question. This is discussed in Chapter 2.

Statement of Preliminary Assumptions

The next step in practice is to acknowledge the implicit assumptions that we have made about the nature and cause of the problem. One such assumption might be in the meaning of terms that we often use in social work, such as *support, depression,* or even a concept as apparently simple as *family.* We all assume meanings for these terms, and these assumptions need to be clearly stated. By doing this, we reduce bias and increase objectivity, thereby upholding basic tenets of the scientific method. These assumptions must also be addressed during the initial stages of the research process. One strategy for accomplishing this is to very carefully state the nature of the question and identify its different components. This will be discussed in Chapter 3.

Selection and Collection of Information

Although we are often tempted to stop at this stage and jump in with an intervention assessment, Johnson (1989) states: "There is a need to determine and accumulate relevant evidence about the situation, and this evidence needs to be related to the salient features of the situation and to the presented concern of need" (p. 79). In research this step is also critical and can be divided into three tasks: data collection, sampling, and design. These steps will be discussed in Chapters 4, 5, 6, and 7.

Analysis of Information Available

In practice, analysis includes examining the information and data that have been collected and reaching some conclusions about those findings. This step is often referred to as assessment. Analysis in research can involve the use of statistical techniques or other strategies. As with practice, the analysis step needs to be carried out systematically and conscientiously to avoid misinterpretations of the results. Specific techniques to maintain objectivity are employed. Johnson (1989) says that in practice the process of analysis generates new information. This also occurs in research. The results often generate new questions and issues. Organization of the data and data analysis will be discussed in Chapters 8, 9, 10, and 11.

Development of a Plan

In practice, the social worker takes the results of the assessment and develops a plan of action that often involves formulating goals. The comparable step in research is writing the report that formally presents the analyzed results along with a description of the research methods. The research report includes recommendations for further research, a logical extension of the new questions that derived from the analysis of the results. Report writing is discussed in Chapter 12.

Implementation of a Plan

This is the active step of social work practice, and it represents the intervention stage. Often in research this step is downplayed. Research findings are of little use unless they are utilized in some way. Chapter 13 discusses various utilizations for research findings.

Evaluation of the Plan

The last step in practice is evaluation, and perhaps because it is last, it is often given little attention. Unfortunately, we may find ourselves simply moving on to the next case. The final step in the research process is also often overlooked. It includes evaluating the research by discussing its limitations and generally assessing its overall quality. This step will be discussed in Chapter 13.

To conclude this comparison of the research and generalist practice processes, we need to mention one other important similarity. This relates to the context within which the steps operate. Generalist social work practice is conducted within a context of two basic elements: **social work ethics** and human diversity. By **human diversity** we mean to include the whole spectrum of differences among people, including (but not limited to) gender, ethnicity, age, and sexual orientation. Research operates within a similar framework. Consequently, throughout this book these two elements—ethics and human diversity—will be discussed as they relate to each step of the research process.

In sum, research and practice employ parallel processes in approaching a problem. Research methods presented in this way are far less intimidating. We all know that practice can be frustrating; in truth, so can research. However, just as practice has its great rewards, so does research.

Summary

There are different types of explanation: values, intuition, experience, authority, and the scientific approach. The scientific approach consists of theories and research methods and involves, among others, the principles of systematic steps, causality, provisionality, and objectivity. There are variations in the scientific approach.

The relationship between theory and research methods involves inductive and deductive strategies for knowledge building. Some are more empirically based than others.

There are ethical and accountability issues involved in research in generalist practice. The roles of consumer and producer can address these issues.

The steps of generalist social work practice parallel the steps of research.

Study/Exercise Questions

1 List and discuss three reasons why you are not interested in carrying out any type of research in social work. Then give counterarguments for each of these three reasons that demonstrate the importance of social work research.

2 List the five different types of explanation presented in this chapter and discuss how you use each of them in your social work practice.

3 Select a theory used in social work and discuss the extent to which this theory has a research base.

4 Discuss some of the ways in which you may find yourself engaged in research as a generalist social worker.

Further Reading

Davis, L. V. (1986). A feminist approach to social work research. *Affilia, 1*, 32–47.

> One of the first articles that specifically discusses the principles of the feminist approach to research in social work.

Guba, E. G. (Ed.). (1990). *The paradigm dialog.* Newbury Park, CA: Sage Publications.

> A good discussion of some different paradigms that have dominated the social services.

Hoffman, K., & Sallee, A. (in press). *Generalist social work: Bridges to change.* Boston: Allyn & Bacon.

> This is one of the most recent textbooks on generalist practice and proposes the Bridge and Crystal models as a way of conceptualizing the knowledge, skills, and roles of the generalist social worker. This book also emphasizes the important role research plays in generalist practice.

Hoover, K. R. (1988). *The elements of social scientific thinking* (4th ed.). New York: St. Martin's Press.

> A brief introduction to social science thinking and research.

Kaplan, A. (1963). *The conduct of inquiry.* New York: Harper & Row.

> A classic discussion of the logic of science; includes a good description of themes, values, and the scientific process. Very readable.

Katzer, J., Cook, K. H., & Crouch, W. W. (1991). *Evaluating information.* New York: McGraw-Hill.

> An excellent consumer's guide to social science research. Useful for each stage of the research process.

Kuhn, T. (1970). *The structure of scientific revolutions* (2nd ed.). Chicago: University of Chicago Press.

> A landmark book that provided a new perspective for conceptualizing science. This short book is exciting and very informative.

Liu, W. T. (1982). *Methodological problems in minority research.* Occasional Paper No. 7. Pacific/Asian American Mental Health Research Paper.

> One of the few books that discusses the implications of carrying out research with various minorities. Includes research with African Americans, the National Chicano Survey, Korean immigrants, Asian minorities, and Pacific/Asian American communities.

Reinharz, S. (in press). *Feminist methods in social research.*

> Examines the wide range of feminist research methods.

References

Anderson, J. (1981). *Social work methods and resources.* Belmont, CA: Wadsworth.

Baer, B. L., & Federico, R. C. (1978). *Educating the baccalaureate social worker.* Cambridge, MA: Ballinger.

Carlson, R. (1972). Understanding women: Implications for personality theory and research. *Journal of Social Issues, 28,* 17–32.

Davis, L. V. (1986). A feminist approach to social work research. *Affilia, 1,* 32–47.

Fraser, M., & Taylor, M. J. (1990). *An assessment of the literature in social work: Utah project.* Unpublished raw data.

Gelles, R. J. (1989). Child abuse and violence in single parent families: Parent absence and economic deprivation. *American Journal of Orthopsychiatry, 59,* 492–501.

Guba, E. G. (Ed.). (1990). *The paradigm dialog.* Newbury Park, CA: Sage Publications.

Hoffman, K., & Sallee, A. (1990, March). *Follow-up study of BSW social workers: Implications for education and generalist practice.* Paper presented at the Council on Social Work Education Annual Program Meeting, Reno, Nevada.

Hoffman, K., & Sallee, A. (in press). *Generalist social work: Bridges to change.* Boston: Allyn & Bacon.

Johnson, L. (1989). *Social work practice: A generalist approach* (3rd ed.). Boston: Allyn & Bacon.

Katzer, J., Cook, K. H., & Crouch, W. W. (1991). *Evaluating information.* New York: McGraw-Hill.

Kuhn, T. (1970). *The structure of scientific revolutions* (2nd ed.). Chicago: University of Chicago Press.

Liu, W. T. (1982). *Methodological problems in minority research.* Occasional Paper No. 7. Pacific/Asian American Mental Health Research Paper.

Mangan, J. (1978). Piaget's theory and cultural differences: The case for value based modes of cognition. *Human Development, 21,* 170–189.

National Association of Social Workers. (1980). NASW Code of Ethics. *NASW News, 25,* 24–25.

Pincus, A., & Minahan, A. (1973). *Social work practice: Model and method.* Itasca, IL: Peacock Publishers.

Reid, W. T., & Epstein, L. (1972). *Task centered casework.* New York: Columbia University Press.

Rubin, A., & Babbie, E. (1989). *Research methods for social work.* Belmont, CA: Wadsworth.

Schatz, M. S., & Jenkins, L. E. (1987). *Differentiating generic foundation, generalist social work perspective, and advanced generalist practice in the generalist perspective.* Final report of a national Delphi study. Fort Collins: Colorado State University, Department of Social Work.

Schatz, M. S., Jenkins, L. E., & Sheafor, B. (1990). Milford redefined: A model of initial and advanced generalist social work. *Journal of Social Work Education,* 26(3), 217–231.

Deciding on the Question 2

"**H**ow do I know if this is a *real* research question? Is this what a research question should look like? I can't quite pin down what it is I need to find out." You will find yourself asking these kinds of questions when you are first confronted with the task of deciding on the research question. As a generalist social worker, we may not participate in deciding on the question; this is often done within the agency prior to our involvement in the research. However, we need to be familiar with the procedure involved in deciding the question so that we can understand (as in practice) how one step in the process leads to the next. We also need to learn this research stage so that we can evaluate our own practice, which is described later in this chapter.

As we discussed in Chapter 1, the first step of the research process—deciding on the question—is equivalent to the first practice step of developing a preliminary statement of the problem. This research step, as in practice, is one of the most challenging. Often, it involves continuously reworking and reevaluating the question. However, to facilitate this step we will break down the process into the following substeps:

1 Research strategies

2 Sources of questions

3 Types of questions

4 The literature review

5 The agency and deciding on the question

6 Ethical issues in deciding on the question

7 Human diversity issues in deciding on the question

Each of these steps will be examined in turn in this chapter.

Research Strategies

Before we embark on the actual formulation of the question, we need to be able to identify the general research strategy that our question will adopt. The research strategy is determined by two factors: (1) the intent or goal of the research, and (2) the amount of information we already have on the topic to be investigated. Three main strategies can be identified: exploratory, descriptive, and explanatory.

Exploratory Research

Exploratory research questions are excellent means of breaking new ground and generating exciting insights into the nature of an issue when we know very little about the problem area. Exploratory research often determines a study's feasibility and raises questions to be investigated by more extensive studies. For example, you might suspect that the ethnicity of the group leader is an important determinant of success in a support group you organized for children of alcoholics. The group leader is Puerto Rican. Consequently, you interview some of the clients in the group to get their opinions. The Puerto Rican clients were more likely than the other clients to claim success for the group. Based on these results, you could then undertake further research.

Exploratory research questions are often extremely useful in social work because we know so little about what works with whom and with what types of problems. In addition, exploratory research allows you to add richness and depth to your investigation, elements that may not be possible with some of the other strategies.

With exploratory research, it is difficult to take the findings and then apply them to other situations. This is known as **generalizing** the findings. In the above example, you cannot conclude definitively that in support groups for children of alcoholics, clients who are the same ethnicity as the group leader are more likely to report a successful experience. This may have only happened in this one group. You would need to carry out further research involving the experiences of clients in other support groups and examining the effect of matching clients and leaders of other ethnic groups besides Puerto Rican.

Exploratory research would not be a strategy to adopt if you were asked to demonstrate the effectiveness of a program to justify its establishment in other communities. Here you would need to be able to apply the findings to other situations. However, we will see later in this chapter that exploratory research is a useful strategy for evaluating our own practice.

E X A M P L E

Exploratory Research

Martinez-Brawley and Blundall (1989) carried out an exploratory study of the attitudes and preferences of farm households toward help, helping, and helpers. The researchers investigated how families viewed the process of giving and receiving help from natural helpers and from formal agencies and how their attitudes changed relative to financial stress. They also explored preferences on the sponsorship and location of social services.

A study of this nature was called for in part because of increased concern regarding the U.S. farm crisis and because of our lack of understanding about why farm families tend not to participate in human service programs.

Descriptive Research

Descriptive research describes, records, and reports phenomena as objectively as possible. Descriptive research can provide important fundamental information for establishing and developing social programs, but it is not primarily concerned with causes. Many surveys that try to determine the extent of a particular social problem—for example, the extent of child sexual abuse—are descriptive. In fact, there is an entire approach to research called **survey research** that focuses on describing the characteristics of a group. Sociologists often use this term. Another term associated with descriptive research is **ethnography.** This term, which is often applied in anthropological research, refers to a method of describing a culture or society. (We will discuss ethnography further in Chapter 4.) Another example of descriptive research is students' recording their initial observations of an agency or case by keeping a log or journal.

You will encounter descriptive research in social work journals. A considerable amount of policy evaluation/analysis is of this type. As a generalist practitioner, you may also be engaged in descriptive research. You could be asked to present some descriptive data relating to your agency (number of clients served, types of problems, and so forth) or of your community (the proportion of the population living below the poverty line, for example). Your supervisor may also require you to keep a journal describing your activities in the agency.

E X A M P L E

Descriptive Research

Lockhart and Wodarski (1989) used descriptive research to examine the extent of AIDS (acquired immunodeficiency syndrome) among children and adolescents. Their article describes the incidence of AIDS by age, race, and ethnicity, according to the Center for Disease Control statistics.

Explanatory Research

Explanatory research aims at providing explanations of events to identify causes. This type of research requires the formulation of **hypotheses:** testable statements about the relationships between certain factors. They usually have an "if X then Y" structure: From an earlier example, "If the ethnicity of the group leader is the same as the client, then success in the group will be more likely." We can accept or reject hypotheses depending upon the evidence produced through the research process.

E X A M P L E

A Hypothesis

A study by Marlow (1990) examined the management of family and employment responsibilities by Mexican-American and Anglo-American women. Three hypotheses were proposed:

1 Mexican-American employed women experience more problems coping with family and work responsibilities than do Anglo-American employed women.

2 Mexican-American employed women are more likely than Anglo-American employed women to prefer informal supports (such as family) over formal supports (such as physicians or counselors).

3 Mexican-American employed women are less likely than Anglo-American employed women to request formal services (such as counseling and child care).

The following conditions need to be met in order to establish **causality.** First, *two factors must be empirically related to one another.* For example, we might determine that there is a relationship between the grade B.S.W. students received in the practice class and their grade in the field. However, this does not mean the practice grade caused the success in the field. The other conditions of causality also need to be met. The second condition is that *the cause precedes the effect in time.* In the practice field example, we would need to demonstrate that students completed their practice courses prior to entering the field. The third element of causality is that *the relationship between the factors cannot be explained by other factors.* In the above example, it is possible that at least one other factor, such as past experience, has as much impact on field performance as the practice course grade.

In each step of the research process, explanatory research tries to address these conditions of causality. In reality, this is often extremely difficult to achieve, and the best we can expect is that only one or two of the conditions are met. Additionally, explanatory research can be problematic because as we attempt to establish causality, we may lose the detail and richness that is produced in the other research strategies.

This type of research is found in the social work literature, and, as generalist practitioners, we may be directly involved in such research. Usually, you would not undertake such research alone but would participate as a member of a team, for example, in determining the effectiveness of a particular program or agency.

E X A M P L E

Explanatory Research

Ezell and Gibson (1989) tested the following hypothesis: "Those elderly without informal social support will report a greater present need for services than those with support" (p. 6). The authors found that the elderly without informal support express greater service needs than those supported by informal networks, but these differences were not great and definitive conclusions could not be reached.

Table 2.1 summarizes the characteristics of exploratory, descriptive, and explanatory research strategies.

Sources of Questions

The research problem or question for generalist social workers usually derives from the agency at which they are employed and is directed at solving problems that arise in practice, and produces pratical outcomes. This type of research question is known as **applied research.** When research is instead aimed primarily at satisfying our intellectual curiosity, it is known as **pure research.**

TABLE 2.1 *Characteristics of exploratory, descriptive, and explanatory research in generalist practice*

Strategy	Definition / Purpose	Application
Exploratory	Little is known about the topic; develops hypothesis to be tested	Evaluating own practice
Descriptive	Describes, records, and reports; not concerned with causality	Conducting surveys of agencies or communities
Explanatory	Provides explanations to identify causes; requires formulation of hypotheses	Usually participates as a team member in examining effectiveness of a program

Let's look at an example to clarify this definition. We are employed in an agency in which a large proportion of the clients are spouse abuse victims, and we see this as a growing problem. A pure research question would be involved with investigating the causes of spouse abuse per se. However, as generalist social workers employed in the agency, we would ask applied research questions—such as one concerned with evaluating how well our agency serves the victims or one determining what other services are needed by this client population.

Personal experiences also come into play in formulating research questions. For example, if we find that a number of our clients are physically challenged young adults, we may determine that there is a need to establish specialized housing for these clients. After consultation with our supervisor, we may decide that it would make sense to carry out a survey to establish the extent and type of need in the community. However, part of our interest in this problem may have stemmed from the fact that we have a physically challenged family member.

Types of Questions

This section will explore the different types of applied research questions that we ask in generalist practice. The following are three examples of applied research questions that were presented in Chapter 1:

▶ Are my visits to Mrs. Garcia and the provision of other support services really helping her recover from the death of her husband?
This question is evaluating the effectiveness of our individual practice.

▶ Program X received additional funding for next year. How can we show that *our* program is effective and deserves more money?
This question is concerned with evaluating the effectiveness of a program.

▶ Bob is a teenage father in our community, and I don't know about any kinds of support programs for him. Is Bob unique in his need for services, or are there lots of Bobs in the community? And what kinds of services do they need?
This question involves describing the extent of a social problem.

Each question represents a different type of applied research that generalist social workers often encounter in their practice. Although these questions appear diverse, they can be equated with the three purposes of generalist social work as described by Baer and Federico (1978):

▶ To enhance people's problem-solving, coping, and developmental capacities

▶ To promote effective and humane operation of systems that provide people with resources and services

▶ To link people with systems that provide them with resources, services, and opportunities

The question that evaluates individual practice is the one asking about visits to Mrs. Garcia. This question directly examines our ability to enhance people's (in particular, Mrs. Garcia's) problem-solving, coping, and developmental capacities. The program evaluation question addresses the issues of the effective and human operations of systems that provide people with resources and services. The third question, a needs assessment question about teenage fathers, is involved with linking people to resources. We will now discuss the different types of questions in more detail.

Evaluation of the Effectiveness of Individual Practice

One type of research question that often occurs in social work practice is concerned with the effectiveness of an individual social worker's practice. As mentioned above, it directly relates to the enhancement of people's problem-solving, coping, and developmental capacities. This type of question often results in a **single-system study** or design. Single-system studies usually involve only one case/subject or client system and require social workers to use specific criteria and methods in monitoring their own practice cases. For the generalist social worker, these cases include individuals, families, groups, or communities. Whatever the type of client system, only one is evaluated in a single-system study.

Increasingly, single-system studies are being recognized as an integral element of social work practice. In part, this has resulted from social workers seeking a method of evaluation that could be relatively easily integrated into their practice. In addition to their ease of integration into practice, the single-system study offers the generalist practitioner the advantages of low cost and availability of immediate feedback to both the social worker and the client. Single-system studies will be discussed fully in Chapter 7.

E   X   A   M   P   L   E

A Single-System Study

Berlin (1983) provides an account of a single-system study. This case involved a young woman who suffered from depression. By following the client over a period of 10 weeks, employing a measuring instrument for depression repeatedly during this period, a reduction in the client's depression level was recorded. Berlin argues that this systematic effort to evaluate practice can enhance immediate intervention and contribute to our knowledge about practice.

Program Evaluation

Program evaluation research questions are asked extensively in generalist social work practice and involve assessing a program's overall functioning rather than the effectiveness of an individual practitioner. This type of question relates directly to the generalist social work function of promoting the effective and humane operation of the systems that provide resources.

Program evaluations play an increasing role in today's social work practice. As a result of the federal government's War on Poverty in the 1960s and early 1970s, funding for social programs was high. Unfortunately, however, there was little accountability to funding sources regarding their effectiveness in meeting client needs.

Fischer (1976) conducted a review of the casework practice in social work. He concluded that approximately half of the clients receiving casework services either deteriorated to a greater degree or improved at a slower rate than did subjects who did not participate in the programs. Fischer's study jolted social workers and others into acknowledging that just because a program had adequate funding did not ensure that it would be effective. Fischer's work also disclosed that many of the studies he reviewed contained various methodological problems. As a result, the profession realized the necessity for more sophisticated research methods in assessing service effectiveness and conducting program evaluations so that findings—positive or negative—could be upheld.

Program evaluation is primarily concerned with determining the effectiveness of a program, and this can be accomplished by adopting different strategies: formative, summative, or cost-benefit approaches. First, the **formative program evaluation,** or process analysis, examines the planning, development, and implementation of a program. This type of evaluation is often performed as an initial evaluative step.

E X A M P L E

A Formative Program Evaluation

Rounds, Galinsky, and Stevens (1991) report on an innovative method for bringing services to people with AIDS in rural communities. Support groups are brought into the homes of rural residents through telephone conference technologies. The goals of the group are to increase information and social support, reduce feelings of isolation, and enhance the coping of individuals living with AIDS.

 Although the authors briefly discuss an evaluation that is being done to assess the outcomes of the program, the focus of the article published in *Social Work* is upon describing the development and implementation of the program.

 The **summative program evaluation,** or outcome analysis, determines whether goals and objectives have been met and the extent to which program effects are generalizable to other settings and populations.

E X A M P L E

A Summative Program Evaluation

Koroloff and Anderson (1989) report in *Social Work* an evaluation of an alcohol-free living center for homeless alcoholics. The results indicate that generally the goals of the program were met. Clients who completed the program were admitted less often to both sobriety services and short-term detoxification and spent significantly fewer days in short-term detoxification. These reductions occurred whether or not the clients successfully completed a treatment plan while living at the center. By the end of the program, there were also client changes in employment status, income, and perceived employability.

 Finally, cost-benefit and/or cost-effectiveness analysis can be conducted. A **cost-benefit analysis** compares the program costs to the dollar value of the program results and computes a ratio of costs to benefits. A **cost-effectiveness study** compares program costs to some measure of program output and calculates a cost per unit.

 The most comprehensive program evaluations combine a study of the implementation, outcomes, and cost benefit aspects of a program.

E X A M P L E

A Cost-Benefit Analysis Program Evaluation

Maiden (1988) reports in *Employee Assistance Quarterly* on a cost-benefit and cost-effectiveness evaluation conducted by the U.S. Department of Health and Human Services Employee Counseling Service Program. A cost-benefit result was that for every dollar spent, there was a return in 6 months of $1.29. The author states that ultimately the program should attempt to realize a $7 return per dollar invested in the program. One cost-effectiveness finding is that the average cost per client served was approximately $951.

Needs Assessment

Needs assessment questions are concerned with discovering the nature and extent of a particular social problem to determine the most appropriate type of response. This is also known as survey research. This type of question is related to the practice function of linking people with systems.

An example of this type of needs assessment is: "I have talked to a couple of clients who need an alternative living situation for their adult developmentally delayed children. I wonder if there is a great enough need in the community to start a group home for the adult developmentally delayed?"

Reporting hearsay, citing individual cases, or simply acting on a hunch does not provide enough evidence for the people who are responsible for funding programs. Usually a funding source—whether a voluntary organization, a private foundation, or a state government—requires documentation of the need for the program with evidence that the needs assessment has been performed scientifically.

E X A M P L E

A Needs Assessment

Biegel, Cunningham, Yamatani, and Martz (1989) report in *Social Work* a needs assessment that examined the impact of unemployment in a blue-collar urban community in Pennsylvania, with the goal of understanding how community members define their needs and seek assistance. The findings indicate that there were two major needs:

1   To systematize availability of health care for those who no longer can afford it

2   To create opportunities for young people to keep them in the community, perhaps in partnership with area schools

TABLE 2.2 *Connections between type of question, research strategy, and function of social work practice*

Type of question and definition	Research strategies	Function of social work practice
Evaluation of individual practice; assessment of the practice of individual practitioners: single-system studies	Usually exploratory	Enhance people's problem-solving, coping, and developmental capacities
Program evaluation; assessment of program effectiveness	Usually explanatory	Promote the effective and humane operation of systems that provide people with resources
Needs assessment; assessment of nature and extent of social problems	Usually descriptive	Link people with systems that provide them with resources, services, and opportunities

Earlier we established the connection between the different types of research questions generalist social workers ask and the different functions of social work practice. Another link can be made between the different types of questions and the different research strategies: exploratory, descriptive, and explanatory. Evaluations of individual practice are generally exploratory in that they are limited in their generalizability but provide rich accounts of the particular practice. Needs assessments are usually descriptive in nature. Program evaluations strive to be explanatory so that they can establish the impact of services on the clients—at least this is the case for summative and cost-benefit program evaluations. This relationship between research strategy and question type does not always occur this way (for example, some program evaluations can be formative or descriptive as discussed earlier), but it can give us a frame of reference for understanding the relationships between different facets of social work. Table 2.2 illustrates some of the connections between the type of question, the research strategy, and the functions of social work practice.

Although the types of research questions appear quite different, they all follow essentially similar research steps and strategies. Some differences in approach are sometimes required. For example, we will see later that when a needs assessment is conducted there is usually no type of comparison group, whereas program evaluations are strengthened by the addition of a comparison group. Throughout the book we will indicate when different approaches are required according to the type of research question that is being asked.

The three types of research questions we have described here are not the only types of research questions social workers ask. If you look through any social work journal, you will find other types of research questions. You may find some pure research questions or historical studies. In addition, there may be articles that are not empirical in nature but that are theoretical and conceptual.

In this book we focus upon evaluating individual practice, program evaluation, and needs assessment questions simply because these are the types of research questions you will be most likely to encounter as *generalist* social workers. However, remember that many other types of questions are possible in social work.

The Literature Review

When we conduct applied research—whether a program evaluation, a needs assessment, or an evaluation of our own practice—we need to consult other sources of information. Sometimes we can gain information from colleagues who have had experience with the questions we are trying to answer. However, our usual information source is the existing written material.

The **literature review** involves consulting the written material relevant to our research problem. This written material can be found in a variety of places, including:

▶ Libraries, public and private
▶ City, state, and federal buildings
▶ Social agencies
▶ Private collections
▶ Political, professional, social, and interest group organizations (e.g., NASW)

In this section we will discuss the specific uses of the literature review and accessing the information.

Use of the Literature Review

The literature review assists with formulating the question by (1) question generation, (2) connecting the question to theory, (3) identifying previous research, and (4) giving direction to the project. (Consulting the literature is also helpful in guiding practice, particularly if the literature is research based. This is the focus of Chapter 13.)

Question Generation

We explained earlier how the generalist social worker is usually assigned a research project or question, and we noted that these questions derive directly from issues pertinent to the agency. However, sometimes you may be given considerable freedom in your choice of question—for instance, if you are asked to conduct a research project for a class. Here it would make sense to consult the literature for ideas. Often research articles include suggestions for future research. For example, in a needs assessment study examining the patterns of use and needs for social services by family caregivers in multigenerational households, one of the recommendations was the need for further exploration of the ethnic patterns of family caregiving (Cox, Parsons, & Kimboko, 1988).

Connecting the Research Question to Theory

In pure research, connecting a question to theory is a fairly obvious step. For example, if we are investigating the causes of spouse abuse, we need to be apprised of the human behavior theories that attempt to explain spouse abuse.

This theoretical base is sought in the existing literature. However, in applied research this step is not so obvious and can be easily overlooked. To clarify, we will now look at how the literature review can be used to connect each of the applied research questions to theory.

Evaluations of Individual Practice   When evaluating our own practice, we need to have an understanding of the theoretical base underlying our use of a particular intervention. For example, if we are using positive reinforcement in helping a parent learn disciplining skills, we need to be sure we are familiar with the theory behind positive reinforcement, that is, behavior theory. This can be found by referring to the behavioral science literature. In addition, we need to understand the theoretical link between the use of positive reinforcement in disciplining children and its appropriateness and effectiveness for this purpose. Again we turn to the literature for this information.

Program Evaluation   You recall that program evaluation can take several forms: summative, formative, or cost-benefit analyses. For each form, we need to consider how the research question links to theory. Perhaps we examine whether our agency is meeting its goal in providing support services to homebound elderly. The literature is consulted to determine the theoretical basis for providing this type of care, and we consult studies of this type that have already been performed. We may also find some of this material in the initial program proposal.

Needs Assessment   When assessing the need for a program, the literature can also be consulted to provide some theoretical substance. For example, in conducting a needs assessment to determine the number of homeless women and children in our community, a theoretical perspective and context can be gained by consulting the literature and determining the risk factors and problems experienced by homeless women and children.

E X A M P L E

Connecting the Research Question to Theory

Darmstadt (1990), in his description of a community-based child abuse prevention program, states in the abstract to the article:

> *Prematurity, congenital abnormalities, intrauterine growth retardation, and perinatal illness often impair parent-infant attachment, which can contribute to subsequent child abuse. Enhancement of parent-infant relationships, parental coping skills, and social support systems through parent education and home visitation has been shown to reduce the incidence of abuse and is emphasized in the child abuse prevention program proposed in this article. (p. 487)*

Darmstadt (1990) cites the literature to support this statement and to provide rationale for the program.

Identifying Previous Research

When we choose or are assigned a research question, it is useful to find out if a similar or identical question has already been answered. If so, we may want to reconceptualize our research question. For example, in conducting our needs assessment we may find a report on a survey that was conducted in our community two years previously. This will probably be useful information as the survey took place so recently. However, if the survey had been conducted 10 years ago, we would need to **replicate** or repeat the study to reduce error. Similarly, in a program evaluation, we may find that other evaluations of comparable programs have been conducted that would result in our evaluation not necessarily contributing new and useful knowledge. Alternatively, we may find that the evaluations were conducted in very different communities from the one our agency serves, which would suggest that another survey would be useful.

E X A M P L E

Identifying Previous Research

Rosenthal, Groze, and Curiel (1990) carried out an assessment of special needs adoption. They surveyed intact special needs families and looked at their characteristics. Early in their article they state:

> *As special needs adoption increased in frequency, so did adoption disruption and the breakdown of adoption prior to legal finalization. . . . A recent five-state study estimated the special needs disruption rate at 13 percent. . . . Research on disruption has been substantial, but the 87 percent of special needs placements that remain intact have seldom been studied. (p. 532)*

Giving Direction to the Research Project

Although we have been concerned here primarily with the role of the literature review in the formulation of the research question, the literature review can also give direction and guidance to the entire research project. You can, for example, review the literature to find out how researchers set up comparison groups in similar projects, or to give you ideas about how samples can be selected. Using the literature review in this way, particularly early on in the formulation of the question, can save considerable time later and prevents us from reinventing the wheel. The specific role of the literature review in each step of the research process will be referred to in the respective chapters.

Accessing Information

As we mentioned previously, there are several literature sources available to the social worker. Agencies and public and private organizations often maintain collections of materials. One good example is the National Association of Social Workers. However, the most extensive resource locations are libraries. If you can find your way around a typical university library, you should have little trouble accessing information in other locations. Consequently, we will focus here on locating information in a library.

Use of Computers

Information retrieval has been revolutionized by the computer. Now literature reviews can be performed in a fraction of the time it used to take. The general principles of conducting a search using computerized information is similar from library to library. The author and/or title and/or subject are entered, and a list of potential sources of information is retrieved by the computer. Guidance regarding subject heading can be found by consulting the three-volume *Library of Congress Subject Headings*. Some examples of subject headings include:

CHILD WELFARE WORKERS

WOMEN SOCIAL WORKERS

Most libraries now have on-line catalogs that allow you to access information on those books and journals in the library. This information used to be available (and still is in some libraries) in card catalogs. Cards provide the full citation and location of the materials. Card catalogs need to be consulted when a computerized on-line system does not exist, which may be the case for older materials.

Dictionaries and Encyclopedias

A good starting point for a literature review is to consult dictionaries and encyclopedias. They can provide general background information to help narrow or broaden the topic, define unfamiliar terms, and offer bibliographies of other sources. If there is an index, it should be used for gaining initial access to a subject. Dictionaries and encyclopedias of use to social workers can be found in Appendix A.

Journals

Journals often provide the primary source of information for social work research. Major journals in social work are listed in Appendix A.

Although journal articles give the most up-to-date and thorough information on many topics, it is difficult to determine which articles are appropriate by using the main catalog, which simply provides the title of the journal, not specific titles of articles. However, many libraries do offer special data bases for the retrieval of journal articles.

Indexes and Abstracts

Indexes and abstracts can also provide invaluable sources of information. Sometimes they are computerized, but if not, they can be located in the library and consulted for sources of information on specific topics. The main indexes and abstracts for social workers are listed in Appendix A.

Bibliographies

Bibliographies can also be consulted. Examples of bibliographies often referred to by social workers are listed in Appendix A.

Government Documents

Government documents, often included in university libraries, provide another source of information. Usually, they must be located through an indexing system separate from the main catalog. Government documents do not have the same type of call number system as other materials in the library; instead, they are organized by the Superintendent of Documents (SuDoc) classification system. The first letters in the call number represent the issuing agency. Increasingly, these documents are becoming available through computerized systems. Some examples of these documents are listed in Appendix A.

Statistical Sources

Main sources of statistics are listed in Appendix A.

Interlibrary Loan

One important resource that is often overlooked is the interlibrary loan facility in many libraries. If a library does not house a particular book, journal, or document, it is possible to borrow these from other libraries through your library. Find out how to use interlibrary loan. Usually interlibrary loan takes some time, so do not leave this until the last minute.

A final note: Do not forget to fully use another resource in the library—the library staff. They are there to help you. See Table 2.3 for a summary of accessing the information.

The Agency and Deciding on the Question

As we discussed earlier, except when conducting single-system studies, we have little or no choice in the research we will be doing as generalist social workers and the question formulation stage has already been carried out. Instead, you find yourself required to conduct a needs assessment to help build a case for the development of a new program in your community. Or, your program's funding source demands that an evaluation be undertaken for funding to continue. There is little room in these cases for deciding on research strategies or types of questions.

TABLE 2.3 *Summary of accessing the information*

1	State the topic, limit the range, and list all relevant synonyms.
2	Locate a good, general introductory text on the topic—one that includes a selected bibliography of the basic books and studies.
3	Try to locate a literature review about the specific topic and the general research area.
4	Locate all relevant books; be sure to use the Library of Congress *Subject Headings* to identify relevant subject terms and use them while searching the card catalog.
5	Using indexes and abstracts, locate relevant journal articles and other research reports; make a list of the indexes and abstracts that seem pertinent to the area of study.
6	Locate other relevant material—published and unpublished—such as government documents, theses, and dissertations.
7	If statistics or other pieces of discrete information are needed in the research, ask the reference librarian how to use the library to obtain such data.
8	If a computer search of such abstracting services and indexes as *Psychological Abstracts, Index Medicus, Sociological Abstracts,* or ERIC is worthwhile, consult a reference librarian for search sources and search profile methodology. Start early; these searches take from three to five weeks.
9	Know the procedures for interlibrary loan and begin the literature search immediately; interlibrary loan takes time.
10	Ask a reference librarian for suggestions about other indexes, abstracts, or research tools—either in the local library or in other libraries.

Source: From M.L. Arkava & T.A. Lane, 1983

Despite this tendency for you to have little choice about your research, in many respects you are in an ideal position for conducting applied research. The social work literature consistently calls for cooperation and collaboration between researchers and scientists (Fanshel, 1978; Hermalin & Weirich, 1983). As an agency-based generalist social worker who is knowledgeable about research and familiar with the workings of the agency and the concerns of the community, you are well situated to conduct relevant research. You can also act as a resource person for outside researchers; when the opportunity arises, you may assist them in conducting research that is beyond the scope of your immediate responsibilities in the agency.

However, if you are asked to initiate a research study from the ground up, you must recognize that research is almost always a team effort. This is particularly the case at the deciding on the question stage. Consult with agency staff and/or the community to determine what they want from the evaluation or needs assessment. Don't forget to confer with those who are providing the funding for the project. We will discuss the importance of consultation in developing the question in the next chapter.

Ethical Issues in Deciding on the Question

Three ethical issues are central to the deciding on the question stage of the research process: (1) the applicability of the question to social work practice; (2) giving credit to those who have contributed to the research; and (3) the role of funding.

Applicability of the Question to Social Work Practice

One concern we need to bear in mind when we are deciding on a research question is if and how the answer to the question is going to contribute to the field of social work. Usually, this is not too much of a problem, particularly as generalist social workers, because most questions derive directly from our practice in an agency. However, if our question has evolved from our personal experiences, we must ask whether this is a question that is really going to assist the clients we serve. To determine the appropriateness of the question, we can consult the literature and discuss it with colleagues.

Giving Credit to the Contributors

When we draw on information that has been generated by others (for example, using a literature review or even consulting with colleagues), we need to give credit to these sources of information when we write the research report. The technicalities of how to do this are discussed in Chapter 12. If we use someone else's ideas and we do not give them credit, particularly if they are written ideas, we are guilty of plagiarism.

Availability of Funding

In agencies, research projects may be conducted because there is available funding for these projects. Certain issues may be a priority at the local, state, or federal level and funds consequently become available. We should be aware of why we are conducting research on these particular issues; that is, in part because of the availability of funds. Presumably, it has already been established that this topic is a deserving one, but we need to realize that other issues are probably equally deserving and should not be ignored because of the convenience of funding. In other words, we should continue to act as advocates for those issues, regardless of the extent to which they are receiving fiscal support.

In addition, you may sometimes want to confirm for yourself whether a research program deserves an investment of time and money. Again, the best source of this type of information is the literature and colleagues.

Human Diversity Issues
in Deciding on the Question

During the deciding on the question stage, we need to pay attention to human diversity issues. We should be aware that published materials on human diversity are scarce and may contain biases, that agencies may also reflect biases, and that our research question must include different types of populations and address the concerns of these groups.

Bias in the Literature

Before we use materials to help us guide a particular research project, we need to be aware of bias in the literature. Literature relating to human diversity issues is scarce, even though it is beginning to grow.

A study undertaken by Lum (1986) of social work practice texts between 1970 and 1983 reported only minimal text content on ethnic minorities and related areas—3% (195 out of 7,688) of the pages were devoted to the combined subjects of ethnicity, culture, and minorities.

We need to remember when consulting the literature that most of the published research was conducted by white middle-class males. The views of this segment of the population, to the exclusion of almost all others, represent a clear bias. Research questions formulated by other groups may have a very different focus. For example, until relatively recently, there were few studies conducted on the relationship between women's work and family lives, particularly minority women and families. Presumably, this relationship was not considered an important issue for the majority of male researchers.

E X A M P L E

Bias in the Literature

Greif and Bailey (1990) point out in their article in *Families in Society* that the literature on fathers is scarce. They reviewed 5 major social work journals during a 27-year period. Fathers tended to be portrayed as perpetrators, missing, and as embattled. The authors suggest that if the social work profession is committed to working with families, attention should be given to changing patterns of fatherhood.

Bias in the Agencies

Most of our research questions do not derive from the literature but rather from practice in agencies. We need to be aware that bias can also exist there and that this bias can influence the formulation of the research question. We have already discussed the fiscal bias issue. However, other biases that relate to human diversity issues can also exist.

For example, an agency's homophobic attitudes may result in ignoring the needs of lesbian clients even though the group may require substantial social supports. Your request to carry out a needs assessment of this particular group may be dismissed by your supervisor. Watch for these biases; be aware that your agency's operation may be influenced by presuppositions and prejudices.

E X A M P L E

Including Diverse Populations and Their Issues in the Research Question

Arnold (1990) examined the early childhood, adolescent, and adult experiences of black women incarcerated in jail and prison. The research goal was to reveal the process of victimization, labeling, and subsequent criminalization of these women. Arnold concludes:

> If we are to witness a drop in the numbers of imprisoned women, legislators and policy makers need to reevaluate what happens to young girls who are victimized by gender, class, and race, and stop blaming the victim by processing and labeling her as deviant and/or criminal. (p. 163)

Summary

Three research strategies are described: exploratory, descriptive, and explanatory. There is a distinction between applied research and pure research. Generalist social workers usually engage in three types of applied research: evaluating their own practice, program evaluation, and needs assessment.

The literature review can be used to generate questions, connect the question to theory, identify previous research, and give direction to a project. There are different strategies for accessing information.

Usually in agencies research questions have already been decided. Ethical issues in deciding on the question include assessing the applicability of the question to social work practice, giving credit to contributors, and availability of funding. Human diversity issues are awareness of bias in the literature and in the agencies.

Study/Exercise Questions

1   Look through a social work journal such as *Social Work Research and Abstracts* or *Affilia* and identify studies that adopt the research strategies de-

scribed in this chapter (needs assessments, program evaluations, and single-system studies). Discuss in class the reasons for your decisions.

2   Take a tour or orientation of your university library. Learn how to use the computerized data bases and access information in the government documents section (if your library has one).

3   Select a topic of interest, preferably one that is related to an agency with which you are familiar. Some examples are social workers' involvement in employee assistance programs, the provision of programs to teenage fathers, the effectiveness of programs in supporting foster parents, and so on. Use a computerized data base in your library—for example, the *Social Science Index* or *Social Work Research and Abstracts*—to locate at least five references on your topic.

4   If you are enrolled in a practicum or field placement, ask your supervisor about program evaluations or needs assessments conducted by the agency. Find out why the evaluations or needs assessments were performed. Who suggested them? Who was involved in those decisions? Present the results of this discussion in class.

Further Reading

Alter, C., & Evens, W. (1990). *Evaluating your practice: A guide to self assessment.* New York: Springer.

> A good discussion of the ways in which practice can be evaluated. Includes excellent examples of how to assess different-size client systems and is consequently very appropriate for the generalist social worker.

Austin, M. J. (1982). *Evaluating your agency's programs.* Beverly Hills, CA: Sage Publications.

> A good introductory book on program evaluation.

Beasley, D. (1988). *How to use a research library.* Oxford: Oxford University Press.

Mendelsohn, H. N. (1987). A guide to information sources for social work and the human services. Phoenix: Oryx Press.

> These are two useful sources on library use; they describe the organization of libraries and access to information in reference books, public documents, journals, books, statistical and legal sources.

Neuber, K. A., Atkins, W. T., Jacobson, J. A., & Reuterman, N. A. (1980). *Needs assessment: A model for community planning.* Beverly Hills, CA: Sage Publications.

> An introduction to needs assessments that is particularly suited to the generalist social worker.

See Appendix A for a listing of journals in social work and related disciplines. Familiarize yourself with these journals. They are an invaluable resource in conducting research.

References

Arkava, M. L., & Lane, T. A. (1983). *Beginning social work research*. Boston: Allyn & Bacon.

Arnold, R. A. (1990). Processes of victimization and criminalization of black women. *Social Justice, 17*, 153–166.

Baer, B. L., & Federico, R. C. (1978). *Educating the baccalaureate social worker*. Cambridge, MA: Ballinger.

Berlin, S. (1983). Single-case evaluation: Another version. *Social Work Research and Abstracts, 19*, 3–11.

Biegel, D. E., Cunningham, J., Yamatani, H., & Martz, P. (1989). Self-reliance and blue-collar unemployment in a steel town. *Social Work, 34*(5), 399–406.

Cox, E. O., Parsons, R. J., & Kimboko, P. O. (1988). Social services and intergenerational caregivers: Issues for social work. *Social Work, 33*(5), 430–435.

Darmstadt, G. L. (1990). Community-based child abuse prevention. *Social Work, 35*(6), 487–489.

Ezell, M., & Gibson, J. W. (1989). The impact of informal social networks on the elderly's need for services. *Journal of Gerontological Social Work, 14*, 3–18.

Fanshel, D. (1978). The future of social work research: Strategies for the coming years. In D. Fanshel (Ed.), *Future of social work research*. (pp. 3–18). Washington, DC: National Association of Social Workers.

Fischer, J. (1976). *The effectiveness of social casework*. Springfield, IL: Charles C Thomas.

Greif, G. L., & Bailey, C. (1990). Where are the fathers in social work literature? *Families in Society: The Journal of Contemporary Human Services, 71*(2), 88–92.

Hermalin, J. A., & Weirich, J. W. (1983). Prevention research in field settings: A guide for practitioners. *Prevention in the Human Services, 2*, 31–48.

Koroloff, N. M., & Anderson, S. C. (1989). Alcohol-free living centers: Hope for homeless alcoholics. *Social Work, 34*(6), 497–504.

Lockhart, L. L., & Wodarski, J. S. (1989). Facing the unknown: Children and adolescents with AIDS. *Social Work, 34*(3), 215–221.

Lum, D. (1986). *Social work practice and people of color*. Monterey, CA: Brooks/Cole.

Maiden, R. P. (1988). Employee assistance program evaluation in a federal government agency. *Employee Assistance Quarterly, 3*(314), 191–204.

Marlow, C. (1990). Management of family and employment responsibilities by Mexican American and Anglo American women. *Social Work, 35*(3), 259–265.

Martinez-Brawley, E. E., & Blundall, J. (1989). Farm families' preferences toward the social services. *Social Work, 34*(6), 513–522.

Rosenthal, J. A., Groze, V., & Curiel, H. (1990). Race, social class and special needs adoption. *Social Work, 35,* 532–539.

Rounds, K. A., Galinsky, M. J., & Stevens, L. S. (1991). Linking people with AIDS in rural communities: The telephone group. *Social Work, 36*(1), 13–18.

Developing the Question

3

Suppose you were asked by your supervisor to carry out a needs assessment to establish a health promotion program for a local business. You have some implicit assumptions about what the program will include, namely, seminars and information dispersal on wellness. However, after consulting with the staff of the business, you find that they are defining a health promotion program more broadly; their idea of a health promotion program includes other services such as health insurance revision, discounts to local health clubs, counseling information and referral, and so forth.

In this chapter we will describe the research stage of developing the question. This is the equivalent of the statement of preliminary assumptions stage in practice. Developing the question involves clarifying the research question once it has been initially formulated. Our clarification will make explicit some initial assumptions inherent in research (which is also what we need to do in practice).

Here we will examine the question more closely and include a discussion of

▶ Units of analysis
▶ Naming the variables and values
▶ Identifying independent and dependent variables
▶ Defining and operationalizing the variables
▶ Use of focus groups
▶ Levels of measurement
▶ The agency and developing the question
▶ Ethical issues in developing the question
▶ Human diversity issues in developing the question

As discussed in the last chapter, often the question has been decided prior to your involvement. For example, the agency may have been asked by one of their funding sources to carry out an evaluation of the services, and you have been asked to help with the planning and implementation of the study. Similarly, it may be that many of the stages we discuss in this chapter will have already been completed. However, it is still important for you as a participant in the project to understand the rationale behind these stages, and, if you have the opportunity, to develop them yourself.

Units of Analysis

After selecting our general research question, one of the first things we need to clarify is the unit of analysis for the study. The **unit of analysis** refers to what or whom we are studying, or the unit "that we initially describe for the ultimate purpose of aggregating their characteristics in order to describe some larger group or explain some abstract phenomenon" (Rubin & Babbie, 1989, p. 88).

There are three types of units of analysis used in social work research: individuals; groups, which may include organizations, communities, or societies; and social artifacts.

Individuals are the most commonly used units of analysis in social work. Descriptions of individuals are often aggregated to explain social group functioning. For example, in conducting a needs assessment for a community youth center, we interview individual youths to assess their needs. This information is then aggregated to document the needs of this group, that is, youths in the community.

E X A M P L E

The Individual as a Unit of Analysis

In a study by Beckett (1988) of how people are affected by plant closing, the unit of analysis was individuals or, more specifically, workers. She pooled the information she gained from the workers and concluded that older workers were most negatively affected by plant closings.

Groups can also be the unit of analysis. Groups are of various shapes and sizes, and include families, organizations, and communities. Families are often the unit of analysis used in social work. For example, you are engaged in an evaluation investigating the impact of a program on family cohesion. Although you will be studying individuals (in families), it is the family group that would make up the unit of analysis in the study. In other words, it is the family unit that will be aggregated with other family units to explain the impact of the program.

E X A M P L E

The Family as the Unit of Analysis

Tracy (1990) examined the social support resources of 45 families at risk for disruption through out-of-home placement. Among other findings, there were indications of a relationship among concrete support, emotional support, and informational support in the families.

Social artifacts are behaviors or products that result from human activity. In social work, social artifacts might include books, divorces, birth practices, or ethical violations suits. Suppose you are asked by your state NASW chapter to investigate unethical social work practice behavior. In the study, you look at the characteristics of those charged with such behavior—whether they are B.S.W.'s or M.S.W.'s, in what field of practice they are employed, and so on. Here the unit of analysis is unethical social work practice.

E X A M P L E

The Social Artifact as the Unit of Analysis

One interesting study used cartoons from *Playboy* as the unit of analysis. Matacin and Burger (1987) report research in *Sex Roles* concerning themes in *Playboy*. Cartoons from all the 1985 issues of *Playboy* were coded for the presence or absence of certain themes. The findings indicated that there were major differences between how men and women were depicted according to these themes. For example, females were more likely to be depicted as objects of unwanted seduction than males.

This is not as complicated as it sounds. Usually social work research projects involve individuals as the unit of analysis. However, we must ensure that this is, in fact, the case. Otherwise, we may commit what is referred to as the **ecological fallacy**: reaching conclusions about individuals when the study's unit of analysis is a group or social artifact, or vice versa. For example, a state study compared the numbers of referrals for child abuse and neglect in different counties. The results indicated that counties with a higher percentage of minorities had higher child abuse and neglect referral rates than those with lower proportions of minorities. We cannot know from this conclusion whether or not minorities are more likely than nonminorities to be referred for child abuse and neglect. Here the unit of analysis was a group—counties—and the study's conclusions can consequently only relate to counties not to individuals. That is, county A is more likely to refer minorities than county B.

Naming the Variables and Values

After defining the unit of analysis, we need to understand what is meant by a variable. A **variable** is a characteristic of a phenomenon, and it is something that varies. Some common examples of variables in social work research are income, ethnicity, and stress level. These characteristics vary or have different qualities, and these different qualities of variables are referred to as **values.** (Note that our use of *value* in this context is not our usual meaning for *value* in social work practice, such as the social work value of self-determination.)

Using the above examples, possible values of income might include:

under $15,000/year
$15,000–$19,999/year
$20,000–$24,999/year
$25,000–$29,999/year
$30,000 and over/year

Ethnicity attributes might include:

white (non-Hispanic)
Hispanic
African American
Native American
other

Stress level values might include:

high
medium
low

Both the variables and values that are used in research studies differ from study to study. In conducting a survey to assess the need for a day care center for developmentally delayed preschoolers, one variable might be income so that we could assess the extent to which parents could pay for such a service. If we were carrying out the needs assessment in rural Kentucky, we might anticipate that incomes would be low. Consequently, the values included on the survey instrument would also be low; the levels presented in the above example might be too high. However, if the needs assessment were being performed in

Santa Barbara, California, this categorization might be too low, and we would need to add much higher income levels. Sometimes we do not determine the values at the beginning of the study, but they become apparent as the study proceeds. We discuss how this happens in the next chapter. Remember, however, that the values for variables usually differ from research study to research study.

In the same survey, ethnicity might also be considered a factor that would influence service need, and consequently should be included in the study. As a variable, ethnicity is restricted in terms of the values that may be included, but there are still some choices. For example, if the study was carried out in New Mexico, the values listed above for ethnicity would include most of the state's population. Alternatively, if the study was conducted in Chicago, more values should probably be added—for example, Asian American. Again, the values included depend on the purpose and context of the study.

One note of caution on the decision regarding the variables to be included in the study: Beware of what is referred to as **reductionism,** or the extreme limitation of the kinds and numbers of variables to be considered as explaining or accounting for broad types of behavior.

For example, in a study on spouse abuse you may take many perspectives to explain this phenomenon. You might focus on economic factors, biological factors, family dynamics factors, or psychological factors, to name a few; according to the literature, all of these appear to play some role in contributing to spouse abuse. Time and money constraints often force us to consider only one group of factors. In this case, we may opt for the economic factors because our literature review disclosed these as being in need of further investigation. Choosing economic factors above the others is not, in itself, necessarily a problem; however, if we then suggest that these are the *only* factors in explaining spouse abuse, we would be guilty of reductionism. It is important to recognize that when you select the variables for a study, these variables may represent only one perspective on the explanation, and in discussing your results you need to acknowledge this. Social workers study human behavior, and human behavior is very complex. We cannot expect to come up with a complete explanation; we need to be aware of this limitation from the early stage of question development to the final stages of writing the report.

Identifying Independent and Dependent Variables

Variables have different functions in a research study. The major distinction we need to make is between the roles of the *independent* and *dependent* variables.

The **independent variable** is the presumed causal variable in a relationship. If we were studying the impact of social isolation on child sexual abuse, the independent variable would be social isolation. In a program evaluation, the independent variable is the program itself.

We can think of the **dependent variable** as the outcome variable that has presumably been affected by the independent variable. In a summative program evaluation where we are interested in whether the goals of the program are being met, the dependent variables would be the goals of the program. In the example of the study attempting to identify the factors leading to child sexual abuse in a community, child sexual abuse would be the dependent variable. For each study, there may be a number of independent and dependent variables. In the study of child sexual abuse, income level (in addition to social isolation) may be another possible independent variable, and different types of child sexual abuse might be identified as different dependent variables.

As in the case of different values, variables are not fixed as dependent or independent; the nomenclature depends upon the purpose and context of the study. Although child abuse is identified as a dependent variable in the above example, in a study examining the factors that determine teenage pregnancy, child sexual abuse might well be identified as an independent variable.

One final note concerning variables: Independent and dependent variables are of primary concern in explanatory studies where specific variables are being identified as contributing to specific outcomes. They can also be identified in exploratory studies where the intent might be to gain a beginning understanding of how certain factors—for example, those related to an intervention—impact on certain client outcomes. In descriptive studies, however, such as a needs assessment, independent and dependent variables are often not identified as such.

E X A M P L E

Independent and Dependent Variables

A study by Lieberman, Hornby, and Russell (1988) examined the relationship of educational level to preparedness for practice in public child welfare work. The educational level—highest and type of degree earned—was the independent variable; preparedness for practice was the dependent variable.

The results indicated that B.S.W.'s felt they were consistently better prepared than their non-social-work-trained counterparts, and M.S.W.'s felt better prepared than any other group.

Defining and Operationalizing the Variables

Definitions

Once we have identified the variables in the research question, we need to formally *define* them. This is sometimes referred to as conceptualizing the variables. The variables need to be described in a clear, unambiguous manner, in much the same way as we need to define concepts in practice.

Many of the variables used in social work practice tend to be vague; they may seem open to a number of different interpretations depending on who is using them. In my first field practicum in a psychiatric hospital in Chicago, I was confused by such terms as *ego strength, depression,* and *independent living skills*. The definitions of these terms were not provided, or if they were, they varied, depending on who was doing the defining. We have to be careful in social work practice that we do not use terms that cannot be clearly defined, otherwise confusion can result. A worker and client may both think they know what is meant by *independent living,* but unless it is explicitly defined they may have very different understandings. The client may have in mind "living in my own apartment with no supervision," whereas the worker may mean "living in her own apartment with close supervision." In this example, no matter which definition is accepted, the term *supervision* will also need to be defined. Supervision might be defined as "the client reporting to the social worker twice a week."

As in practice, we need to define the variables clearly when we start our research project. If we were to research a program's impact on clients' ability to engage in independent living, we would again need to define independent living. In defining the variables, we can use our own definitions or ones that we find in the literature.

Operationalizations

Once the variables have been formally defined, we must **operationalize** them. This means specifying the manner by which the variables are to be measured. Operationalizing becomes easier once variables have been formally defined, although even after definitions have been accepted some ambiguities remain. To continue with the above example, measuring the extent to which independent living has been achieved would involve clarifying the reporting issue. Is this a telephone call or a face-to-face visit? How long would the client need to live independently in order for this to be regarded as successful? What kinds of financial expectations are included in the concept *independent living?* These are only a few of the questions that need to be answered before a satisfactory operational definition of the variable can be achieved.

Measuring a variable could entail simply recording the presence or absence of a phenomenon. If reporting is defined as a telephone contact, either the contact was made or it was not. Or measurement might involve more elaboration, such as specifying the nature of the telephone contact. For example, if a prior arrangement was made regarding the time of the call and who was to initiate it, were these conditions fulfilled?

Operationalizing variables can be a challenge. It may seem overwhelming to the social worker to measure a concept like depression. A useful strategy in operationalizing a variable is to look in the literature and determine how others operationalized this concept. Many variables in social work research we refer to frequently. Depression is a good example; there are many depression measures available in the literature, including the Generalized Contentment Scale (Hudson, 1990), the Hamilton Rating Scale (Hamilton, 1967), and the CES-ED Scale (Radloff, 1977). Many of these measures can be adopted by social workers for evaluating their own practices.

Nevertheless, it may be that none of these measuring instruments are appropriate for the aspect of depression that you are interested in examining. *Depression* is generally a label applied to specific behaviors that are being exhibited, and to operationalize a variable like depression, often we must consider the behaviors that led to the label's original application. These behaviors might include excessive sleeping, loss of appetite, and so forth. Excessive sleeping then becomes easier to measure than an overall concept of *depression.* Excessive sleeping could be measured by the length and times of sleep each day.

The processes of defining and operationalizing the variables are closely related and can become circular. After defining a variable the social worker may find that it is still difficult to operationalize the variables, and consequently it needs to be redefined. In fact, this circular process characterizes the entire research process in the same way that it characterizes practice.

E X A M P L E

The Variable That Is Difficult to Define

Seaberg's (1990) article in *Social Work* is devoted exclusively to the difficulties of defining an often-used concept in social work: child well-being. According to the literature, he states that the concept includes aspects of family functioning, healthy/normal families, social indicators and quality of life, child protective service guidelines, moral philosophy, and the child well-being scales. Seaberg concludes:

> *Because it [child well-being] is highly abstract and value based, caution must be exercised in using the concept child well-being and in allowing it to become institutionalized in policy and decision making about families. . . . the likelihood of ever developing a specific conceptualization of child well-being that would achieve a high level of consensus throughout U.S. society seems remote (p. 271)*

We should keep this issue in mind when we consider some frequently encountered social work concepts. Global terms, such as *child well-being,* can be defined in many different ways.

Goals and Activities: Defining and Operationalizing

One type of defining and operationalizing that demands a separate discussion is when the generalist social worker conducts a summative program evaluation to determine if the outcome of a program has been achieved. This type of research requires a specific strategy that involves defining and operationalizing the goals and activities of the program to be evaluated.

First, we need to specify what we mean by *goal* and *activity*. People use these terms in different ways, which further confuses the matter. A *goal* usually refers to the end product, "an end that one strives to obtain" (*Webster's*, 1980). Occasionally, people use the terms *goals* and *objectives* synonymously, or they use *goals* to refer to a long-term end product and *objective* to refer to a short-term end. An *activity*, at least in this context, refers to the means by which the goal is achieved.

In a program called Adolescent Family Life, the goals of the program might be to

▶ Reduce the rate of high-risk babies born to adolescents

▶ Reduce the rate of child abuse and neglect among teenage parents

The activities may include

▶ Providing prenatal care to adolescents

▶ Providing parenting classes to teenage parents

The next step is to define and operationalize these goals and activities. The first goal—reduce the rate of high-risk babies born to adolescents—requires us to define *adolescents* and *high risk*. We might decide to define *adolescent* as 18 years and under and *high risk* as low birth weight and/or premature. Of course, we would then need to operationalize these latter two terms—*low birth weight* perhaps as under 5½ pounds at birth and *premature* as less than a 32-week pregnancy. We would continue defining and operationalizing the other goal and the activities in a similar manner.

Use of Focus Groups

A **focus group** is a special group formed to help develop the research question. It is made up of people who are informed about the topic under study. The focus group helps develop the question by making suggestions about the definitions of the question, ways of collecting the data, and other issues related to planning the research. A focus group can be particularly useful in the designing stage of a program evaluation or needs assessment.

> *A focus group can be defined as a carefully planned discussion designed to obtain perceptions of a defined area of interest in a permissive non-threatening environment. It is conducted with approximately seven to ten people by a skilled interviewer. The discussion is relaxed, comfortable, and often enjoyable for participants as they share their ideas and perceptions. Group members influence each other by responding to ideas and comments in the discussion. (Krueger, 1988, p. 18)*

The focus group is informal. The researcher asks participants focused questions with the emphasis on sharing information. Sometimes the focus group can be a study in itself, rather than a precursor to the other data collection methods.

Levels of Measurement

Another step in the development of the research question is considering the level of measurement. The **level of measurement** refers to the extent to which a variable can be quantified and subsequently subject to certain mathematical or statistical procedures. Quantification involves establishing a number to a variable, and it depends, as you might guess, on how the variable is being operationalized. Using our example of measuring depression, we could count the number of hours the client sleeps each night, use an already developed measure such as the Generalized Contentment Scale, or have the client simply note each day whether or not she was depressed. Each measure involves us assigning numbers in different ways, and consequently they result in different levels of measurement. Four different levels of measurement can be identified: nominal, ordinal, interval, and ratio (see Table 3.1).

The **nominal** level of measurement classifies observations into mutually exclusive categories, with no ordering to the categories. Phenomena are assigned to categories based on some similarity or difference (for example, ethnicity, gender, marital status). Numbers are assigned to nominal categories, but the numbers themselves have no inherent meaning. For example, 1 is assigned to Hispanic and 2 to African American, but the numbers could be reversed and no meaning would be lost. The use of numbers with nominal data is arbitrary. In our example of depression, the client recording the absence (no) or presence (yes) of depression each day would result in a nominal level of measurement, as would other yes/no responses to questions.

The **ordinal** level of measurement classifies observations into mutually exclusive categories that have an inherent order to them. An ordinal level of measurement can often be used when we are examining attitudes. Respondents to a survey may be asked whether they agree with a particular statement, and the alternatives might be as follows:

strongly agree

agree

disagree

strongly disagree

These responses are ordered in sequence from strongly agree to strongly disagree (or vice versa) and are numbered 1 to 4. Nevertheless, although these values are placed in sequence and are meaningful in that sense, the distance between each of the values is not necessarily equal and may be somewhat arbitrary.

Interval measurement classifies observations into mutually exclusive categories with an inherent order and equal spacing between the categories.

TABLE 3.1 *Levels of measurement*

Level of measurement	Definition	Example
Nominal	Data are assigned to categories based on similarity or difference.	Ethnicity, marital status, yes / no responses
Ordinal	Data are sequenced in some order.	Many attitude and opinion questions
Interval	Data are sequenced in some order, and the distances between the different points are equal.	IQ, GRE scores
Ratio	Data are sequenced in some order, the distances between the different points are equal, and each value reflects an absolute magnitude. The zero point reflects an absence of the value.	Years of age, number of children, miles to place of employment

This equal distance differentiates the interval level from the ordinal level of measurement. A good example of an interval scale is the IQ test: The difference between an IQ of 120 and 130 is the same as that between 110 and 120. Nevertheless, the interval level of measurement does not allow one to make any statements about the magnitude of one value in relation to another. It is not possible to claim that someone with an IQ of 160 has twice the IQ of someone with an IQ of 80.

The **ratio** level of measurement possesses all the characteristics of the interval level of measurement along with reflecting the absolute magnitude of the value. Put another way, the zero point reflects an absence of the occurrence of that value. Measurements of income, years of education, the number of times a behavior occurs all constitute examples of ratio levels of measurement. In the depression example, counting the number of hours of sleep each night would result in a ratio level of measurement.

Note that most variables can be defined to allow for different levels of measurement. Our example of depression is one case; anger is another. For example, a variable such as anger can be measured at various levels. If the question is posed "Do you think your child is angry?" with the possible responses of yes or no, this constitutes a nominal level of measurement. If the question was "To what extent do you think your child is angry?" and the respondent is offered a scale:

very aggressive

aggressive

not aggressive

this would be an ordinal level of measurement. If anger is measured as one component in a personality test such as the Minnesota Multiphasic Personality Inventory (MMPI), the resulting level of measurement would be interval. Finally, if anger is defined in behavioral components, for example, the number of times the child hit another in an hour, it would be possible to use a ratio level of measurement.

These levels of measurement have important implications for the statistical analysis of research results. We will examine these implications in Chapters 9 and 10. For now, remember to strive for the highest level of measurement, that is, ratio level. But, as may already be apparent, many of the variables used in social work research are difficult to measure at this level.

The Agency and Developing the Question

Sometimes much of the development of the research question occurs before we are involved. Often, variables have already been identified, defined, and operationalized by those who initially conceived of the research question: our supervisors, the agency administrators, the funding organization, or individuals or groups in the community.

Don't be discouraged if this happens. Work with what you have, and remember that this is only the beginning of the research. Often you can enhance the future development of the project through your research knowledge and your skills as an agency-based generalist practitioner. Don't forget that research is a team endeavor.

Ethical Issues in Developing the Question

Inclusion of Relevant Variables

The major ethical issue at the developing of the question stage of the research process is determining what variables and their values to include in the research question. We need to be certain we have included all the variables in the study that are important. In a needs assessment, it might be tempting to leave out some factors that we think may not support the need we are trying to document. In surveying a community to assess the need for an elder day care center, we may want to leave out variables such as transportation need because if these needs are high, this might jeopardize the eventual funding of the project. However, all variables that are perceived to be important to the study should be included.

Avoiding Reductionism

An associated issue that we discussed previously is reductionism. We need to avoid looking at only one type of variable (for instance, economic factors) and claiming, if an association is found, that it is only this variable that is responsible for the particular outcome. This can be a danger when carrying out program evaluations because we will be tempted to look only at the variables associated with the program, rather than considering others. For example, if we are evaluating a program that is intended to enhance self-esteem among high school dropouts, we will undoubtedly include the program-related variables such as length of time in the program and so on. However, we may not consider measuring outside factors that could also influence self-esteem, such as involvement in a local sports activity. These other factors may turn out to have more impact than the program itself, but we may be reluctant to include them because they jeopardize the demonstrated efficacy of the program. In our discussion of group design in Chapter 6 we look at some ways to consider other factors. For now, simply take note of this possible source of bias and begin to think about what some of these other factors might be.

Human Diversity Issues in Developing the Question

In developing the question, we must look carefully at human diversity issues to ensure that we are not building in biases against certain groups. This involves us being familiar enough with the nature of the units of analysis and the nature of the research question to be able to include the relevant variables and operationalize them appropriately in ways that do not exclude certain groups. In part, this issue underlies the argument for encouraging more minorities and diverse groups to conduct research that has implications for themselves.

As we discussed in the last chapter, traditionally there has been a predominance of studies conducted by white middle-class men, resulting in an inherent bias not only in the selection of the types of research questions but also in the researchers, as outsiders, not understanding the issues. Consequently, the necessary variables are not included in the studies. As Becerra and Tambrana (1985) state in their article on methodological approaches to research on Hispanics, "Clearly, the major advantages of having Hispanics conduct research on Hispanics is that, it is assumed, Hispanic researchers will be sensitive to and understand the cultural norms and language" (p. 43). However, the authors also point out that simply "being Hispanic" does not ensure cultural sensitivity or knowledge; an awareness of subgroups should also be considered (for example, some Hispanic subgroups are Cuban, Mexican American, Spanish, Puerto Rican), as well as the level of acculturation and social economic class.

Bowman (1983) addresses the issue of who conducts research, particularly with African Americans, by using two concepts: significant involvement and functional relevance. Significant involvement is when the members of the group under study have a central role in the research, including the decision making at each stage of the research process. Functional relevance refers to studies that promote the expressed needs and perspectives of the study population. Significant involvement need not necessarily result in functional relevance and vice versa. Bowman argues that both of these concepts need to be considered in conducting research with minorities to ensure that minority concerns are addressed in research studies.

Similar arguments are presented in support of more women-centered research. Women tend not to conduct research in social work (Davis, 1986). Consequently, certain questions are not asked, and the content of research questions is not necessarily relevant to women. For example, when studies were conducted on work satisfaction, it was unusual to include variables that related to family issues, which are often of primary concern for women but traditionally have not been for men. Thus, a biased picture was portrayed, depicting women's lives in a male framework.

To broaden the idea of diverse group representatives conducting research, community members at large need to be involved as much as possible in the development of projects to enhance the responsiveness of the evaluation as a means of empowerment. The Cornell Empowerment Project (1989) suggests that evaluation should be as *inclusive* as possible, involving

▶ People who develop and use the program (for example, funders, agency boards, program staff)
▶ Direct and indirect beneficiaries of the program
▶ People who suffer a disadvantage related to the program (for example, groups at a political disadvantage)

A final point concerning who conducts the research relates to the potential problem of people studying themselves. This becomes an issue when we have members of an organization or agency evaluating their own performance or members of a particular ethnicity or culture studying themselves. Although this can provide some important insights, these types of evaluations need to be counterbalanced by evaluations and assessments of outsiders. Focus groups can be an excellent means of at least partially ensuring that a number of people from diverse groups have an impact on the design and implementation of the research.

E X A M P L E

A Focus Group

Foster (1988) examined the opinions of low-income black men and women concerning whether or not they could earn their way out of poverty and how they might do so. The author used four focus groups of employed and unemployed men and women from the Washington, D.C., area. Although the results from this study were used for policy development rather than for the immediate development of a planned research study, focus groups can provide important insights for the design and implementation of a larger study because they directly reflect the opinions of the subjects.

Summary

The unit of analysis is what or whom we are studying. We use units of analysis to aggregate their characteristics in describing some larger group or abstract phenomenon. Units of analysis can be individuals, groups, or social artifacts. We must distinguish between variables and values. The definition and operationalization of variables includes defining goals and activities. Focus groups can be helpful in developing research questions. Another step in developing the question involves the level of measurement: nominal, ordinal, interval, and ratio. We should strive for the ratio level of measurement.

Often the generalist social worker does not have much influence on developing the research question. Ethical issues include ensuring the identification of relevant variables and avoiding reductionism. Human diversity issues are emphasizing and encouraging the participation of diverse groups in the development of the question.

Study/Exercise Questions

1 Look at some research articles in *Social Work* and identify the unit of analysis used in the study. Also identify the independent and dependent variables when appropriate.

2 You are involved in an evaluation of a support group for parents of children with developmental disabilities.

   a Identify some possible goals and activities of the group.

   b Name at least five variables you would need to include in the evaluation.

   c Define and operationalize these variables.

3 You have been asked to assist in designing and implementing a needs assessment for an elder day care facility in your community. Who would you consult in the early stages of developing the assessment?

4 If you are in a field placement, talk to your supervisor. If not, talk to someone who is employed in a supervisory position in an agency in your community. Find out how he or she has involved others in research projects in the agency.

Further Reading

Burgess, R. G. (Ed.). (1986). *Key variables in social investigation.* London: Routledge & Kegan Paul.

   Presents 10 of the most commonly used social science variables and discusses their underlying concepts and the ways in which they have operationalized.

Krueger, R. A. (1988). *Focus groups: A practical guide for applied research.* Newbury Park, CA: Sage Publications.

> A thorough coverage of the use of focus groups in research. Topics include when to use them, how to form them, and how to use them as a research tool.

References

Becerra, R. M., & Tambrana, R. E. (1985). Methodological approaches to research on Hispanics. *Social Work Research and Abstracts, 21*(2), 42–49.

Beckett, J. O. (1988). Plant closings: How older workers are affected. *Social Work, 33*(1), 29–33.

Bowman, P. J. (1983). Significant involvement and functional relevance: Challenges to survey research. *Social Work Research and Abstracts, 19*(4), 21–26.

Cornell Empowerment Project. (1989). Evaluation consistent with the empowerment process. *Networking Bulletin.* Ithaca, NY: Cornell University, Cornell Empowerment Project.

Davis, L. V. (1986). A feminist approach to social work research. *Affilia, 1,* 32–47.

Foster, J. M. (1988). *Getting ahead: What poor people think about their chances of earning their way out of poverty.* Washington, DC: Greater Washington Research Center.

Hamilton, M. (1967). A rating scale for primary depressive illness. *British Journal of School and Clinical Psychology, 6,* 178–296.

Hudson, W. (1990). *The multiproblem screening inventory.* Tempe, AZ: Walmyr Publishing.

Krueger, R. A. (1988). *Focus groups: A practical guide for applied research.* Newbury Park, CA: Sage Publications.

Lieberman, A. A., Hornby, H., & Russell, M. (1988). Analyzing the educational backgrounds and work experiences of child welfare personnel: A national study. *Social Work, 33,* 485–489.

Matacin, M. L., & Burger, J. M. (1987). A content analysis of sexual themes in *Playboy* cartoons. *Sex Roles, 17*(3/4), 179–186.

Radloff, L. (1977). The CES-ED Scale: A self-report depression scale for research in the general population. *Journal of Applied Psychological Measurement, 1,* 385–401.

Rubin, A., & Babbie, E. (1989). *Research methods for social work*. Belmont, CA: Wadsworth.

Seaberg, J. R. (1990). Child well-being: A feasible concept? *Social Work, 35*, 267–272.

Tracy, E. M. (1990). Identifying social support resources of at-risk families. *Social Work, 35,* 252–258.

Webster's New Collegiate Dictionary. (1980). Springfield, MA: G. & C. Merriam Co.

Collecting the Data

4

Now that the research question has been determined, how do we gather the information? Do we got out and interview people directly? Do we use forms and questionnaires to collect this information? Or maybe we need to observe the problem?

After defining and conceptualizing the problem in generalist practice, we must decide how information will be collected. This information is referred to in both practice and research as **data** (singular, **datum**), and the way in which they are collected is known as the **measuring instrument** or the **data collection method.** These methods include questionnaires, observation, logs/journals, interviews, and secondary data. All of these will be described in this chapter.

As a generalist social worker, you may or may not actually collect the data. The plan and perhaps even the data collection may have already been implemented. Often you will be brought into the research at this stage to help with the data collection. Even if you don't direct the collection of the data, you will still find it useful to understand why a certain measuring instrument is being used and what the strengths and the weaknesses are of the different data collection methods.

This chapter will include a discussion of

- ▶ Quantitative and qualitative approaches
- ▶ Ways of collecting the data
- ▶ Who collects the data
- ▶ Combining data collection methods
- ▶ Determining reliability and validity
- ▶ The agency and data collection

▶ Ethical issues in collecting the data

▶ Human diversity issues in collecting the data

Quantitative and Qualitative Approaches

Before we embark on a discussion of the different ways in which data can be collected, we need to distinguish between two research methods that in part determine both the types of data that are collected and the ways in which the data are collected and then analyzed. These two approaches are the quantitative and qualitative methods (see Table 4.1).

The **quantitative** method creates categories of the phenomenon under study prior to investigation and assigns numbers to these categories, that is, quantifies and then carries out statistical analyses. Generally, the quantitative approach uses data collection methods such as questionnaires or very structured interviews and observations. We will discuss these in detail in the following chapters. For example, in assessing the success of a support group, you might use such quantitative measures as the number of groups attended by the clients or their satisfaction scores on a questionnaire. This approach is useful when we need the responses of many subjects (for example, over 30) to a set of questions and particularly when we are conducting explanatory research. Until relatively recently, this quantitative approach has been regarded as the best and most rigorous way to conduct scientific research.

The **qualitative** method involves the nonnumerical examination of phenomena. It focuses on the underlying meanings and patterns of relationships. The qualitative method may only look at one or two cases, and it uses unstructured interviews or observations to collect the data. Using the qualitative ap-

TABLE 4.1 *A comparison of quantitative and qualitative methods*

Quantitative	*Qualitative*
Create categories prior to investigation	Categories emerge as a result of the investigation
Use of a large number of subjects (e.g., over 30)	Use of a small number of subjects (e.g., sometimes only 4 or 5)
Use statistical techniques to analyze the results	Use narrative techniques to analyze the results
Usually collects data with questionnaires, structured interviews, observation	Usually collects data with unstructured interviews, observation, logs / journals

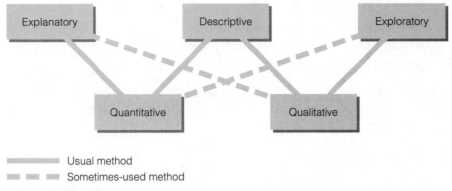

Usual method
Sometimes-used method

FIGURE 4.1 *The relationship between quantitative and qualitative methods and type of research strategy*

proach on the support group example, you might interview the group members about the ways in which they found it beneficial or not beneficial. Recently in social work research we have seen increasing interest in the qualitative approach to research methods.

In Chapter 2 we introduced the term *ethnography*, defining it as a way of describing a group or culture. We need to note here that some argue this term is synonymous with qualitative research methods. However, for our purposes we will keep the terms distinct; we adopt the position that qualitative methods include those characteristics discussed above and that ethnography may involve both qualitative and quantitative methods.

Each of the three types of research questions we have been considering could use a qualitative or quantitative (or a combination) strategy. For example, for a program evaluation in which we are especially interested in understanding the internal dynamics of the program (we referred to this type of program evaluation earlier as the *summative* type), we ask such questions as: What makes this program work? How do the staff and clients interact? and so forth. Here a qualitative approach may be more effective because the answers can provide a detailed description of the program. If, however, the program evaluation question is specifically concerned with whether the goals of the program have been met—including the number of clients who have been successful in the program—then a quantitative approach might be more appropriate.

Thus, the choice of a qualitative or quantitative approach in part depends on the nature of the research strategy and research question. We must stress that we use qualitative or quantitative methods interchangeably to answer different types of questions. However, there is a certain link between explanatory strategies and the use of quantitative methods and exploratory strategies and the use of qualitative methods. Descriptive strategies may use either qualitative or quantitative methods (see Figure 4.1). Additionally, sometimes we use both qualitative and quantitative methods in the same study.

E X A M P L E

Combining Qualitative and Quantitative Methods in a Program Evaluation

Fraser and Haapala (1987–88) conducted an evaluation of a family preservation program by using qualitative data collection methods to describe the treatment intervention and quantitative data collection methods to measure outcome.

The qualitative data were collected from mothers, children, and therapists, who identified what they considered to be critical incidents in the treatment intervention: interruptions, practice of new skills, moments of insight, and so on. The quantitative outcome measure was whether or not the children were placed out of home.

The findings indicated that specific interventions such as the provision of concrete assistance to families and the number of treatment session interruptions were positively associated with successful outcomes.

Although we may consider whether a qualitative or quantitative method will be used early on in the research project, it is not until the data collection phase that this decision really has an impact.

Ways of Collecting the Data

Five major methods of collecting data, or measuring instruments, will be described in this section (see Figure 4.2):

◗ Interviews

◗ Questionnaires

◗ Observation techniques

◗ Logs/Journals

◗ Secondary data

We will discuss the scales that can be used in conjunction with any of the above methods. Each of the five methods will also be assessed for objectivity and applicability as we describe them.

Objectivity, one of the characteristics of the scientific method, entails being free of attitudes, opinions, and points of view. However, as we discussed in Chapter 1, research cannot be completely objective; instead, it is constantly influenced by the wider context of the research. Nevertheless, we still strive for as much objectivity as possible. To a large extent, the degree of objectivity is

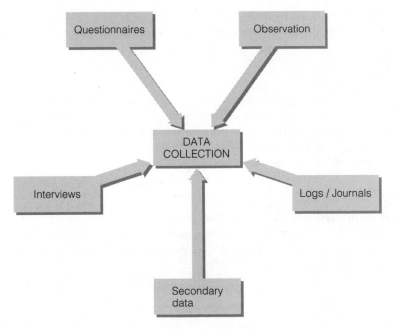

FIGURE 4.2 *Methods of data collection*

dependent upon the type of measuring instrument or data collection method selected. Some instruments allow us to be more objective than others.

Although it is important to consider the potential objectivity of a measuring instrument, it is also necessary to assess the *applicability* of a measuring instrument, that is, whether or not it is appropriate and suitable for a particular type of problem. For example, observation would typically not be a useful method to employ if we were collecting information on child abuse, but would be suitable for collecting information on child behavior problems. Each data collection method will be described, along with a discussion of both its strengths and weaknesses in terms of objectivity and its relative applicability for the kinds of research questions we encounter as generalist social workers.

Interviews

As a generalist social work student, you are already quite skilled at conducting interviews. Interviews are structured, semistructured, or unstructured. Often, the questions may be very similar, but the interviews are distinguished based on how they are conducted.

Structured Interviews

In a **structured interview,** the interviewer knows in advance the questions to ask and in many cases is simply administering a verbal questionnaire. Often this questionnaire has already been developed by the agency. The structured interview is probably the most common method of collecting data for generalist social workers.

Semistructured Interviews

In a **semistructured interview,** the interviewer has more freedom to pursue hunches and can improvise with the questions. Semistructured interviews often use interview schedules consisting of the general types of questions to ask, but they are not in a questionnaire format. Sometimes semistructured interviews are referred to as open-ended interviews.

Unstructured Interviews

Completely **unstructured interviews** can also be used. This type of interview is similar to a conversation except that the interviewer and interviewee know that an interview is being conducted and that the interviewee is privy to information of interest to the interviewer.

E X A M P L E

A Structured Interview

Surber, Dwyer, Ryan, Goldfinger, and Kelly (1988) examined medical and psychiatric needs of the homeless. Researchers interviewed the homeless at shelters and at a food line using a standardized questionnaire. In this study, the researchers seemed to have specific questions in mind, presumably questions drawn from previous research of the homeless. Obviously, the questionnaire could not be mailed, so face-to-face administration of the questionnaire was the chosen data collection method.

E X A M P L E

A Semistructured Interview

Lusk, Peralta, and Vest (1989) conducted a study of street children of Juarez, Mexico. They collected data from 103 children using a combination of direct observation and semistructured or open-ended interviews. They asked questions relating to the general characteristics of the street children, type of employment, school attendance, drug abuse, gang membership, and child abuse history.

Objectivity   Although structured and semistructured interviews are more objective than unstructured interviews (because asking specific questions minimizes some bias), in general, the objectivity of interviewing is limited. We know that we respond differently to different people depending on how we are approached. With the question, "Do you think there is a need for a Y in this community?" the answer will be influenced by several factors: the interviewer's age, gender, ethnicity, and dress; the context in which the interviewer approaches the interviewee; the manner in which the interviewer speaks; and so forth. In addition, these characteristics will not have a constant effect on all the interviewees. Instead, each interviewee will respond differently to these characteristics depending on previous experiences. In fact, there will be a **reactive effect**: the interviewer will influence the interviewee, the interviewee will respond in a particular way, which will then cause a feedback effect on the interviewer. Consequently, objectivity is unlikely.

E X A M P L E

A Possible Reactive Effect

In the Surber and colleagues (1988) study on medical and psychiatric needs of the homeless, interviewers noticed that the men were generally cooperative and friendly and the women were fearful, suspicious, and hostile. The researchers suspected that this might be due to the gender of the interviewer, which could be producing a reactive effect. However, they found that these reactions held true regardless of whether the interviewer was male or female.

Some of the problems undermining the objectivity of interviews can be overcome by training the interviewers. They can be given an explicit protocol or format that they are required to follow. As a generalist social worker, you may be required to conduct interviews of this type. Also, audio recordings of the interviews allow review of them. However, recordings can sometimes inhibit the interviewees, resulting in a distortion of their responses.

The advantage of interviews is that they allow ambiguous questions to be clarified, thus increasing objectivity. This opportunity does not exist when questionnaires are administered, particularly by mail. Then respondents interpret the questions in their own way, which may be very different from the intention of the researchers when they developed the questions.

Interviewing also has a positive effect on the **response rate**: the proportion of people who respond to the questions in either a questionnaire or interview. We have all been asked to participate in research—on the telephone, on the street, or through the mail. Sometimes we agree and sometimes we refuse to participate. For researchers, a problem arises when many people refuse to participate because these people might turn out to be very different from those who do. For example, if we send out 100 questionnaires asking about people's experiences of childhood sexual abuse and receive back only 25—all of whom state they were not abused as children—we have no way of knowing if the non-respondents were all abused and were reluctant to disclose this on their questionnaire, or were not abused and decided not to respond, or were distributed between abused and not abused. Because we do not know which of the preceding cases holds, the results will be biased and will lack objectivity. However, interviews generally ensure a high response rate. This is particularly true for face-to-face interviews, less so for telephone interviews.

Nevertheless, the high response rate of even face-to-face interviews is not always assured. Again, referring to the Surber et al. (1988) study of medical and psychiatric needs of the homeless, 20 percent of the men and 50 percent of the women refused to participate. The response rate does not only depend on the method of data collection; other factors include the characteristics of the subjects, the purpose and nature of the research question/project, and the characteristics and training of those applying the data collection instruments. For example, First, Roth, and Arewa (1988) may have obtained a higher response rate (90 percent) with their study of minority homeless because

> *Interviewers were selected for their ability to engage subjects, to be comfortable in settings where homeless persons could be found, and to develop rapport with homeless persons. All 42 interviewers had at least a bachelor's degree and most had considerable social science training. (p. 121)*

Applicability   Interviewing can be used in preference to other techniques when we are interested in the following:

▶ A high response rate.

▶ Finding out as much as possible about an issue. Qualitative research studies often use this approach to fully explore all the dimensions of a phenomenon.

▶ Anonymity is not of primary importance. If you research involves a sensitive issue—such as the incidence of spouse abuse in a community—and the sample consists of individuals with whom we have never had any previous contact, interviewing would not be an appropriate data collection method. People are usually reluctant to share such sensitive information.

▶ Time and money are of no great object. Interviews are time consuming, particularly if we are interested in getting responses from a large geographic area. In addition, interviewers often need to be trained. Consequently, this data collection method is expensive. If the budget is low and the sample large, interviewing would not be the data collection method of choice.

▶ The respondent is not comfortable with writing or is illiterate.

Questionnaires

In general, questionnaires have many advantages that interviews do not have; at the same time, they lack the strengths of interviews. There are several types of questionnaires.

Mailed Questionnaires

Mailing questionnaires is a popular method of distributing questionnaires. Agencies often use this method to survey their clients as part of a program evaluation or needs assessment.

E X A M P L E

A Mailed Questionnaire

Peterson (1990) carried out a survey of 476 members of NASW to determine their characteristics, educational background, and perceptions of the field of aging. A mailed questionnaire was used to collect the data. Respondents perceived that the field of aging would be much larger and more important in the future, and they recommended increased gerontological preparation for all social work students.

Face-to-Face Questionnaires

Face-to-face questionnaires may be administered similarly to structured interviews. Structured interviews can be thought of as verbally administered questionnaires.

E X A M P L E

A Face-to-Face Questionnaire

In the Surber et al. (1988) study of the homeless, interviewers administered a standardized questionnaire at the shelters and at the food line.

Group Questionnaires

These questionnaires are administered to groups. For example, if you are interested in getting feedback on a foster parent training session, you might administer the questionnaires to the entire group at one time.

E X A M P L E

A Group Questionnaire

In a study by Anderson, Kann, Holtzman, Arday, Truman, and Kilbe (1990), students completed self-administered questionnaires in their classroom under the direction of trained data collectors. The questionnaires were part of an effort to gather information on HIV (human immunodeficiency virus) and AIDS knowledge and sexual behavior of high school students.

Bilingual Questionnaires

These are essential in many communities and with certain populations.

E X A M P L E

A Bilingual Questionnaire

Salgado de Snyder, Cervantes, and Padilla (1990) examined gender and ethnic differences in psychosocial stress and generalized distress in 593 Hispanic immigrants, Mexican Americans, and Anglo Americans. They administered the data collection instrument (a demographic checklist, an inventory, and a scale) either in Spanish or English, depending upon the language proficiency of the respondents.

Objectivity   Questionnaires are relatively objective. Interviewer bias is absent, and the responses are clear and usually unambiguous. However, the objectivity of the responses depends a great deal on the care with which the questionnaire has been constructed. Ambiguities can be minimized by stating questions as clearly and simply as possible. This includes avoiding double-barreled questions, such as "Do you have children, how many of your children are under the age of 12?"

Just as interviews generally have high response rates, questionnaires—particularly those that are mailed—have low response rates. However, we can take some precautions to help improve the response rate, including length, structure of the questions, content of the questions, format of the questionnaire, cover letter, and follow-ups.

Length   Make the questionnaire as short as possible and eliminate unnecessary questions. When constructing a questionnaire, for each question ask yourself, "How is this question relevant to my research question?" If you cannot come up with a good answer, drop the question.

Structure of the Questions   Questions can be structured in two ways: closed-ended and open-ended. A **closed-ended question** only gives the respondent a certain number of categories to respond to as answers. An example of a closed-ended question is

> *How many children under the age of 12 are*
>
> *presently living in your home?*   _____ 0
>   _____ 1
>   _____ 2
>   _____ 3 or more

These are easy for the researcher to understand once the questionnaire is returned, but it is important to ensure that all possible categories are included for the respondent.

An **open-ended question** leaves it up to the respondent to create a response. No alternatives are given. An example of an open-ended question is

> *What kinds of improvements would you suggest the day care center*
>
> *make in this next year?* _____.

Open-ended questions can be intimidating to respondents and they may be put off by them, but this type of question ensures that respondents can answer in ways that accurately reflect their views, that is, they are not forced to respond within the researcher's categories. Open-ended questions are particularly useful when we do not know a great deal about the subject that we are investigating, that is, in exploratory research. They also provide a way of collecting qualitative data.

Content of the Questions   One strategy for increasing the response rate is to limit sensitive questions, or if they have to be included, embed them within the questionnaire. The same holds true for many demographic questions such as gender and educational level. Instead of starting the questionnaire with these questions, place them at the end. It can be discouraging if these are the first questions because they do not interest most respondents.

Format of the Questionnaire   The response rate can also be enhanced by the overall packaging of the questionnaire. Make sure it is free of typographical and spelling errors. Ensure that the layout is clear and uncluttered.

Cover Letter   If you are mailing the questionnaire, include a cover letter that very briefly describes the purpose of the study and encourages the person to respond. You may want to include a small incentive, such as a quarter, coupons, or a pen. Of course, the person should never be coerced to respond. Also, emphasize in the cover letter that responses will be kept confidential. An example of a cover letter is shown in Figure 4.3.

We would like to ask you to take a few minutes to complete this questionnaire. This is part of a study being carried out by the Department of Social Work on women and employment. Your answers will help in the planning of services and programs in order to assist working women like yourself.

Please do not write your name on the questionnaire as your answers will be completely confidential.

This questionnaire will be picked up tomorrow.

If you have any questions about the study, please ask the person who is distributing the questionnaire, or call me at 646-2143.

Christine Marlow, Ph.D.
Associate Professor of Social Work

P.S. If you are interested in receiving results from this study (available in about 6 months) or would be willing to be interviewed in person so that we can obtain more detailed information, please complete and return the following section.

☐ Yes, I would like to receive the results of this study

☐ Yes, I would be willing to be interviewed

Name _____

Address _____

_____

Telephone _____

Return this to the person who picks up the questionnaire or mail to me at:

Department of Social Work
New Mexico State University
Las Cruces, NM 88003

THANK YOU

FIGURE 4.3 *Example of a cover letter*

Follow-ups   Second mailings can enhance the response ratio of mailed questionnaires by about 10%. However, they do add to the cost of the project.

Even with careful design and administration of the questionnaire, response rates can still suffer. As we discussed in relation to interviews, other facts can influence the response rate besides the structure of the instrument or the way it is administered. These factors include the topics and variables included in the research itself.

E X A M P L E

Factors Influencing the Response Rate

As part of a follow-up study on clients who had received surveys from an agency, Sirles (1984) found that certain factors could be identified as influencing the response rate, factors that apparently had very little to do with the instrument itself. These factors included the client's counselor, the reason for termination, the number of sessions, and the amount of improvement as assessed by the counselor.

Applicability Questionnaires can be used in preference to other data collection techniques when:

- ◗ A high response rate is not a top priority
- ◗ Objectivity is critical
- ◗ Anonymity is important
- ◗ Budgets are limited, although extensive mailings of questionnaires can also be expensive
- ◗ The respondents are literate

Observation

Not all phenomena can be measured by interviews or questionnaires. Examples of these types of phenomena include illegal behaviors or children's behavior. If we are interested in a child's behavior in the classroom, interviewing or administering a questionnaire to the child would probably not elicit objective responses. As a social work student, you have probably already realized that observation is an integral part of social work practice, and you have probably already learned to be a good observer. Observation can be structured or unstructured.

Structured Observation

This observation occurs when the behaviors are known and categorized prior to the observation. If a quantitative approach is adopted, structured observation is the method of choice. In **structured observation,** behaviors are categorized prior to the observation according to their characteristics, including their *frequency, duration,* or *magnitude.* These categories can then be quantified.

Let's take the example of trying to measure a child's inattention in the classroom. First, *inattention* needs to be clearly defined, perhaps as "talking with other children without permission from the teacher." Frequency would measure the number of occasions during a specified period of time (for example, one hour), the child talked with other children without permission. Duration would note the length of time the child talked, and magnitude would record how loudly the child talked within a specified period of time. Clearly, the selection of the method of observation depends on what behavior is being measured, how the behavior is defined, and how often it occurs.

E X A M P L E

An Observational Approach

Bales Interaction Process Analysis (1950) has been used extensively for research in social interaction. This instrument codes interactive verbal and nonverbal behaviors into different categories, including "shows solidarity," "agrees," and "asks for opinion." This instrument can be used in studying group work.

Unstructured Observation

Unstructured observation is used when little is known about the behaviors being observed and so is appropriate for exploratory research. Unstructured observation is used extensively in anthropology for studying unfamiliar cultures. This type of observation provides qualitative data.

The observer interacts to varying degrees with those being observed. When the observer fully submerges him- or herself to become one of the observed group, this is known as **participant observation.** A classic example of participant observation in social work is having the observer become a member of a gang in order to observe gang behavior.

E X A M P L E

Participant Observation

Kibria (1989), when studying the patterns of Vietnamese refugee women's wagework, used participated observation along with in-depth interviews and the administration of a questionnaire. The findings indicated that Vietnamese-American women play an important part in familial economic strategies. The author urges that further investigations in this area continue to use less conventional methods of data collection, including participant observation, "in order to capture the full range of women's informal and formal wagework experiences" (p. 320).

Objectivity   Observation varies in its objectivity and depends a great deal on the type of observation, level of training, and control for reactivity.

Type of Observation   Generally, structured observation is more objective than unstructured. This is because the behaviors are defined beforehand. With unstructured observation, there is not this clarity of definition. In addition, in unstructured observation, the observer's involvement in the behavior can further bias the observation.

The Level of Training   The more training the observers receive regarding the procedures to be followed for the observation, the greater the objectivity. Often, particularly in structured observation, the categories are not immediately apparent, no matter how much care was taken in their development. Observers may need to be instructed in what is meant by, for example, "asks for opinion."

Control for Reactivity   Reactivity, or the reactive effect, refers to the problem of the observer's behavior inhibiting or affecting the subject's behavior in some way. (We discussed this problem earlier in regard to interviewing.) We can partially control reactivity by using one or more of the following four strategies: videotapes, one-way mirrors, time with observer, and participant observation. A videotape recorder can be used to record behavior, however, this may further inhibit the subject. Second, sometimes one-way mirrors can be used, although we must be sure to obtain consent from those being observed. A third method for controlling reactivity is for the observer to spend some time with the subject so that the subject can become more comfortable with the observation. For example, if you want to observe classroom behavior, sit in the classroom for some time before you actually make the observation. Finally, we can overcome some reactivity effects with participant observation.

One further comment regarding objectivity is that observation need not always be visual. Sometimes enough information can be gained by listening to audio recordings. Maybe you have already used this method of observation as a means of improving your practice. However, it is important to remember that without the nonverbal interaction, objectivity can be decreased due to possible misinterpretation of the communication.

Applicability   Observation can be used in preference to other data collection techniques when:

▶ Behaviors are difficult to measure using other techniques.

▶ Observers and funds are available for training.

▶ Objectivity is not a priority (as is the case with participant observation).

Logs/Journals

Sometimes logs, journals, or diaries can be used to collect data. These could be considered forms of self-observation but really warrant a separate discussion

---

SOCIAL WORKER'S JOURNAL RECORD OF A HOME VISIT TO A CLIENT
Thursday, February 15

Tonight I visited Art A. again. The house looked dark when I pulled up, and I felt kind of uneasy. I went through all the safety precautions I had learned previously and then went to the door and knocked. My stomach felt jittery. Finally, after several minutes, I heard footsteps inside and Art opened the door. He looked kind of disheveled and I sensed that he was upset about something, but he asked me very politely to come in and sit down. The house was so dark! I asked him to turn on some lights, and I sat near the door, just in case. Something just didn't feel right. Then it hit me—his dog Spike hadn't barked when I knocked and that dog was his constant companion. I didn't want to ask him about Spike because I was sure it was bad. I felt a lump forming in my throat. What a great social worker I am! I'm supposed to be calm, cool, and collected! I guess if I didn't empathize though, I wouldn't have been there in the first place. Sure enough, Spike was dead—he'd been run over by a car.

CLIENT'S LOG OF DRINKING BEHAVIOR
Monday

10:00   I took my break at work and had a couple of sips of George's beer (he brings it in his lunch pail).

12:00   Drank 2 beers with lunch.

5:00   Stopped after work at Charlie's Grill and had 3 beers and 2 or 3 shots of whiskey, which my friends bought for me.

7:00   Jack Daniels before dinner (on the rocks).

8:00   3–4 beers watching the Broncos whip the Cowboys.

11:00   Went to buy cigs and stopped at Fred's bar, had a couple of beers.

1:00   Had a shot of whiskey before bed to help me get to sleep.

FIGURE 4.4 *Examples of journal and log recordings*

from observation. Logs, journals, or diaries—as with observation—can be structured or unstructured.

The client may record his or her own behavior, or the social worker may record the client's behavior. Logs and journals are also used by social workers to record their own behavior. In Figure 4.4, the social worker is assessing her feelings and reactions in a home visit by recording in a journal. Logs are typically unstructured and can allow for a stream of consciousness type of data collection.

Objectivity   Objectivity can be fairly limited, particularly if the logs or journals are not structured or guided in some way. Objectivity can be enhanced by the use of more structured journals/logs so that the client or worker responds to specific questions. It is also helpful to encourage the client to record behaviors as soon as they occur rather than relying too much on retrospective information.

Applicability   Logs and journals can be used in preference to other data collection techniques when:

▶   Conducting an exploratory evaluation of our practice.

Secondary Data

Secondary data are forms of information that have been previously collected. These data can then be used for other research purposes. With computers, secondary data have become more accessible even to the most humble of researchers. We use secondary data all the time in generalist practice—by consulting case records that have been written by others and by referring to agency statistics when writing up reports. In fact, case records provide an important secondary data source for agency-based social work research. There are two kinds of secondary data: direct sources and indirect sources.

Direct Sources

Direct sources include statistics that are generated with the intention that they will be used for a multitude of research purposes and by a variety of different organizations. These can be at the local, state, or national level. U.S. census data is an example of a direct source; statistics are provided on all three levels.

E X A M P L E

Secondary Data Use

A study by O'Grady-LeShane (1990) uses data from the U.S. Bureau of the Census to illustrate the problem of older women and poverty. By examining these data, she found that older women's economic position depends largely on marital status. Widows and other women living alone are among the most poor.

Agencies—both private and public—are creating data banks in increasing numbers and storing information about their operations, including the number of clients served, types of target problems, outcomes, staffing patterns, and budgets. Additionally, information can be obtained on crime rates, child abuse and neglect rates, and so forth.

These types of data are particularly useful when conducting a needs assessment. Two strategies can be adopted using secondary data in a needs assessment: rates under treatment and social indicators. **Rates under treatment** approach uses existing data from agencies to determine the needs of a community. The problem with this approach is that utilization of existing services may not, in fact, reflect unmet needs.

E X A M P L E

Rates Under Treatment

Charping and Slaughter (1988) review various voluntary energy assistance programs in the United States as a means of demonstrating that the energy requirements of the poor need to be addressed. They also present the various ways in which such programs could be set up. The programs reflect the different states' treatment of energy—either as a social entitlement or as an economic commodity.

The **social indicators** approach selects demographic data from existing public records to predict a community's needs. Statistics relating to the spatial arrangement of people and facilities in a community, housing patterns, crime patterns, and so on can help us determine where, for example, to place a community center.

E X A M P L E

Social Indicators

Plotnick (1989) uses U.S. Bureau of the Census data on poverty among U.S. children as a means of demonstrating the need for alternative strategies to address child poverty. He suggests tactics such as an expanded earned income tax credit, child-support system reforms, and a medical insurance plan.

Indirect Sources

Indirect sources refer to information that can be used for research but that was initially collected for some other purpose. Indirect sources include case records, newspapers, and other media reports. For example, we may be interested in studying an agency's attitudes toward the developmentally disabled, and in doing so, we may consult case records on this topic. The most common way of dealing with indirect sources is to subject it to content analysis. **Content analysis** refers to a method of coding written communication to a systematic quantifiable form. This will be discussed further in Chapters 8 and 11.

Objectivity   When using secondary data, we need to be aware that sometimes these data have limited objectivity. This is particularly true for indirect sources, which can often be extremely biased because they were not initially collected for research purposes. For example, there may be gaps in a record that we are using. In addition, because the case records were recorded for a purpose other than for our purpose (for example, gathering information on agency attitudes toward the developmentally disabled), information relating to our research question may be missing.

Direct sources are more objective, but the researcher needs to verify the exact form of the questions that were initially asked. This is because the form of the questions asked later by the secondary researcher may be different, and we need to know what this difference is. For example, you may be interested in the number of juveniles seen by the local juvenile probation office who had a previous record of substance abuse. You may be interested primarily in alcohol use whereas the data collected did not distinguish between alcohol and other types of substance abuse. When using secondary data, you cannot assume that the first researcher's questions are similar to your own.

Colby (1982) discusses some of these problems in her article on secondary analysis. She also points out that secondary analysis is especially valuable for the study of women because theories about women, and women themselves, have undergone substantial change. Consequently, it is important to reanalyze data to determine the extent to which different results are due to a different interpretation or to, in fact, changes that have occurred over time.

Applicability   Secondary data can be used when:

▶ The data are available; this is not always the case.

▶ The definition of the secondary data variables and the form of their questions are the same (or similar) to yours. If not, you must at least be aware of the differences.

▶ A needs assessment is required and the budget is limited.

▶ You are interested in conducting a historical study (for example, the history of an agency or of the way a particular problem has been addressed in the past).

Scales

Before ending this section on different data collection methods, we need to discuss the ways in which complex and multifaceted variables can be measured. Most variables are not clear-cut and cannot be contained in one question or item; instead, they are composed of a number of different dimensions or factors. Level of functioning, marital satisfaction, and community attitudes are all of this complex type. Consequently, we need composite measures consisting of a number of items; these are referred to as **scales**. Scales can be used in interviews and questionnaires, and sometimes even in structured observation.

Scales are composed of several items "that have a logical or empirical structure to them" (Rubin & Babbie, 1989, p. G7). The most common form for social science research is the **Likert scale**. The respondent is shown a series of statements and is then asked to respond using one of five response alternatives, usually: "strongly agrees," "agrees," "no opinion," "disagrees," "strongly disagrees," or some variant of these (see an example in Figure 4.5).

Below are examples of three Likert scale questions that were used in a survey of M.S.W. students at New Mexico State University.

1. How difficult has it been for you to balance your school and personal time? (circle one)

1	2	3	4	5
Extremely difficult	Very difficult	Difficult	Somewhat difficult	Not difficult at all

2. How did you feel about the pace of your courses last semester?
   ☐ 1. The pace was far too slow. (I was bored.)
   ☐ 2. The pace was too slow.
   ☐ 3. The pace was about right for learning the material presented.
   ☐ 4. The pace was a little too fast.
   ☐ 5. The pace was far too fast. (I felt overwhelmed.)

3. How did you feel about the in-class presentations that you were required to complete last semester (the ones you did yourself or in a group)?
   ☐ 1. I feel that I learned a lot from preparing for and giving these presentations.
   ☐ 2. I feel that I learned some from preparing for and giving these presentations.
   ☐ 3. I feel that I didn't learn much from preparing for and giving these presentations.

FIGURE 4.5 *Likert scales*

Sometimes you may need a scale to measure a specific variable—for example, child well-being or aggression. Whenever possible, as with other types of data collection methods, try to use *existing* scales. This will eliminate considerable work.

Three specific types of scaling are commonly used in social work research, particularly in single-system designs: target problem scales, goal attainment scales, and rapid assessment instruments.

Target Problem Scales

We use **target problem scales** as a means of tracking the changes in a client's target behavior. This type of scale is particularly useful when actual outcomes are difficult to identify. The scale involves identifying a problem, applying an intervention, and then repeatedly rating the extent to which the target problem has changed (Mutschler, 1979). One such target problem scale is shown in Figure 4.6. This example includes a global improvement scale that summarizes the amount of change that actually took place in the target problem.

TARGET PROBLEM (rated by client)	TARGET PROBLEM RATING					GLOBAL IMPROVEMENT
	Degree of Severity				Degree of Change	
	Session #					
	1	2	3	4	Month	
Difficulty in talking about feelings	ES	ES	S	S	S	3
Getting to work on time	ES	S	S	NVS	NP	5
Fear of leaving house in daytime	ES	S	S	NVS	NP	5
			TOTAL			13 / 3 = 4.3
						Somewhat to a lot better

Severity Scale			Improvement Scale		
NP	=	No problem	1	=	Worse
NVS	=	Not very severe	2	=	No change
S	=	Severe	3	=	A little better
VS	=	Very severe	4	=	Somewhat better
ES	=	Extremely severe	5	=	A lot better

The global improvement rating is obtained by totaling the change scores and dividing by the number of target problems. This yields a number that reflects the client's overall improvement on all problems.

FIGURE 4.6 *Example of a target problem and global improvement scale for one client*

Goal Attainment Scale

Goal attainment scales (GAS) reflect the achievement of outcomes and are used to both set client goals and to assess if the goals have been met. Kiresuk and Lund (1977) were among those who first suggested using these for social work research. Goal attainment scaling involves four steps:

1 Identify the problem

2 Specify the areas where change is desired

3 Make specific predictions for a series of outcome levels for each area

4 By a set date, score the outcomes as they are achieved (five possible outcomes are designated from the least favorable to the most favorable)

Goal attainment scales can be used for a wide variety of problem situations. Figure 4.7 shows a modification of a goal attainment scale used by the

Family Name: ___Vin___   Social Worker Name: _Remington/Drake_
Goal Number: ___1___   Goal: _To increase knowledge of parenting_
skills to reduce the family's need for the services of the Human
Services Department.
_____

Statement of problem: The client is requesting new methods or
                      techniques to help parent her children.

Date Goal Scaled: _During first week_ Date when scored: _Weekly_
Rating of Client when goal was first scaled: _____−2_____
Rating of Client when goal was last scored: _____+2_____
Whose goal?: _Client and Family Preservation Services team_

Outcome Categories	Client's Attainment Criteria
Most unfavorable outcome thought likely* (−2)	The client totally disregards her parenting skills or tools when interacting with her children.
Less than expected success (1)	The client listens to and understands new parenting skills and techniques presented but does not follow through with applying them.
Expected level of success (0)	The client learns a new parenting skill or technique suggested by Family Preservation Services.
More than expected success (+1)	The client applies one new skill or technique suggested by Family Preservation Service.
Best anticipated success* (+2)	The client applies two new skills or techniques suggested by Family Preservation Services.

*Unlikely, but still plausible.

FIGURE 4.7 *Example of a goal attainment scale*

New Mexico Human Services Department. In identifying the problem, positive terms should be used, as has been done in this example. Instead of stating that the client lacks parenting skills, it is stated that she would like to learn new methods or techniques for parenting. The 0 level is the expected outcome for this goal, with two less successful (-2, -1) and two more successful ($+1$, $+2$) possible outcomes, with their respective criteria for attainment. At the initial time of scoring, this client was scored at a -2, or the most unfavorable outcome; but at a later date, the score was $+2$, indicating the client had achieved the best anticipated successful outcome for this goal. The GAS is an excellent way for both social worker and client to monitor progress and to determine the desirability of specific outcomes.

Rapid Assessment Instruments

Rapid assessment instruments (RAI's) are a standardized series of structured questions or statements administered to the client to collect data in single-system studies. They are short, easy to administer, and easy to complete (see Levitt & Reid, 1981). Some examples include the Beck Depression Inventory, the Rathus Assertiveness Schedule, and the Multi-Problem Screening Inventory (Hudson, 1990). The MPSI can be used in conjunction with practice to collect data on several variables, including generalized contentment and marital satisfaction. These scales are computerized. Other types of scales can be found in the sourcebooks listed in Further Reading.

Who Collects the Data

As with the other decisions to be made concerning data collection, the decision about who should collect the data depends greatly on the type of research question asked. We tend to think of the researcher as the only person who should collect the data, and this is true in many cases (for example, when interviewing or administering a questionnaire).

Apart from the researcher, the client or subject can also collect the data. Journals or diaries can be used in this way. Questionnaires can be self-administered (mailed questionnaires being the obvious example). Clients can also observe and record their own behavior using scales or checklists. Engaging the client in the data collection process is particularly valuable in conducting single-system studies, and as we will see in Chapter 7, can provide opportunities for feedback on changes in the client's behavior.

Earlier we mentioned the reactivity effects in interviewing or observation when the subject changes behavior as a result of the data being collected. This reactivity effect can also be a problem when the client collects data on his or her own behavior or uses **self-monitoring.** This reactivity can be quite strong, resulting in self-monitoring being used as an intervention device. Kopp (1988) conducts an interesting review of the literature that examines how self-monitoring has been used both as a research and as a practice tool in social work.

Chapter 4

Combining Data Collection Methods

Methods and instruments can and should be used in conjunction with one another. Often the methods complement one another, and qualitative and quantitative methods can be combined.

E X A M P L E

Using Multiple Measures

A study of the maltreatment of school-age children was carried out by Wodarski, Kurtz, Gaudin, and Howing (1990). Measures included:

▶ Caseworker report, including child well-being scales
▶ Child behavior checklist
▶ Child interview schedule
▶ Child's permanent school record
▶ Jesness Inventory (self-report measure for delinquency)
▶ Parent interview schedule
▶ Piers-Harris Children's Self-Concept Scale
▶ Scales of independent behavior
▶ Composite adjustment indices

Through these instruments, the researchers were able to collect data on the children's school performance, socioemotional development, adaptive behavior, as well as for control and demographic variables.

Combining measures can enrich your study and can help ensure that you are tapping a maximum number of dimensions of the phenomenon under study.

Determining Reliability and Validity

Before a measuring instrument is used in the research process, it is important to determine its reliability and validity. Both of these terms refer to different aspects of objectivity. We will see that we can assess reliability and validity for most of the measuring instruments we use.

Reliability

Reliability indicates the extent to which a measure reveals actual differences in what is being measured, rather than differences that are inherent in the measuring instrument itself. Reliability refers to the consistency of a measure. A wooden foot rule is a reliable measure for a table. However, if the rule is made of elastic, this would not provide a reliable measure because repeated measures of the same table would differ due to the rule expanding and contracting. Or, if a client is chronically depressed and we measure the degree of depression at two points in time, the instrument is reliable if we get close to the same score each time, provided the level of depression has not in fact changed. Clearly we need to establish the instrument's reliability before we can determine true changes in the phenomenon under study.

As generalist social workers, we need to assess the extent to which our data collection instrument is reliable. There are two major ways to do this: assessing sources of error and assessing the degree to which the instrument's reliability has actually been tested. Each of these will be discussed in turn.

Sources of Error

When assessing the reliability of an instrument, we need to determine if there is evidence of certain sources of error. The following are major types of error: unclear definition of variables, use of retrospective information, variations in the conditions for collecting data, and structure of the instrument.

Unclear Definition of Variables   In the discussion of variables, we mentioned the difficulty of their definition because many terms used in social work tend to be vague. If a variable is not clearly operationalized and defined, its measurement lacks reliability: The possible outcome can be interpreted differently by different social workers. Unclear definitions of variables can often occur in questionnaires due to the wording of questions. A question might be phrased in such a way that two individuals interpret it differently and provide two different answers even though the behavior on which they are reporting is the same. For example, in the question "Do you often use public transportation in the city?" people may interpret *often* in different ways.

Use of Retrospective Information   This information is gathered through subject recall, either by a questionnaire or an interview. These data are almost inevitably distorted. Case records are one form of retrospective data collection, and they are consequently subject to considerable error. Case records usually reflect the idiosyncratic recording practices of the individual social worker. The worker will select certain aspects of the case to be recorded, resulting in a lack of reliability.

Variations in the Conditions for Collecting Data   When we use interviews to collect data, the interview conditions can also affect reliability. The subject may respond differently depending on whether the interviewer is male or female. (This is the reactive effect we discussed earlier.) Similar problems may arise due to the ethnicity and age of the interviewer. Where the interview is conducted may also cause disparities in responses. Even with questionnaires (for example, mailed questionnaires) lack of control over the conditions under which they are administered can result in low reliability.

Structure of the Instrument   Certain aspects of the data collection method itself may enhance or decrease reliability. An open-ended questionnaire that requires that responses be categorized and coded can present reliability problems.

Testing Reliability

In addition to identifying the sources of error in an instrument, we can also assess the extent to which the instrument's reliability has been tested. As generalist social workers, we will usually not test the reliability of instruments ourselves, but we need to be able to understand what, if any, reliability tests have been carried out by others.

Reliability is determined by obtaining two or more measures of the same thing and seeing how closely they agree. There are four methods that are used to establish the reliability of an instrument: test-retest, alternate form, split half, and observer reliability.

Test-Retest   **Test-retest** involves repeatedly administering the instrument to the same set of people on separate occasions. These people should not be subjects in the actual study. The results of the repeated administrations are then compared. If the results are similar, reliability of the instrument is high. A problem associated with this method of testing reliability is that the first testing has influenced the second. For example, during the second testing the individuals may be less anxious, less motivated or interested, or simply may remember their answers and repeat them. In addition, they may have learned from the first testing; this is particularly the case with attitude questions. To avoid these problems, some have suggested (Bostwick & Kyte, 1988) that measuring instruments that are strongly affected by memory or repetition should not be tested for reliability using this method.

Alternate Form   With **alternate form** tests, different but equivalent forms of the same test are administered to the same group of individuals—usually close in time—and then compared. The major problem with this approach is in the development of the equivalent tests, which can be time consuming. In addition, this approach can still involve some of the problems associated with the test-retest method.

Split Half   With the **split half** method, items on the instrument are divided into comparable halves. Then the scores from the halves are combined to produce an overall score. This testing method looks at the internal consistency of the measure. The test is administered and the two halves are compared. A major problem with this approach is ensuring that the two halves are equivalent.

Observer Reliability   **Observer reliability** involves comparing administrations of an instrument to administrations done by different observers or interviewers. To do this effectively, the observers need to be thoroughly trained.

Each of these methods of testing for reliability involves comparing two or more results. Usually this comparison uses some kind of **correlation coeffi-**

TABLE 4.2 *Criteria for assessing the reliability of measuring instruments*

1	Is the variable clearly defined?
2	Is retrospective information avoided?
3	Are there controlled conditions under which the data are collected?
4	Is the question format closed?
5	Are reliability tests used? If so, is the correlation coefficient greater than 0.5?

If the answer is yes to most of these questions, then the instrument is probably reliable.

cient. This is a statistic that measures the extent to which the comparisons are similar or not similar, that is, the extent to which they are related or correlated. We will discuss the concept of correlation in more detail in Chapters 9 and 10. For our purposes now in assessing reliability, the correlation coefficient can range from 0.0 to 1.0, the latter reflecting a perfect correlation or the highest level of reliability possible. Table 4.2 summarizes the criteria that can be used to assess an instrument's reliability.

E X A M P L E

Instruments with High Reliability

The scales included in the Multi-Problem Screening Inventory developed by Hudson (1990) all have test-retest and split half reliability correlation coefficients of at least .90. The computerized scales were developed to measure a variety of behaviors, including child problems, guilt, work problems, and alcohol abuse.

Validity

The **validity of a measuring instrument** refers to the extent to which we are measuring what we think we are measuring. This is a different idea than reliability. We may have a very reliable instrument—to take the example used previously, a foot rule. If the foot rule is used to measure the dimensions of a table, this is a reliable and valid instrument. However, if we use the foot rule to measure ethnicity, the instrument still maintains its reliability but is no longer valid. We would not be measuring ethnicity but some other variable (for example, height), which has no relationship to ethnicity as far as we know.

Validity is not as straightforward as reliability because there are different types of validity, and each one is tested in a different way. The three main types of validity are criterion validity, content validity, and construct validity. Each type of validity relates to different aspects of the overall validity of the instrument, and each provides different dimensions of the problem of ensuring that what is being measured is what was intended to be measured. We will discuss these types of validity along with the ways in which each can be tested.

Validity testing can be quite complex, and sometimes entire articles in the social work literature are devoted to testing the validity of specific instruments. For example, Guttmann and Brenna (1990) assessed the validity of the Personal Experience Inventory (PEI), an instrument for assessing the level and nature of substance abuse in adolescents. Seaburg (1988) examined the validity of the Child Well-Being Scales and concluded that due to the complexity of the concept of *child well-being,* the validity of the scales is somewhat questionable and should be used cautiously. As generalist social workers, we do not usually test the validity of an instrument ourselves, but (as with the testing of reliability) we need to know how testing is conducted so that we can assess the validity of the instrument we propose to use.

Criterion Validity   **Criterion validity** refers to the extent to which a correlation exists between the measuring instrument and another standard. To validate an instrument developed to assess a program that helps pregnant teenagers succeed in high school, a criterion such as SAT scores might be used as a comparison. Similarities in scores would indicate that criterion validity had been established.

Content Validity   **Content validity** is concerned with the representativeness of the content of the instrument. The content included in the instrument needs to be relevant to the concept we are trying to measure. For example, the content validity of an instrument developed to measure knowledge of parenting skills could be obtained by consulting with various experts on parenting skills— perhaps social workers who run parenting groups and a professor at the department or school of social work. They could then point out areas in which the instrument may be deficient. Clearly, content validity is partially judgmental and depends upon the knowledge of the experts who are available to you.

Construct Validity   **Construct validity** refers to the extent to which an instrument measures a theoretical construct. A measure may have criterion and content validity but still not measure what the researcher intended it to measure. This type of validity is the most difficult to establish, because as we mentioned earlier many of the variables may be difficult to define. Constructs used in social work include aggression, sociability, and self-esteem to name just a few. With construct validity, we are looking not only at the instrument but also at the theory underlying it.

For example, in testing the construct validity of an instrument to measure aggression in preschoolers, the associated theoretical explanations need to be examined by referring to the literature and research on the topic. One explanation that may be found is that the highly aggressive children will not be

TABLE 4.3 *Criteria for assessing the validity of measuring instruments*

1	Was the instrument tested for criterion validity?
2	Was the instrument tested for content validity?
3	Was the instrument tested for construct validity?
4	Is the variable defined as clearly and concretely as possible?

If the answer is yes to most of these questions, then the instrument is probably valid (that is, if the findings from the tests support the validity of the instrument).

achieving well in the classroom. If the instrument does not reflect this dimension of the topic, the instrument probably does not have construct validity.

IQ tests provide an example of a measure with low construct validity. IQ tests were created to measure intelligence. However, since their development, it has become apparent that they measure only one dimension of intelligence—the potential to achieve in a white middle-class academic system. Other dimensions of intelligence remain untapped by IQ tests, resulting in their limited validity for measuring intelligence.

One way of more fully ensuring construct validity is to define the construct using small, concrete, observable behaviors (Duncan & Fiske, 1977). This helps avoid some of the wishy-washiness associated with many constructs used in social work practice. For example, both the verbal and nonverbal behaviors of preschoolers are recorded, and certain patterns of these behaviors become apparent in those children previously labeled "aggressive." Consequently, we can be more fully assured that our label "aggressive" does in fact have construct validity.

Once we are familiar with this information on validity and the ways it can be tested, we are in a position as generalist social workers to assess the validity of the measuring instruments that we read about or that we propose to use. Table 4.3 presents a checklist that can be used to assess the validity of instruments.

The Agency and Data Collection

As generalist social workers, we often do not have much of a choice when it comes to selecting a data collection method. You may be asked to help develop a questionnaire for a needs assessment, in which case the decision about the data collection has already been made.

Because of time and money constraints, some of the more complicated and time-consuming data collection techniques—such as lengthy questionnaire and scale construction, participant observation, and extensive interviews—

cannot be considered by the generalist social worker engaged in research. Instead, consider using rapid assessment instruments, case records, and self-observation (by the client) as much as possible.

Ethical Issues in Collecting Data

When collecting data for a research study, there are two ethical issues with which we need to be concerned: potential harm to the subjects and anonymity and confidentiality.

Harm to the Subjects

Clearly, we need to avoid harming the subjects in any way. The NASW Code of Ethics states: "The social worker engaged in research should consider carefully its possible consequences for human beings. . . . The social worker engaged in research should protect participants from unwarranted physical or mental discomfort, distress, harm, danger or deprivation." As simplistic as this sounds, on closer examination we realize that it is easier said than done. When asking questions in whatever form—whether interviewing or using a questionnaire—we are often requiring the subjects to examine and assess their own behavior. If we are asking questions relating to childhood abuse, this may be painful for the respondent. Other questions that are difficult to answer concern income and the ability to pay for a proposed service.

Consequently, assessing the extent of discomfort for the subject can be difficult. Some projects—for example, federally funded research and research conducted at universities—require the proposed research to be reviewed by human subjects committees and the researcher to answer specific questions regarding potential harm to the subjects. Even when an outside review is not required, we have to depend on our own sensitivity to the impact of our data collection method on the subject.

Anonymity and Confidentiality

Both anonymity and confidentiality help participants avoid harm. Again, the NASW Code of Ethics states: "The social worker who engages in the evaluation of services or cases should discuss them only for professional purposes and only with persons directly and professionally concerned with them. . . . Information obtained about participants in research should be treated as confidential."

Anonymity means that the researcher cannot identify a given response with a given respondent. We mentioned previously that an interview can never be anonymous, and when we put identification numbers on questionnaires to facilitate follow-up and increase the response rate, anonymity is also jeopardized. Ensuring anonymity not only reassures the subjects but can also enhance the objectivity of the responses. For example, if you are asking questions about deviant behavior, the respondent is more likely to give a response that accurately reflects the behavior if anonymity can be assured.

Confidentiality means that the researcher knows the identity of the respondents and their associated responses but ensures not to disclose this information. Obviously, confidentiality becomes particularly critical when conducting interviews for which anonymity is impossible to ensure. The principle of confidentiality should be explained to respondents either verbally or in a cover letter accompanying the questionnaire. Do not confuse confidentiality and anonymity; they are different and are both extremely important.

Human Diversity Issues in Collecting the Data

Awareness and knowledge of human diversity issues are critical during the data collection stage of the research process. Some of the central issues to which we need to pay attention are:

▶ The selection of the data collection method for diverse populations

▶ The relevance of the content of the data collection method to diverse populations

▶ The application of the data collection method to diverse populations

The Selection of the Data Collection Method for Diverse Populations

We need to seriously consider the extent to which data collection methods may or may not be applicable to certain groups within a population. Some groups may be uncomfortable with the notion of being administered a questionnaire or being interviewed; we need to be sensitive to the ways in which different cultural groups might regard different methods.

For example, Myers (1977) recommends the use of in-depth interviews instead of questionnaires with certain groups, including respondents who are poor, of an ethnic or racial minority, or are socially distant from the researcher. As a result of using in-depth interviews rather than other data collection methods, the validity of the responses can be enhanced. Myers suggests that sometimes, because of the time-consuming nature of this approach, in-depth interviews can be combined with more structured questionnaire methods.

Feminist researchers have also suggested departing from more traditional research methods, including specific data collection techniques. Gilligan's (1982) analysis of the development of men's and women's resolutions of moral conflicts concluded that women develop a mode of thinking that is "contextual and narrative" and their understanding is based on the individual in the context of their relationship with others. This way of thinking is contrasted with men's, which is seen as focusing on autonomy and separation from others.

As a result of these different ways of thinking, authors (e.g., Davis, 1986) have suggested that this requires different approaches to research, particularly different data collection techniques. Male research methodology—the traditional approach—emphasizes the abstract and formal and lends itself to quantification, whereas the female approach with an emphasis on connection lends itself more easily to qualitative approaches. Approaches in which the researcher and subject explore the topic together, each contributing to the process, result in the data remaining "in context." Davis (1986, p. 38) states, "the researcher and subject can work in different ways to explore a 'truth' that they mutually create and define."

We should recognize that the feminist approach to research results in data that cannot be considered objective in the way we discussed previously in this chapter.

> *The researcher and subject are interconnected in an ongoing relationship that influences the data that are produced. No "objective" data can be collected because all data depend on the specific individuals and their relationship with one another. (Davis, 1986, p. 37)*

Thus, when using this approach to data collection, we must acknowledge that "objectivity" will be lost; however, we will be gaining other types of information that may be equally beneficial to our understanding of the phenomenon under study.

The Relevance of the Content of the Data Collection Method to Diverse Populations

Apart from considering the appropriateness of a particular data collection instrument, we also need to consider the content of that instrument and its appropriateness to the group under study.

Certain words or phrases—whether in interview or questionnaire form or whether conducted under the auspices of a feminist or traditional research approach—may be interpreted by the respondent in a different way from that intended by the researcher. In many cases, this is due to a lack of understanding or insensitivity to a cultural group that is being studied. For example, asking about your mother may be interpreted by some groups as including your mother-in-law. This can lead to serious validity problems, that is, the researcher is thinking of *mother* in one sense, and the subject is defining *mother* very differently. Reliability problems also arise.

Another perhaps less obvious problem might occur when conducting, for example, a research project concerned with methods and problems of discipling children. We would need to acknowledge the methods and problems experienced by gay and lesbian parents (unless we purposefully *intend* to exclude them) in addition to those of heterosexual parents because some of the problems they encounter might be different. Consequently, we would need to include questions relevant to this group so as not to exclude problems that might be characteristic of this group and so jeopardize the validity of our findings.

We have already discussed the usefulness of rapid assessment instruments and other instruments that have already been developed. However, check to see if they have been used with diverse populations, and if their reliability and validity have been tested with these groups.

Many of these issues are an extension of our discussion in Chapter 3 when we addressed the need to include relevant variables in the study. Here we are simply emphasizing the importance of not only including certain variables but also being aware of human diversity issues in the phrasing or construction of the data collection instrument.

The Application of the Data Collection Method to Diverse Populations

The data collection method and the structure and content of this method may be sensitive to the needs of diverse populations, but the way in which the instrument is administered may not.

For example, we may be carrying out a needs assessment for socially isolated recent immigrant Asian women. To obtain valid and reliable information, we would not only need to include questions that are relevant to this population, but we would also need to ensure that the interviews were conducted in such a way that they would elicit the information required. This necessitates the use of interviewers, administrators of questionnaires, and/or observers who are sensitive to the population under study. For example, with the Asian women an interviewer would need to be familiar with this group's language, gender roles, and intergenerational role expectations in order to engage the subject in the interview *and* to obtain valid and reliable data.

Summary

Quantitative approaches create categories of the phenomenon under study and assign numbers to these categories. Qualitative approaches examine the phenomenon in more detail. Data collection methods include interviews, questionnaires, observation, logs/journals, and secondary data. Scales can measure complex variables. There are several techniques for checking the reliability and validity of data collection methods.

When collecting data in an agency, data collection methods that are compatible to the practice need to be used. Ethical issues include considering potential harm to the subjects and the issue of confidentiality and anonymity. When considering human diversity issues, the selection, relevance, and application of the data collection method need to be considered.

Study/Exercise Questions

1 Develop a questionnaire to assess the campus needs (e.g., parking, day care, and so on) of students in your class. Include both open and closed questions.

   a How do you decide what questions to include?

   b How would you administer the questionnaire?

2 Have another student in the class critique your questionnaire and comment on its reliability and validity.

3 Using the sourcebooks listed in this chapter and others located at the library, find a suitable instrument to measure the self-esteem of adolescents.

   a Report on its validity and reliability.

   b Are there any groups for which the instrument may not be reliable or valid?

4 Your agency has asked you to participate in planning a program for adults with a history of childhood sexual abuse.

   a How would you collect data that would demonstrate a need exists for such a program?

   b How would you ensure confidentiality?

5 Design a structured interview to assess the satisfaction of clients who have just finished receiving services from a family service agency.

   a Conduct this interview with a classmate.

   b Would other methods of data collection be more reliable or valid in this case?

6 Design a way of observing a Headstart student who is reported to be disruptive in the classroom. How would you check the validity and reliability of this method?

Further Reading

Bainbridge, W. S. (1989). *Survey research*. Belmont, CA: Wadsworth.

> An excellent sourcebook for survey research with a good chapter on constructing questions.

Beere, C. A. (1990). *Women and women's issues: A handbook of tests and measures.* San Francisco: Jossey-Bass.

A collection of instruments that have been used for studies concerned with women and women's issues.

Corcoran, K., & Fischer, J. (1987). *Measures for clinical practice: A sourcebook.* New York: Free Press.

A collection of scales for research and practice.

Gordon, R. L. (1987). *Interviewing: Strategy, techniques and tactics* (4th ed.). Homewood, IL: Dorsey Press.

A useful reference book on research interviewing.

Hudson, W. (1990). *The multi-problem screening inventory.* Tempe, AZ: Walmyr Publishing.

Irwin, D. M., & Bushness, M. M. *Observational strategies for child study.* New York: Holt, Rinehart & Winston.

Includes some exercises to give experience in observation.

Jacob, H. (1984). *Using published data: Errors and remedies.* Beverly Hills, CA: Sage Publications.

Levitt, J., & Reid, W. J. (1981). Rapid assessment instruments for practice. *Social Work Research and Abstracts, 17,* 13–19.

A collection of instruments that can be used in the evaluation of individual practice.

Lockhart, D. C. (Ed.) (1984). *Making effective use of mailed questionnaires.* San Francisco: Jossey-Bass.

Discussion of the design and administration of mailed questionnaires.

Magura, S., & Moses, B. S. (1986). *Outcome measures for child welfare services: Theory and applications.* Washington, DC: Child Welfare League of America, Inc.

A collection of scales for research and practice.

Miller, D. C. (1991). *Handbook of research design and social measurement.* Newbury Park, CA: Sage Publications.

A comprehensive collection of issues in research design and measurement.

Mueller, D. (1986). *Measuring social attitudes: A handbook for researchers and practitioners.* New York: Teachers College Press.

Information on how to construct scales and examples of existing scales.

Rossi, P., Wright, J., & Anderson, A. (Eds.). (1983). *Handbook of survey research.* New York: Academic.

A collection of articles focusing on different aspects of survey research.

Warren, C. A. B. (1988). *Gender issues in field research*. Newbury Park, CA: Sage Publications.

> An excellent little book on conducting field research and on gender issues. Includes chapters on the sexual politics of fieldwork and women's place in fieldwork methodology.

References

Alter, C., & Evens, W. (1990). *Evaluating your practice*. New York: Springer.

Anderson, J. E., Kann, L., Holtzman, D., Arday, S., Truman, B., & Kilbe, L. (1990). *Family Planning Perspectives, 22*(6), 252–255.

Bales, R. F. (1950). *Interaction process analysis: A method for the study of small groups*. Cambridge, MA: Addison-Wesley.

Bostwick, G., & Kyte, N. (1989). Validity and reliability. In R. M. Grinnel (Ed.), *Social work research and evaluation*. (3rd ed., pp. 111–136). Itasta, IL: Peacock Publishers.

Charping, J. W., & Slaughter, M. M. (1988). Voluntary energy assistance programs: Community self-help in action. *Social Work, 33*(2), 161–163.

Colby, A. (1982). The use of secondary analysis in the study of women and social change. *Journal of Social Issues, 38*(1), 119–123.

Davis, L. V. (1986). A feminist approach to social work research. *Affilia, 1*, 32–47.

Duncan, S., & Fiske, D. (1977). *Face-to-face interaction*. Hillsdale, NJ: Erlbaum.

First, R. J., Roth, D., & Arewa, B. Q. (1988). Homelessness: Understanding the dimensions of the problem for minorities. *Social Work, 33*(2), 120–124.

Fraser, M., & Haapala, D. (1987–88). Home-based family treatment: A quantitative-qualitative assessment. *The Journal of Applied Social Sciences, 12*(1), 1–23.

Gilligan, C. (1982). *In a different voice*. Cambridge, MA: Harvard University Press.

Guttmann, D. R., & Brenna, D. C. (1990). The personal experience inventory: An assessment of the instruments' validity among a delinquent population in Washington State. *Journal of Adolescent Chemical Dependency, 1*(2).

Hudson, W. (1990). *The multi-problem screening inventory*. Tempe, AZ: Walmyr Publishing.

Kibria, N. (1989). Patterns of Vietnamese refugee women's wagework in the U.S. *Ethnic Groups, 7*, 297–323.

Kiresuk, T. J., & Lund, S. H. (1977). Goal attainment scaling. In C. C. Attkisson, W. A. Hargreave, M. J. Horowitz, & S. E. Sorenson (Eds.), *Evaluation of human service programs.* New York: Academic Press.

Kopp, J. (1988). Self-monitoring: A literature review of research and practice. *Social Work Research and Abstracts, 24*(4), 8–20.

Levitt, J., & Reid, W. J. (1981). Rapid assessment instruments for practice. *Social Work Research and Abstracts, 17,* 13–19.

Lusk, M., Peralta, F., & Vest, G. W. (1989). Street children of Juarez: A field study. *International Social Work, 32,* 289–302.

Mutschler, E. (1979). Using single-case evaluation procedures in a family and children's service agency: Integration of practice and research. *Journal of Social Service Research, 3,* 115–134.

Myers, V. (1977). Survey methods for minority populations. *Journal of Social Issues, 33,* 11–19.

O'Grady-LeShane, R. (1990). Older women and poverty, *Social Work, 35*(5), 422–424.

Peterson, D. A. (1990). Personnel to serve the aging in the field of social work: Implications for educating professionals. *Social Work, 35*(5), 412–415.

Plotnick, R. D. (1989). Directions for reducing child poverty, *Social Work, 34*(6), 523–530.

Rubin, A., & Babbie, E. (1989). *Research methods for social work.* Belmont, CA: Wadsworth.

Salgado de Snyder, V. N., Cervantes, R. C., & Padilla, A. M. (1990). Gender and ethnic differences in psychosocial stress and generalized distress among Hispanics. *Sex Roles, 22*(7/8), 441–453.

Seaburg, J. R. (1988). Child well-being scales: A critique. *Social Work Research and Abstracts, 24*(3), 9–15.

Sirles, E. (1984). Who responds to follow-up surveys? *Social Casework, 65*(6), 354–356.

Surber, R. W., Dwyer, E., Ryan, K. J., Goldfinger, S. M., & Kelly, J. T. (1988). Medical and psychiatric needs of the homeless: A preliminary response. *Social Work, 33*(2), 116–124.

Wodarski, J. S., Kurtz, P. Q., Gaudin, J. M., Jr., & Howing, P. T. (1990). Maltreatment and the school-age child: Major academic, socioemotional, and adaptive outcomes. *Social Work, 35*(6), 506–513.

5

Sampling

Now that you've decided on your research question and you know how you'll be collecting the data, who are you going to collect it from?

Sampling is equivalent to the second stage of the selection and collection step of generalist social work practice. (The first stage is designing the data collection procedure.) In social work research, **sampling** involves determining who will be the subjects in the study. Sampling is necessary because we usually cannot include everyone in the study. For example, we may be interested in determining the need for a latchkey program in our community, and we must identify and get opinions from all the families in the city who have school-age children age 12 and under. This could be a large number of families in even a small-sized city, and we have a limited budget and only two months in which to complete the project. Consequently, we need to select a smaller group of subjects, or **sample,** from this large group, or **population,** that is made up of all possible cases in which we are ultimately interested in studying (Figure 5.1).

Sampling should be a familiar concept to us as generalist social workers. We often need to collect information relating to a target problem from a large number of people. When, due to time and other constraints, we cannot contact all of the people, we select a sample. In research, there are specific ways to select a sample; the particular method we use depends on the nature and accessibility of the population and the type and purpose of the study we are undertaking.

Again, as with the steps of the research process we have already discussed, we may not be directly involved in sampling decisions. However, knowledge of the process is essential for two reasons: (1) Sometimes we will be involved in the sampling decision, and (2) we need to understand how the sampling can affect how we use the research findings in our practice.

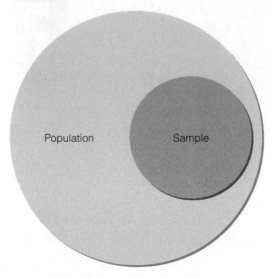

FIGURE 5.1 *Population and sample*

This chapter will discuss:

▶ Key concepts in sampling
▶ Types of sampling methods
▶ Sample size
▶ The agency and sampling
▶ Ethical issues in sampling
▶ Human diversity issues in sampling

Key Concepts in Sampling

One of the key concepts of sampling is the extent to which the sample is representative of the population. A **representative** sample means that the sample accurately represents the distribution of relevant variables in the population. For example, in the above needs assessment, we are interested in making statements about the latchkey program in the entire city, so our sample needs to be representative. Thus, when selecting a sample of the community, it is important that the sample not be biased in any way. One way bias occurs is if only one neighborhood is selected. Neighborhoods tend to have specific socioeconomic and ethnic characteristics, for example, upper-middle-class suburbs, Hispanic barrios, retirement communities. As a result, they are not usually representative of the entire city population, at least not in terms of socioeconomic and ethnic structure. Neighborhood is only one example of possible bias. Other groupings, such as schools and churches, also may not be representative of the larger community.

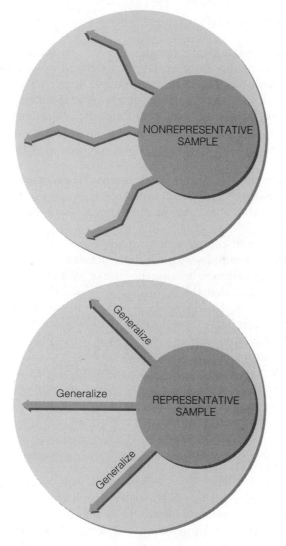

FIGURE 5.2 *Generalizing with representative and nonrepresentative samples*

If our sample is representative of the population, then we can generalize the findings from our sample to that population. When we **generalize,** we claim that the findings from studying the sample can be applied to the population (see Figure 5.2). If we discover in our representative sample of families from city A that 70% express an urgent need for a latchkey program, we then generalize that 70% of the families in city A (that is, our population) will also express this need. In needs assessment studies such as this, it is critical that we are able to generalize our findings. However, in other studies, generalizability and representativeness are not such important issues (for example, when we are conducting exploratory studies).

Before we describe different sampling strategies, we need to become familiar with two other general sampling concepts. First, an **element** in sampling refers to the item under study in the population and sample. In generalist social work research, these items or elements may be the different client systems with which we work—individuals, families, groups, organizations, or communities. Elements may be more specific than these basic systems. In the previous example, families with school-age children age 12 and under is a more specific element than simply families.

The second concept is **sampling frame.** This is the list of all the elements in the population from which the sample is selected. In the above example, the sampling frame would consist of a list of families in the city with school-age children age 12 and under.

As we confront the realities of compiling a sampling frame, we may need to redefine the population. For example, we might have decided on families with children 12 and under as our element because the state in which we are conducting the study legally mandates that this is the age at which children cannot be left without adult supervision. However, when we begin to compile a sampling frame, we run into problems because we find it very difficult to identify families with children of this age and younger. Instead, we discover that we can more easily identify families through the school system, which has children from 1st through 7th grades. We may end up with a few 13-year-olds, but this isn't a problem if we redefine our population as "families with children in the 1st through 7th grades."

Types of Sampling Methods

There are two major ways in which the sample can be selected: probability and nonprobability sampling. **Probability sampling** allows us to select a sample where each element in the population has a known chance of being selected for the sample. This type of sampling increases the representativeness of the sample. This sounds straightforward, and as we discussed earlier, representativeness is a desirable quality in a sample. However, probability sampling is often difficult, particularly in social work research, because this type of sampling requires a sampling frame; sometimes, even if we are willing to change the definition of the element, having a sampling frame is not feasible. In the above example, it may be that the school will not release the names and addresses of the parents with children in 1st through 7th grades. Instead of a probability sampling method, we may have to choose a nonprobability sampling method. **Nonprobability sampling** is limited in terms of sample representativeness in that the probability of each element of the population being included in the sample is unknown. However, it offers some advantages, particularly for exploratory studies. Probability and nonprobability sampling approaches will be presented in this chapter.

Probability Sampling

Probability sampling occurs when every element in the population has an equal chance of being selected; thus, its representativeness is assured. In addition, no subject can be selected more than once in a single sample. There are four major types of probability sampling: (1) simple random sampling; (2) systematic random sampling; (3) stratified random sampling; (4) cluster sampling.

Simple Random Sampling

Simple random sampling is the easiest of the sampling methods, where the population is treated as a whole unit and each element has an equal probability of being selected in the sample. By random, we mean that each element has the same chance of being selected. When we toss a coin, there is an equal chance of it being heads or tails. In the latchkey needs assessment example, a simple random sample would involve assigning identification numbers to all the elements (families with children in 1st through 7th grades) and then using a table of random numbers that can be generated by a computer. Most software packages for the social sciences have the ability to generate random number tables. If we did not have the random numbers table, we could literally put all the identification numbers of each element in a container and pick our sample from this.

E X A M P L E

Simple Random Sampling

Sung (1989) carried out a needs assessment exploring the problems and service needs of American families residing in a large housing project overseas. One of the interesting features of this needs assessment is that the researcher took into consideration needs as expressed by both the consumers (that is, the families) and the providers (human service professionals). Two random samples were used. One consisted of 200 people randomly selected from the 1,400 people living in the complex and the other consisting of 30 American professionals randomly selected from a list of 50 officers and civilians engaged in various types of human services. For both of these groups, lists were available for each of the populations allowing probability sampling to occur.

Although simple random sampling is the most straightforward probability sampling method to use, it has some problems that will become apparent as the other types of probability sampling are discussed.

Systematic Random Sampling

Systematic random sampling involves taking the list of elements and choosing every Nth element on the list. The size of N depends upon the size of the sampling frame and the intended size of the sample. For example, if we had 400 elements in our sampling frame and we needed a sample of 100, every 4th element would be selected for the sample. If we needed a sample of 200, every 2nd element would be selected.

E X A M P L E

Systematic Random Sampling

Rosenthal, Groze, and Curiel (1990)—in a study of race, social class, and special needs adoption—used different sampling procedures with different agencies. With a list of subsidized adoptions from the Illinois Department of Children and Family Services, systematic random sampling was done, with every fifth child being selected for the study.

Generally, systematic random sampling is as random as simple random sampling. However, one potential problem with systematic random sampling arises when the ordering of elements in the list follows a particular pattern. This may result in a distortion of the sample. In the latchkey example, students from the school district may be arranged into class lists of approximately 30 students, and all students who moved to the community within the last 6 months may be placed at the end of each of these lists. In some communities, these recent additions may be made up primarily of migrant workers. Consequently, if we select say every 10th, 20th, and 30th element in each class list, our resulting sample will be made up of a disproportionate number of migrant workers because these students—although consisting of 3 or 4 students in each class—are more likely to occur at each 30th element.

However, problems with the ordering of elements can usually be identified quite easily and precautions can be taken. Systematic random sampling may be easier than simple random sampling when lists are available because it avoids the step of assigning identification numbers.

Stratified Random Sampling

Stratified random sampling is a modification of the previous two methods; in it the population is divided into strata and subsamples are randomly selected from each of the strata. Sometimes we need to ensure that a certain proportion of the elements is represented, and stratified random sampling provides a greater chance of meeting this goal than either systematic or simple random sampling.

In our latchkey program study, we may be concerned that the different ethnic groups of these families with children in 1st through 7th grades are represented. We identify that 10% of the families are Native Americans. With a simple or systematic random sample, our sample *should,* if it is truly representative, include 10% Native American. Unfortunately, due to the workings of probability theory this is not always the case. At this point, we cannot delve into the depths of probability theory. But if we toss a coin 20 times, theoretically we should end up with 10 heads and 10 tails. However, often we don't. We may have six heads and four tails.

The extent to which the values of a sample differ from those of the population is called **sampling error.** Sampling error can be assessed mathematically and depends to a certain extent on the sample size. If our sample size is large enough, the sampling error can be reduced. With 100 tosses, we are much more likely to end up with 50 heads and 50 tails. However, larger samples in social work consume more time and money.

In order to ensure that the Native-American families are representatively included in the sample, we can use stratified random sampling. Stratified random sampling requires two preconditions. First, we must be sure that the group we are concerned about being adequately represented has an impact on the phenomenon we are studying. In the above example, do we think that Native-American families' viewpoints on latchkey programs will differ from those of other families? If not, their representativeness in the sample may not be that important. Second, we need to know the proportion of this group relative to the rest of the population. In this example, we do; 10% are Native American.

Stratified random sampling involves dividing the population into the groups or strata of interest; in this example, we would divide the population into Native Americans and non-Native Americans. (Note that we can create more than two strata if necessary. For example, we might also be concerned that Hispanic families be assured adequate representation in the sample. Knowing they make up 40% of the population, we would then create three strata: Native Americans, Hispanics, and others). After creating the strata, simple or systematic random sampling is then carried out from each stratum in proportion to the stratum's representation in the population. In our example, to end up with a sample of 20, we would randomly select 2 from the Native-American stratum, 8 from the Hispanic stratum, and 10 from the other stratum (see Figure 5.3).

Although under some circumstances stratified random sampling may be an improvement over simple random sampling, the disadvantages are the two preconditions described earlier—that is, the certainty that the characteristics with which you are concerned with impact the outcome and that you know the proportions of these characteristics in the population prior to the sampling.

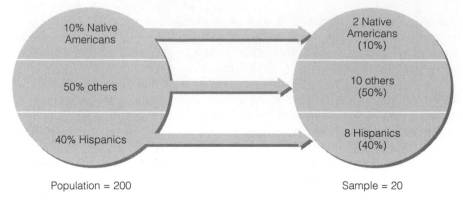

Population = 200   Sample = 20

FIGURE 5.3 *Stratified random sampling*

E X A M P L E

Stratified Random Sampling

Larson, Richards, Raffaelli, Ham, and Jewell (1990) examined the nature of depression in late childhood and early adolescence by using a profile of daily states and activities. The sample consisted of 5th to 9th graders and included 406 randomly selected 5th to 8th graders (ages 10–15) stratified by gender, school grade, community, and time of year of participation. These students were selected from the populations of four Chicago-area schools—two in a working-class community on the edge of the city and two in an outlying white-collar suburb. The 9th graders were selected from the high schools serving the same residential neighborhoods.

Cluster Sampling

Cluster sampling involves randomly sampling a larger unit containing the elements of interest, and then sampling from these larger units the elements to be included in the final sample. Cluster sampling is often done in social work research because it can be used when it is difficult to get a sampling frame, and yet it is still a form of probability sampling. In the latchkey example, suppose that the community is large, and we are required to obtain the lists of students from each school rather than from the school district office. This could present a lengthy undertaking in a large school district with many schools. Or the lists may not be available either from the school or from the school district. In these cases, cluster sampling might provide a feasible solution.

In cluster sampling, a random sample of a larger unit is taken; in this case, the schools in which 1st through 7th graders are enrolled. This random sampling can be either simple, systematic, or stratified. In our example, we use

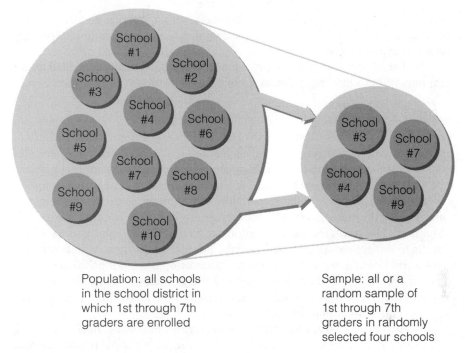

Population: all schools in the school district in which 1st through 7th graders are enrolled

Sample: all or a random sample of 1st through 7th graders in randomly selected four schools

FIGURE 5.4 *Cluster sampling*

simple random sampling to select four schools. Then a random sample (again, either simple, systematic, or stratified) of the 1st through 7th grades in these four schools would be selected (Figure 5.4). Alternatively, if a student list is not available, all 1st through 7th graders in the four schools would be included in the final sample.

An example of cluster sampling that can be useful in an agency setting is when an agency serves a large number of clients over a yearly period (for example, 8,000 clients are referred). Instead of randomly selecting from this large sampling frame, 3 months may be systematically randomly sampled from the 12 months (that is, every 4th month) and the clients referred during those 3 months included in the sample. Each month represents a cluster.

There is one potential problem with cluster sampling. When we sample a small number of units (for example, four schools), there is greater probability of sampling error. The four schools may consist of three white middle-class schools, whereas the students' population (in 10 schools) is a 50-50 mix socio-economically. Consequently, the sample would be biased in favor of white middle-class students and other groups would be underrepresented.

Nonprobability Sampling

As mentioned previously, identifying the sampling frame can be problematic. Nonprobability sampling then becomes an important option and is usually the sampling method employed in generalist social work practice. Sometimes it is the sampling method of choice, particularly if we are conducting exploratory studies or evaluating our own practice.

There are four main types of nonprobability sampling: availability sampling, quota sampling, purposive sampling, and snowball sampling.

Availability Sampling

Availability sampling is used extensively in social work research, particularly in needs assessments and simply involves including available or convenient elements in the sample. Sometimes it is confused with random sampling because superficially it appears to be random. A typical example of availability sampling is interviewing people in a shopping mall in an attempt to get a sample of the community. Alternatively, in an agency you are asked to conduct a program evaluation. The funds for the evaluation are available now, and you have two months to collect the data. You define the population as those clients referred to the agency over a two-month period. Cluster sampling is not possible because of the immediacy and short time frame of the evaluation. Consequently, you decide to include in your sample clients referred to the program during the next 30 days. This is an availability sample.

Availability sampling presents some serious problems. In the shopping mall example, you are only going to be able to include people in your sample who shop at the mall—maybe a small and not very representative sample of the community as a whole. In the program evaluation example, it may be that the clients referred to the agency that month are different from clients referred at other times of the year—December may not be a very representative month of the entire year. Consequently, this results in a biased sample from which it would be difficult to make generalizations to the entire community.

E X A M P L E

Availability Sampling

A study by Schilit, Lie, Bush, Montagne, and Reyes (1991) examined intergenerational transmission of violence in lesbian relationships. The researchers used an availability sample. Probability sampling would have been difficult with this population—lesbians living in the region—because complete lists do not exist. The availability sample consisted of a mailing list for a lesbian organization in Tucson, which contained approximately 350 names and addresses in the Tucson area.

Availability sampling is often the sampling method we use when evaluating our own practice when we select one case and assess the effectiveness of the intervention. We will discuss this type of research in more detail in Chapter 7.

Quota Sampling

In **quota sampling,** a certain proportion of elements with specific characteristics are included in the sample. In some respects, this is similar to stratified random sampling except that there is no randomness in the selection of the elements. In the latchkey example, quota sampling would be appropriate if we wanted to ensure the representation of Native-American families in our sample, but a sampling frame was not available, rendering any type of probability sampling impossible. As with stratified random sampling, we would need to know the proportion of Native Americans in the population. Again, let's assume there are 10% Native Americans in our population; a sample of 100 would, consequently, need to include 10 Native Americans. This sample would be picked using a nonprobability method, either availability or purposive sampling.

The problems associated with this form of sampling, as with stratified random sampling, are that the researcher needs to be sure that the categories or variables selected are important ones and that the proportions of these variables are known in the population. Additionally, quota sampling suffers from the fact that elements from the strata are not randomly selected and consequently cannot be said to represent the population.

E X A M P L E

Quota Sampling

In the Lusk, Peralta, and Vest (1989) study, a form of quota sampling was used. Street children were interviewed in Juarez, Mexico. The researchers used nonprobability sampling and attempted to increase the representativeness of the sample by interviewing the children in different parts of the city and at different times of the day. This is a good example of how you can modify a nonprobability sampling method to increase its representativeness.

Purposive Sampling

Purposive sampling purposively includes in the sample those elements of interest to the researcher. Sometimes we may be less interested in the representativeness of the population and more interested in ensuring that our sample includes elements that are directly relevant to the problem being studied. For example, in the latchkey project you might decide that you are interested in learning about the problems of families who need latchkey care rather than finding out the proportion of families who are in need of latchkey services. Therefore, you decide to focus on those families whom you know have these problems. You select your sample by identifying families who have contacted local agencies or school social workers because their children's afterschool care is a problem. Thus you are purposively selecting the sample rather than attempting a random sample.

A purposive sample differs from an availability sample in that a purposive sample contains elements that possess the characteristic you are interested in studying. An availability sample chooses the sample because of its ease of selection. However, all the elements in the purposive sample may not possess the characteristics you are studying.

E X A M P L E

Purposive Sampling

Gilgun and Connor (1989) studied how perpetrators view child sexual abuse. Their sample consisted of life history interviews with 14 male perpetrators of child sexual abuse. The subjects were recruited from maximum security prisons and community-based treatment programs. Consequently, all the subjects possessed the characteristics that were the focus of the study.

The problem with purposive sampling as with other nonprobability methods is the lack of ability to generalize from these samples. In the latchkey example, we cannot generalize to either all the families in the community with children in grades 1 through 7 (our initial population) or to all parents who experience latchkey projects (a possible alternative population). However, its strength is that for many studies it can ensure the collection of information that is directly relevant to the subject being investigated. Purposive sampling is often the sampling method of choice in qualitative studies. Also, it is often used in single-system studies when we are interested in monitoring the impact of an intervention on a specific target behavior.

Two specific types of purposive sampling that are commonly used for needs assessments are the key informant and the community forum. The **key informant** is someone in the community who is identified as an expert in the field of interest. Essentially, the key informant is a smaller version of a purposive sample.

E X A M P L E

Using Key Informants

Rivera (1990) studied the extent to which knowledge about AIDS has been integrated into Mexican folk medicine (or *curanderismo*). Rivera interviewed three *curanderos* in Mexico and two owners of *botanicas* (healing artifact stores). He states that the three *curanderos* had respected reputations, were well known where they lived (Guadalajara, Oaxaca, and close to Mexico City). The two owners of *botanicas* lived in barrios in Colorado and Texas.

The **community forum** involves publicizing a meeting or series of meetings where the individuals are briefed on the issues and then asked for input.

E X A M P L E

A Community Forum

Rothman (1988) reports on the development of programs and facilities for runaway and homeless youths in Los Angeles County. After a survey of 42 knowledgeable individuals in the county (a purposive sample), a report on how the services and programs should be organized was presented and discussed at a series of community meetings or forums "to encourage feedback from informed and interested parties in the community. Its aim was to develop dependable, new program initiatives having wide support" (p. 15).

Snowball Sampling

Snowball sampling involves identifying some members of the population and then having those individuals contact others in the population. This is a very useful strategy to adopt with less accessible populations, for example, the homeless. In the latchkey example, if we were interested in those families who have experienced problems as a result of a lack of latchkey services rather than simply being interested in the proportion of families who need such services, snowball sampling might be appropriate, particularly if it is difficult to identify the families with problems. We might identify and contact a few families and then ask those families to contact others whom they think are having problems.

E X A M P L E

Snowball Sampling

Danziger and Farber (1990) conducted a study investigating young black women's personal experiences, level of school success, and the kinds of supportive resources they receive. The researchers conducted in-depth interviews with 162 young women who live in the inner-city communities of Milwaukee and Detroit. In Milwaukee, a number of women were contacted who had participated in an earlier survey. From this core, snowball sampling was used to get referrals from other potential participants. In Detroit, referrals were received from agencies along with snowball sampling.

Sample Size

Statisticians have devoted a considerable amount of energy to determining how large or small samples should be. Some of the kinds of research that generalist social workers usually conduct do not require us to make a decision about sample size because the sample is fixed, namely, when evaluating a small program or in evaluating our own practice.

The size of the sample in part depends on its homogeneity, or the similarity between the different elements. If we can be assured that the characteristics of the sample elements are similar on the dimensions in which we are interested in studying, then the sample can be smaller. In our latchkey example, if all the children are similar in terms of ethnicity, socioeconomic status, and family configuration and these are characteristics in which we are interested, then the sample size can be small. If, however, we are interested in comparing the latchkey program needs of different types of families—for example, across family configuration, income, and so on—then we would probably need a larger sample in order to ensure that we had enough subjects in each category. We will see in Chapter 10 that a minimal number of cases is required in each category to allow certain statistical analyses to occur.

There are a number of quite complicated formulas that can assist in determining sample size. A guide to sample size is anywhere from 30 to 100. If you have concerns about the size of your sample, consult with a statistician or refer to a good statistics text (see Chapters 9 and 10 for some references).

The Agency and Sampling

As generalist social workers engaging in research, we may need to use sampling methods that are not textbook examples. Two cases of these modifications are discussed in this section.

Typically, an integral part of a needs assessment is the ability to generalize the findings to an entire community, county, or larger area. Unfortunately, we often cannot obtain representative samples due to most agencies' time and money constraints. However, sometimes it is possible to obtain a limited probability sample—for example, from a neighborhood or agency—and then compare the characteristics of this sample with the characteristics of a sample drawn from a larger population. In this way, some tentative generalizations of the findings can be made.

Sometimes similarities are not found between the smaller and larger samples. For example, in the Schilit and colleagues (1991) study on lesbian violence discussed earlier, the authors found that when they compared the ethnicity, income, and education of their subjects to these characteristics in the population of Tucson, there were large differences, thus limiting any generalizations.

E X A M P L E

A Limited Probability Sample

Smith and Kronauge (1990), in their study of who is involved in the decision making surrounding abortion, drew a random sample from those women who received abortions through one agency in St. Louis, Missouri. The researchers then compared two characteristics of this sample—marital status and age—with a national sample and found them similar, which allowed them to tentatively generalize the findings from their sample to the wider population.

This method of expanding generalizations suffers from some problems similar to those of stratified random sampling: the assumption that we know what the important characteristics are when comparing a smaller sample with a larger sample. Consequently, this method should be used with caution.

A second modification to textbook sampling, which we may confront when carrying out a program evaluation (particularly a summative type), is that often we do not need to sample at all. This is frequently the case in rural areas where the number of clients receiving services at one time can be quite small, perhaps 20 or less. Consequently, all could be included in the evaluation. In reality, this does not constitute a sample but rather we are studying the entire population, that is, all those receiving services.

Ethical Issues in Sampling

Two ethical issues relate to sampling; first, responsible reporting of the sampling method, and second, obtaining the subject's consent to the research.

Reporting the Sampling Method

It is the responsibility of the researcher to ensure that the research methods used in the study are described as accurately as possible when reporting the findings of the research—whether in a journal article, a report, or a presentation. Details of reporting will be described in Chapter 12. However, some discussion of this issue is necessary here because the sampling method is often the source of inaccuracies and ambiguities in the research report.

Sometimes authors write about random methods of sampling that are really availability or some other form of nonprobability sampling. When reading reports and articles, look for an explicit description of the sampling method along with a frank description of the generalization limitations, particularly if it is a nonprobability sampling method.

In the Gilgun and Connor (1989) study on perpetrators' views of child sexual abuse, the researchers used a purposive sample. However, they clearly

TABLE 5.1 *Sampling methods and generalization of findings*

Sampling method	Generalizability
Probability Simple random	Can generalize; limitations minimal
Systematic random	Can generalize; limitations minimal—note how the elements are listed in the sampling frame
Stratified random	Can generalize; limitations minimal—make sure the strata involved are reflected in the analysis of the data
Cluster	Can generalize but some limitations possible—note the characteristics of the elements because there is a possibility of sampling error with this type of probability sampling
Nonprobability Availability	Generalizations very limited
Quota	Generalizations limited
Purposive	Generalizations very limited
Snowball	Generalizations very limited

described the sample as well as the rationale for using a nonprobability sample, with its limitations and strengths.

> *This was a volunteer sample that was not randomly selected. Researchers widely acknowledge that random samples cannot be obtained in perpetrator research because most sexual abuse is undetected. The sample, therefore, is skewed towards known perpetrators, who could be quite different from perpetrators whose abuse is not detected. Data from such skewed samples, however, can provide insight into how some abusers think about sexual abuse. (p. 249)*

Table 5.1 summarizes the sampling methods discussed in this chapter and the extent to which the findings from the resulting sample can be generalized.

Subject's Consent

There is one ethical issue described by the NASW Code of Ethics (1980) that directly relates to sampling. This ethical issue addresses the subject's consent to the research:

> *The social worker engaged in research should ascertain that consent of participants in the research is voluntary and informed, without any implied deprivation or penalty for refusal to participate, and with due regard for participants' privacy and dignity. (pp. 24–25)*

Whenever any type of social work research is undertaken, it is critical that no coercion is exerted. If questionnaires are being mailed to the subjects, the cover letter needs to explain to the potential subjects the nature and the purpose of the research.

Many ethical guidelines present us with dilemmas. We may feel that by disclosing information about the research project to the subject we will be jeopardizing the results of the research. For example, if observation is being used to collect data about a specific behavior and if the subjects know they are being observed, their behavior might change considerably—in other words, reactivity may occur.

Another problem that arises when we inform subjects that their participation is voluntary is that a certain number may choose not to participate. The researcher then does not know whether the results from the subjects who agreed to participate are different from those who refused. The response rate may be affected and the results may have limited generalizability. (We discussed response rates in Chapter 4 with respect to mailed questionnaires.)

Sometimes (although the *sometimes* must be stressed) the voluntary participation ethical standard may need to be modified. If this is necessary, we must clearly understand and explain the reasons. In particular, we must be careful that researchers do not use their power and/or authority to exploit the subjects. Suppose a professor who is carrying out research on students' experiences of sexual harassment requests that all the students in her class complete a questionnaire that she estimates will take about 15 minutes. She states that participation is voluntary, but those who choose not to participate will be required to write a five-page research paper. This is clearly a form of coercion with the professor using her authority to force subjects to participate. A similar situation can be envisioned with a social work researcher requiring the participation of individuals who are dependent upon the social worker for services. Consequently, the decision to violate the subject's consent must be very carefully considered to ensure that no blatant coercion is occurring.

Another way of viewing the issue of the subject's consent is to modify our perspective as to the distinction between researcher and subject. The relationship between researcher and subject can be seen as egalitarian rather than the traditional stance in which researchers wield power and authority over subjects. By adopting an even footing, the question of the subject's consent becomes a nonissue. Instead, researchers make their research skills accessible to the subjects and the subjects become active contributors in the research and each gains from their involvement. This process has been discussed as one characteristic of feminist research. The subjects' direct participation and contribution to the research is based on the argument propounded by Gilligan (1977) that the female voice emphasizes connectedness whereas the male's emphasizes autonomy. Emphasizing the egalitarian relationship between researcher and subject is one way of incorporating this connectedness into research methodology. This type of relationship can be created by using sampling methods such as the key informant and the community forum in which community members have an opportunity to serve both as participants and as contributors (Humm-Delgado & Delgado, 1986).

When evaluating individual practice, the way the research is presented to the client is important and can also affect the researcher–subject relationship.

If you present the research as something special, different, or separate, then the client will see it that way and often resist being involved (or used) in a research project. But if you stress the integration between research and practice and point out how the client will benefit from the feedback on the relative effectiveness of the intervention, then you will be more accurately depicting the whole idea of evaluating practice. In addition, you will be engaging in a true partnership with the client, benefiting all involved.

Breaking down the distinction between researcher and subject has other advantages apart from the issue of the subject's consent. First, it addresses the concern that research is not always responsive to the needs of oppressed groups. This was discussed in Chapter 3; by creating a partnership between researcher and subject, responsiveness is more assured. Second, the validity of the research may be enhanced. The more traditional relationship between researcher and subject, which emphasizes separateness, may result in a greater likelihood of the subject giving invalid responses due to a lack of understanding of intent of the researcher. This problem is avoided by building the partnership. Third, this approach seems to be particularly compatible to social work practice where an emphasis is placed on establishing a relationship with the client.

Creating an egalitarian relationship between subject and researcher thus seems to be a reasonable approach to adopt and one that offers several advantages. However, as a final note we should add that in practice this can sometimes be difficult to achieve. Srinivasan and Davis (1991) comment on this in their article that reports on the organization of a women's shelter. This study, incidentally, is a good example of the application of feminist research principles. They state:

> *Although my intent was to establish egalitarian relationships with all participants in the study, I was not always successful in this regard. The staff readily accepted and treated me as another volunteer, but the residents had more difficulty accepting me as an equal. The residents were skeptical about why I was there. (p. 41)*

Human Diversity Issues in Sampling

Unfortunately, the social science literature, at least prior to the early 1970s, does not provide many examples of studies with heterogeneous samples. For example, Holmes and Jorgensen (1971) found that subjects are males twice as often as females, a ratio that is even more than the use of college student subjects over noncollege student subjects. Not only are the samples homogenous, but also the findings from these samples were generalized to the population as a whole—populations that included noncollege graduates, women, and minorities. These generalizations should never be made because the samples were simply not representative of the populations.

A classic example of this problem is presented by Kohlberg's (1969) study of the development of morality. In his initial study, he selected a sample of Harvard male graduates. Based on this study, Kohlberg developed a model and theory of moral development that he used as a template to assess the moral development of *all* individuals. Moreover, as a result of applying this model to women, he concluded that women often did not reach the higher level of moral development and were, therefore, deficient morally. Later, Gilligan (1977) challenged these conclusions and studied moral development in a sample of women. She proposed alternative moral developmental stages for women, concluding that women were not deviant or deficient in their moral development but simply followed a different course.

Similar assumptions and erroneous generalizations have been made relating to minority populations. White middle-class samples have been studied, and the findings have been generalized and presented as the norm by which to evaluate minorities. This is not always done explicitly by the researchers themselves, but often by others who draw assumptions from the findings and apply them to other groups.

Historically, these assertions have been made about the effectiveness of social programs. Programs are demonstrated to be ineffective with an African-American urban sample, and it is concluded that, consequently, this program will be ineffective with all minorities. It is critical that we recognize diversity within minority groups. Program ineffectiveness with urban African Americans does not mean program ineffectiveness with all minorities nor does it mean ineffectiveness with rural African Americans.

The danger of this occurring can in part be avoided by enhancing the knowledge of the research consumers. This includes you! Researchers, as we discussed in the previous section, can also help by being explicit about the limitations of their sampling method. However, it is often easier to be critical of existing studies than to avoid such pitfalls in our own research. The erroneous assumptions that Kohlberg made almost seem obvious to us now, but that is because we have an increased sensitivity to gender issues. Additionally, we are becoming more aware of ethnic and racial diversity when applying research methods. Be cautioned that there are other dimensions of diversity that are less evident—for example, ageism and homophobia—that are still pervasive even among social workers. Sometimes we are not even aware of what these dimensions of diversity are, and the issue goes beyond whether or not we are consciously excluding a particular group.

Summary

Key concepts in sampling are representativeness and generalizability. The two different types of sampling strategies are probability and nonprobability methods. Probability sampling includes simple random sampling, systematic random sampling, stratified random sampling, and cluster sampling. Nonprobability sampling includes availability sampling, quota sampling, purposive sampling, and snowball sampling.

When conducting sampling in an agency, modifications to sampling methods may need to be made. Ethical issues include the accurate reporting of the sampling method and the subject's consent. Human diversity issues relate to ensuring that the sampling is representative of diverse populations.

Study/Exercise Questions

1   A local agency has asked you to help them conduct a survey to determine if the city needs an elder day care facility. The population of the city is 65,000. About 20% of the city's population lives below the poverty level. All persons over the age of 60 would be eligible for the center.

   a Define the population.

   b Will probability sampling be possible? If not, why not, and if so, what method would you use?

   c Discuss the pros and cons of each of the following suggestions made by various members of the board of the agency:

   i   Interview elders who frequent the local shopping mall early in the morning for exercise.

   ii Mail questionnaires to members of the local branch of the American Association of Retired Persons (AARP).

   iii Conduct a telephone interview using the telephone directory as a sampling frame.

2   Review an issue of *Social Work*. In the research article:

   a What was the sampling method used?

   b What are the limitations to the generalizations of the findings with each of the sampling methods?

   c Were these limitations made explicit in the articles?

Further Reading

Jaeger, R. (1984). *Sampling in education and social services*. New York: Longman.

   An introduction to sampling methods. Also includes information on computer programs for sampling.

Johnson, J. C. (1990). *Selecting ethnographic informants*. Newbury Park, CA: Sage Publications.

   A systematic guide to selecting nonprobability samples. Excellent for the generalist social worker who often cannot use probability samples.

Kish, L. (1965). *Survey sampling*. New York: Wiley.

   The classic work on sampling; extremely comprehensive, and readable, although complex in places.

References

Danziger, S. K., & Farber, N. B. (1990). Keeping inner-city youths in school: Critical experiences of young black women. *Social Work Research and Abstracts, 26*(4), 32–39.

Gilgun, J. F., & Connor, T. M. (1989). How perpetrators view child sexual abuse. *Social Work, 34*(3), 249–254.

Gilligan, C. (1977). In a different voice: Women's conceptions of self and of morality. *Harvard Educational Review, 47,* 481–512.

Holmes, D. S., & Jorgensen, B. W. (1971). The personality and social psychologists study men more than women. *Representative Research in Social Psychology, 2,* 71–76.

Humm-Delgado, D., & Delgado, M. (1986). Gaining community entree to assess service needs of Hispanics. *Social Casework, 67*(2), 80–89.

Kohlberg, L. (1969). *Stages in the development of moral thought and action.* New York: Holt, Rinehart & Winston.

Larson, R. W., Richards, M. H., Raffaelli, M., Ham, M., & Jewell, L. (1990). Ecology of depression in late childhood and early adolescence: A profile of daily states and activities. *Journal of Abnormal Psychology, 99*(1), 92–102.

Lusk, M. W., Peralta, F., & Vest, G. W. (1989). Street children of Juarez: A field study. *International Social Work, 32,* 289–302.

National Association of Social Workers. (1980). NASW Code of ethics. *NASW News, 25,* 24–25.

Rivera, G., Jr. (1990). AIDS and Mexican folk medicine. *Sociology and Social Research 75*(1), 3–7.

Rosenthal, J. A., Groze, V., & Curiel, H. (1990). Race, social class, and special needs adoption. *Social Work, 35,* 532–538.

Rothman, J. (1988). Intervention research: Application to runaway and homeless youths. *Social Work Research and Abstracts, 25*(1), 13–18.

Schilit, R., Lie, G., Bush, J., Montagne, M., & Reyes, L. (1991). Intergenerational transmission of violence in lesbian relationships. *Affilia, 6*(1), 72–87.

Smith, H. W., & Kronauge, C. (1990). The politics of abortion: Husband notification legislation, self-disclosure, and marital bargaining. *The Sociological Quarterly, 31*(4), 585–598.

Srinivasan, M., & Davis, L. V. (1991). A shelter: An organization like any other. *Affilia, 6*(1), 38–57.

Sung, K. (1989). Converging perspectives of consumers and providers in assessing needs of families. *Journal of Social Service Research, 12*(3/4), 1–29.

6

Group Design

Early in the research process you may ask yourself, "How will I know if it's the program that resulted in client change? Maybe it was something else?" To answer this question, we need to develop a research design. This is particularly important when we are conducting a program evaluation. The design and sampling stages are comparable to the selection and collection of the information phase of practice.

The focus of this chapter is **group design,** which means that we are interested in the effect of a variable or variables—the independent variable(s)— on another variable or variables—the dependent variable(s) for a number of different elements or client systems. In a program evaluation, we are often interested in the impact of a program on a particular group of clients. This is to be distinguished from *single-system designs,* which involve understanding the effect of a variable or variables—the intervention(s)—on one client system or element. Single-system designs will be discussed in detail in Chapter 7.

As a generalist social worker, you may not be directly involved in designing the research for a program evaluation. However, at some point your agency will undertake such an evaluation, and it is important that you understand the implications of selecting one type of design over another. In the same way that different sampling methods have their own advantages and limitations, so do research designs.

This chapter will discuss:

▶ Purpose of group design
▶ Validity in group design
▶ Types of research design (strengths and weaknesses)
▶ The agency and group design
▶ Ethical issues in group design
▶ Human diversity issues in group design

Purpose of Group Design

Some forms of research that we have discussed require that *causality* be established. For example, this is critical in summative program evaluations. Causality demands that three basic conditions be met (see Chapter 2): First, the cause precedes the effect in time. Second, the cause and the effect are related to one another. Third, this relationship cannot be accounted for by other factors. These three conditions are established by aspects of research design discussed in this chapter, including the timing of the data collection and the formation of comparison groups. We will also see that these factors affect the generalizability of the findings.

Due to the central role of causality in program evaluation, program evaluations provide the majority of examples in this chapter.

Validity in Group Design

Validity is a central concept in group design. When we discussed validity in Chapter 4, we referred to validity as the ability of the instrument to measure what it was supposed to measure. When we think about the validity of a research design, we are considering two related validity issues: internal validity and external validity.

Internal validity is the extent to which the changes in the dependent variable(s) are a result of the introduction of the independent variable(s) and not some other factor(s). For example, was the reduction in drug use by adolescents a result of their participation in the drug awareness program, or were other factors responsible for this reduction? Here, we are trying to establish causality. In order to ensure internal validity in our drug use question, the three aspects of causality described in the previous section need to be addressed.

The first two conditions—the cause precedes the effect and the relationship between cause and effect—can be met by one aspect of the research design: the data collection time. We may be interested in determining if depressed clients improve as a result of group therapy. We measure their level of depression before and after the group and find that their depression level is high prior to the group and low after the group. This establishes that the group therapy preceded the drop in depression level. Without the first measure of depression (before the group therapy), we would not know whether the low depression measure caused people to join the group or whether the therapy group did, in fact, contribute to the low level.

The two measures also allowed us to establish a relationship between a change in depression levels and participation in the group. For example, 80% of those in the group had low depression after their participation. To decide whether this is a significant or important relationship, we use statistical tests (these will be discussed in Chapter 10). Even if we do determine that the relationship is significant, we still cannot say the group caused a change in depression level as the relationship could be explained by other factors. For example, it may be that at the same time we were measuring the group, a television series

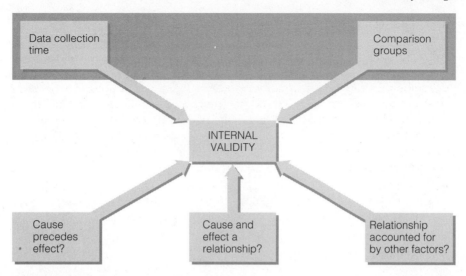

FIGURE 6.1 *Internal validity in group design*

was broadcast on how to cope with depression. Many of our participants may have watched this; in fact, this is what contributed to the lower depression levels rather than participation in the group.

This is where the second aspect of research design as it relates to causality becomes so important: comparison groups. **Comparison groups** are either those who go through another type of program or those who receive no type of bona fide intervention. These comparison groups can help strengthen causality claims. If the decrease in depression level is greater among those who received the group therapy than among those who were in the comparison group, we can begin to narrow down the factors responsible for that change as being the group therapy intervention (see Figure 6.1).

It is important that the comparison groups are equivalent. The most reliable way of ensuring equivalence of the groups is to use random assignment of subjects into an **experimental group** (the group that receives the intervention being evaluated) and a **control group** (the group that does not receive the intervention being evaluated). **Random assignment** means that every subject has an equal chance of being assigned to either group. Equivalency of the groups is important because without it we cannot determine if disparity in outcome between the two groups is due to the treatment or due to the difference between the two groups. Later in this chapter we will discuss some of the problems associated with random assignment and some alternative strategies for setting up comparison groups.

Do not confuse random assignment with random sampling. Random sampling involves creating a sample from a population, not assigning the experimental and control group. Random sampling and random assignment may or may not both be used in the same study. They are independent procedures and have different implications for the findings. Random sampling is concerned

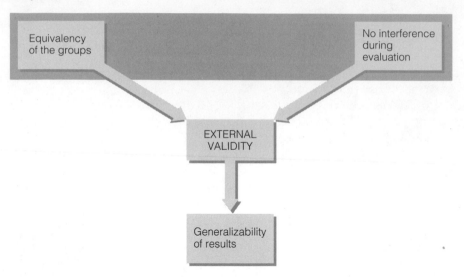

FIGURE 6.2 *External validity in group design*

with the generalizability of the findings and the representativeness of the sample. Random assignment is concerned with the equivalence of the experimental and control groups and with establishing causality. However, we will see in our next discussion that equivalency of the groups can *also* have an effect on the generalizability of the findings.

Group research designs that use randomly assigned controlled groups are **experimental designs,** whereas designs that use comparison groups rather than control groups or no type of comparison or control group are **quasi-experimental** or **preexperimental** designs.

External validity is the other type of validity of concern in group design; it refers to the extent to which the research results are generalizable to the wider population. Internal validity tells us if one treatment is effective with the present client system. External validity tells us if our treatment will be effective with other but similar client systems. As we discussed in Chapter 5, generalizability is influenced by the sampling approach. However, in addition, generalizability depends on two other conditions: first, ensuring the equivalency of the groups, and second, ensuring that nothing happens throughout the course of the evaluation that may jeopardize the equivalence of the groups or the representativeness of the sample (see Figure 6.2).

The first condition for external validity is to ensure the *equivalency of the groups* that are being compared. In the previous example, we may decide that randomly assigning the comparison group is not feasible and that the comparison group should be made up of individuals who were depressed but who chose to be treated in individual rather than group therapy. However, this type of comparison group is problematic in that individuals in the comparison group might possess different characteristics than those who entered group therapy. Consequently, any differences in outcome between the two groups not only would result in lowered internal validity (that is, the causality would be questionable), but in addition the population to which the results could be generalized would be limited. The results could only be generalized to the types of individuals who would choose group therapy over individual therapy, and we may not even be sure what factors lead to this decision.

The second condition that is influenced by the research design and that affects external validity is ensuring that *no interference* occurs during the course of the evaluation that may affect either the equivalence of the groups or the representativeness of the sample. This is sometimes referred to as **treatment diffusion**. A common source of interference is that, in our example, the subjects' lowered depression level after the intervention might be in part affected by their knowledge that they were being evaluated. Again, this not only influences internal validity, but we should also wonder whether subjects who receive the group therapy and who are not being evaluated will have lowered depression levels as well. In other words, the generalization of the initial results to other populations again becomes questionable.

Types of Group Design

In this section we will look at different types of research design with their relative validity problems or threats. We will also comment on how these designs can be useful in program evaluations.

To make this discussion more accessible, we will consider a case example and then apply different designs to it. Assume that you are employed by a clinic that offers adolescents a series of six birth control classes to change attitudes and consequently reduce the number of unplanned pregnancies. You have been asked by your supervisor to evaluate the effectiveness of the program. Now let's work with each design and see how we might apply them to this program evaluation question.

One-Group Posttest-Only Design

The **one-group posttest-only design** consists of one group (that is, no comparison group) with one point of data collection (after the intervention). Figure 6.3 shows how this design might be visualized. Note that although the term *test* is used, this is simply a way of talking about the point at which data collection occurs. The data collection method may be any of the types we discussed in Chapter 4, such as observing a behavior or administering a questionnaire.

The one-group posttest-only design can be extremely useful in gathering information about how a program is functioning. This design can answer two questions; both are fairly basic, but unfortunately neither is routinely asked in agencies. First, how well are the participants functioning at the end of the program? Second, are minimum standards of outcome being achieved? How-

FIGURE 6.3 *One-group posttest-only design*

ever, these questions are elementary, and this design is very limited in its ability to explain or make statements about whether a program was the *cause* of particular outcomes in clients and whether the results can be generalized to other client populations. Consequently, we view this design as having numerous threats to its validity—both internal and external.

E X A M P L E

A One-Group Posttest-Only Design

Marx (1988) describes an "integrative outreach" program designed to meet the needs of adolescents in the Maine State Child Welfare system. The program integrates the experiential education of a wilderness-based adventure program with the psychosocial counseling of a community-based human service agency. Marx's article describes the program in some detail. Measures of outcome include questionnaires administered to the parents and teens at graduation and at the end of the eight-month follow-up.

Threats to Internal Validity

Remember that internal validity refers to whether we can determine if the program caused a particular outcome. With our case example, we need to ask whether it was, in fact, the provision of birth control information that led to any reduction in the pregnancy rate among the adolescent clients.

Using the one-group posttest-only design results in the following threats to internal validity.

Selection   **Selection** refers to the possibility that the kind of people selected for one group may differ from the kind selected for another. It may be that the clients who enrolled in the program were already highly motivated to prevent unwanted pregnancies. There was no pretest to measure this potential predisposition of the clients.

History   **History** involves those events—other than the program—that could affect the outcome. The low pregnancy rate of the participants may be the result of a massive media campaign directed at preventing teenage pregnancy or some other factor that brought about the change. Without a comparison group, this cannot be assessed.

Mortality   **Mortality** refers to subjects dropping out from the groups and so resulting in groups that are not equivalent. Some adolescents may have attended one class on birth control and then dropped out, however they are still considered to be members of the experimental group. This results in the group that ultimately receives the posttest being biased and perhaps showing a higher success rate than would be the case if the success rates of those who dropped out were also monitored. Consequently, the outcome of *all* the participants must be assessed, and if there is no type of pretest, this cannot be done.

Note that mortality and selection have some similarities. With selection we are referring to the bias involved when people initially choose to participate in the program. With mortality, however, we are referring to the bias introduced by those who drop out of the program once they have begun.

Because the data collection only occurs one time (after the intervention) and because of the lack of a comparison group, the extent to which we can say the program caused a change in pregnancy rates is limited with this type of design.

Threats to External Validity

External validity and the generalizability of the results using this type of design include:

Selection–Treatment Interaction   **Selection–treatment interaction** occurs when the ability to generalize is limited because the sample is not randomly selected or there is no pretest, so we cannot determine how typical the clients are. It may be that they are all highly motivated to prevent pregnancy prior to enrolling in the program and, consequently, whether or not they complete the classes is irrelevant.

History–Treatment Interaction   **History–treatment interaction** occurs when other factors may be contributing to the outcome, and so might affect the generalizability of the results (for example, if the positive results were in fact a function of a massive media campaign on pregnancy prevention rather than the program). The program might have a negative outcome if the evaluation were carried out at a different point in time.

One-Group Pretest/Posttest Design

The **one-group pretest/posttest design** is similar to the preceding design except that a pretest is added (Figure 6.4). In our case example, this might consist of a questionnaire given to all clients that asks about their attitudes to unplanned pregnancy prior to their attending the classes. This design not only helps us answer the two questions—How well are the participants functioning at the end of the program? and Are minimum standards of outcome being achieved?—but also, How much do participants change during their participation in the program? This is a useful design, and certainly one that is often used in program

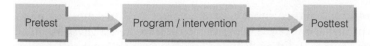

FIGURE 6.4 *One-group pretest/posttest design*

evaluation. However, to what extent can we attribute any decrease in pregnancies to the birth control information when we use this design?

Some additional information can be gained from this type of design. The pretest allows selection to be ruled out as an alternative explanation because any preexisting information on birth control possessed by the adolescents would be identified. However, we will see that in the long run, this design often poses even more threats to validity than the former one.

E X A M P L E

A One-Group Pretest/Posttest Design

Whitman, Graves, and Accardo (1989) describe a program for developmentally delayed parents and their preschool children, a program that includes instruction in parent-child interactions, medical care, hygiene, and home management. Initially, program participants were administered a number of tests prior to implementing the program. The tests included the Communicative Activities of Daily Living Scale (Holland, 1980); an analysis of parent-child interaction; an assessment of the emotional functioning of the parent; a sampling of language; hearing, dental and articulation screening tests; and a physical therapy evaluation. The family was assessed using the Home Observation for Measurement of the Environment Scale. These tests provided a basis for the development of goals for the family and assisted in the program planning. After the 10th month of the program, the assessments and scales were administered again and the results were used to determine change.

Threats to Internal Validity

History   This is still a threat as there is no comparison group.

Maturation   Even though a change may be detected between the pretest and the posttest, this change may not be due to the subjects' enrollment in the program but simply due to **maturation.** In our example, the adolescents would have changed their attitudes regardless of the program. Maturation is a particularly strong threat if the participants are young and/or if there is a long time between the pretest and posttest. A comparison group helps control for maturation effects.

Testing   The **testing** validity threat may occur any time the subjects are exposed to a measuring instrument more than once. If the pretest gave the adolescents the message that their attitude to unplanned pregnancies should change, this effect cannot be separated from the effect of the classes. A comparison group can help control for these testing effects because if they do exist, they exist for both groups; if the attitudes of the clients in the experimental group changed more than those in the comparison group, we would be much more comfortable in concluding that the intervention was responsible for this change rather than the pretest.

Instrumentation   The way in which the variables are measured (**instrumentation**) may change during the course of the evaluation. There may be a change in the questionnaire between its first and second administration. Sometimes, these changes are difficult to avoid. For example, the context in which the questionnaire is administered may change. This change may account for any difference in the results rather than the birth control classes producing this difference.

Regression to the Mean   In our example, some of the subjects may have scored low on the pretest as a result of it being a difficult day for the subject. Most people tend to perform close to their averages, but some days they score particularly high or low. The scores then tend to regress to the average (the mean). The design offers no control for **regression to the mean.**

Interaction of Selection and Other Threats   Even if none of these previously discussed threats to internal validity are applicable to the general population, the threats may be relevant for those subjects selected to participate in the study. To take maturation as an example, it may not be the case that women in general become knowledgeable about birth control as they mature. However, adolescents who express a desire to receive more information through counseling may be as likely to become more knowledgeable just through the function of age. This represents the **interaction of selection and other threats**—in this case, maturation.

Threats to External Validity

History–Treatment Interaction   History–treatment interaction is a problem with this design.

Reactive Effects   Reactive effects can occur when subjects change their behavior if they know they are participating in the study. As a result, the outcomes may be distorted and cannot be generalized to a wider population. These reactive effects are difficult to overcome in any design because we cannot ethically engage in research without gaining the subject's consent. We will discuss this issue later in this chapter.

Static-Group Comparison Design

The **static-group comparison design** is an extension of the posttest-only design and includes a comparison group that also has a posttest (Figure 6.5). In this

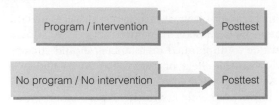

FIGURE 6.5 *Static-group comparison design*

design, the groups are nonequivalent in that the comparison group was not randomly assigned, and there is no way of knowing how the groups are different or similar.

Several strategies can be adopted to achieve some equivalency of the comparison group even if random assignment does not occur. These strategies include baseline comparison, matching, cohort groups, and overflow comparison.

Baseline Comparison

Baseline comparison occurs when the comparison group is composed of cases handled prior to the introduction to the program. The problem with this approach is that it is difficult to determine whether cases identified as eligible in the absence of a program would have actually been referred to such a program.

Matching

Matching involves selecting certain characteristics that are thought to be important in impacting outcomes—for example, gender or ethnicity—and ensuring these characteristics are equally represented in each group. In our example, based on previous research and our own experience, we may think that ethnicity—namely, being Hispanic—is an important factor in determining the effectiveness of the program. Consequently, we make sure the program group has the same proportion of Hispanic adolescents as the comparison group. In a sense, matching is equivalent to quota sampling. Matching can also be combined with random assignment. When combined in this way, it is the equivalent of stratified random sampling. Needless to say, matching has the same problems as stratified or quota sampling. You need to ensure that the variables considered are, in fact, key variables. Often, it is difficult to determine the critical variables because of the lack of previous research or other sources of information to guide these decisions.

Cohort Groups

Cohort groups provide another strategy for compiling comparison groups and are a variation on matching. Cohort groups are composed of individuals who move through an organization at the same time as those in the program being evaluated, but they do not receive the services of the program.

For example, you compare adolescents in the same class at school. Some are enrolled in the program—that is, the birth control class—and others are not. Or one entire class is enrolled and another class is not. Cohort groups can also be combined with matching.

Overflow Comparison

Overflow comparison groups are those people who are referred to a program but because the slots are filled a waiting list is created and this can then serve as a comparison group.

However the comparison group is formed in the static-group comparison design, they are all nonequivalent, that is, not randomly assigned. This design offers one advantage over single-group designs: The threat from history is eliminated because external events that may have an effect on the outcome will be occurring in both groups. However, the design still has other threats to internal and external validity.

Threats to Internal Validity

Selection   This is the major threat to this design's internal validity and is the result of not randomly assigning the groups and having no pretest. Consequently, it is not possible to determine how similar the two groups are to each other; any difference that occurs in the outcome between the two groups may not be due to the presence or absence of the intervention, but to other differences between the groups.

For example, if our experimental group is made up of adolescents who elected to enroll in the birth control classes and the comparison group is made up of adolescents who did not want to attend the classes, there is the potential for this group to be very different from the experimental group. The experimental group may later have a lower pregnancy rate than the comparison group, but this may not be a function of the classes as much as to the fact that the experimental group was more motivated to learn about birth control than the comparison group. We cannot be assured of the equivalency of the groups due to lack of random assignment and lack of a pretest.

Mortality   Mortality is still a problem, again because of the absence of a pretest and the absence of a randomly assigned comparison group.

Threats to External Validity

Selection–Treatment Interaction   Selection–treatment interaction is a problem with this design.

Reactive Effects   Reactive effects threaten the external validity of this design.

Clearly the addition of a comparison group strengthens this design. However, there are two problems that we may encounter in using nonequivalent comparison groups, these are ethical problems and contamination between the groups.

First, ethical problems can arise in the establishment of comparison groups. Gaining the subjects' consent is important as we discussed in Chapter 5, but informed consent may be difficult if the subjects realize that they may only be in a comparison group. You may be tempted to withhold some information to encourage their participation and to maintain the integrity of the comparison and experimental groups. If someone knows she is in the experimental group, the expectations may be higher for a successful outcome; the converse is true for the comparison group, that is, reactivity effects could have an influence. Another ethical issue is the question of whether assignment to a comparison group is ethical in that it could be conceived of as denial of treatment. These and other ethical issues involved in the research design will be examined later in the chapter.

Second, it may be difficult to prevent **contamination** between the comparison group and the experimental group. This is when it becomes difficult to distinguish between the experimental and the comparison group. Contamination can occur in two ways: first, the clients themselves may talk to each other about the program; second, there may not be a clear distinction between the types of intervention provided in the two groups. If the adolescents in our example are typical adolescents, they will probably have contact with each other either in their neighborhoods or in school, and they could talk to each other about the program. One way of overcoming this is to select the comparison group from one community and the experimental group from another, but this can threaten the equivalency of the two groups.

Occasionally, there is not a clear distinction between the program experiences of the clients in each group. With the adolescents, if it is a matter of one class versus six classes, this is not so much of an issue; but if different techniques are used—such as lecturing versus a more interactive style of teaching about birth control—it may become a problem in that there is only a fuzzy distinction between these two approaches. The extent of this problem depends on the nature of the intervention being evaluated. In some cases, it may be necessary to closely monitor the type of intervention each group is receiving. However, this rather structured approach to providing interventions can lead to resistance from the agencies, who may see this rigid structure as depriving them of the ability to respond to individual client needs. This can result in the agency failing to refer clients to the project (Schilling, Schinke, Kirkham, Meltzer, & Norelius, 1988).

We should also note that sometimes it is completely impossible to ensure the equivalency of groups because of some predetermined situation. Sometimes, in fact, research is focused on identifying the factors that distinguish the two groups. For example, Dobrin (1989) examined the different ethical judgments of male and female social workers. Obviously, these two groups are not equivalent. This kind of situation usually arises in pure research rather than the types we have been primarily concerned with in this book. However, matching

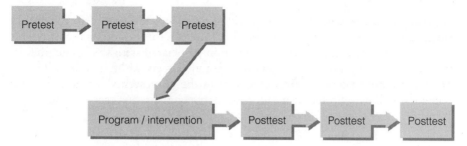

FIGURE 6.6 *Time series design*

often can be used very successfully with this type of pure research study to ensure the equivalence of groups on other factors.

E X A M P L E

Matching

Kiecolt, Janice, Dyer, and Shuttleworth (1988) collected data on social support and need from two matched groups that differed with respect to whether or not they were family caregivers for Alzheimer's disease victims. The two groups were matched on frequency of contact, closeness of relationships, or upset associated with relationships. The caregivers whose relatives had more symptomatic Alzheimer's behavior were more distressed and described their relationships with others as more upsetting.

Time Series Design

A **time series design** overcomes some of the problems of the designs discussed previously, measuring several times before the intervention and then several times after the intervention (Figure 6.6). For example, a test on the adolescents' attitude to birth control might be given to the adolescents several times over the course of several months prior to the counseling. Then it is given several times after the intervention. Depending on the period of time over which the tests are given, we can also view this as a **longitudinal design,** or one that tracks behavior over a significant period of time. A **cross-sectional design,** on the other hand, measures behavior as it occurs at one point in time or over a relatively short period of time.

The advantage of the time series design is its ability to detect trends in the data before and after the intervention. In effect, this discounts the problems of maturation, testing, and instrumentation associated with the single pretest/posttest design because any trends in these effects could be detected. For example, if maturation is having an effect on the adolescents' attitude to birth control it will be reflected by a difference between the pretest scores.

E X A M P L E

A Longitudinal Study

Lurigio and Lewis (1989) conducted a longitudinal study of state mental patients in Chicago by investigating patient adjustment to everyday living outside state hospitals. The subjects were interviewed shortly after their admission to the hospital and 6 and 12 months later. The findings revealed that the patients experienced extensive poverty, homelessness, inadequate aftercare services, and "a dearth of community-based resources to prevent repeat hospitalizations" (p. 88).

Threats to Internal Validity

History   History is a major threat to internal validity in the time series design. This is due to the absence of any type of comparison group, although events external to the evaluation would have to be fairly powerful in order to confound the effect of the treatment.

Threats to External Validity

History–Treatment Interaction   History–treatment interaction is a potential threat to external validity as it interacts with the treatment. An intervention that appears to work under some circumstances may not under others.

Reactive Effects   With repeated testing, reactive effects are also a problem.

Pretest/Posttest Comparison-Group Design

The **pretest/posttest comparison-group design** is a combination of the static-group comparison and the one-group pretest/posttest design (see Figure 6.7). The comparison group is still not randomly assigned, although this design can adopt any of the various methods used to set up comparison groups that are mentioned for the static-group comparison design. By combining the features of both the static-group comparison and the one-group pretest/posttest design, this design becomes less problematic than either of them. History is controlled due to the comparison group, and the pretest identifies to a certain extent differences or similarities between the groups.

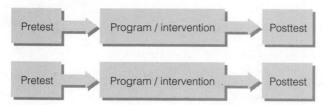

FIGURE 6.7 *Pretest/posttest comparison-group design*

Threats to Internal Validity

Selection and Maturation Interaction   In our example, the pretest may indicate that the group that received classes had more positive attitudes toward birth control than the comparison group, prior to the intervention. If the posttest also indicates this difference between the groups, maturation may have been the cause of the treatment group having even more positive attitudes over time, regardless of whether they had received the classes. This potential problem with internal validity depends a great deal on how the comparison group is selected and what the results indicate.

Threats to External Validity

Selection–Treatment Interaction   Selection–treatment interaction is potentially a problem and can affect the generalizability of the results.

Maturation–Treatment Interaction   Maturation–treatment interaction is potentially a problem.

Reactive Effects   Reactive effects are a problem with this design.

E X A M P L E

A Pretest/Posttest Comparison-Group Design

Workman, Bloland, Grafton, and Kester (1987) compared 36 female community college students who received assertion training with 37 students from the same population who did not receive the group training. The two groups were not formed by random assignment. The Tennessee Self-Concept Scale and the State Trait Anxiety Scale were administered pretest and posttest. The results indicated that the group who received the training increased significantly in the dependent variables of assertiveness, internal locus of control, and self-concept, and that there was a significant reduction in state and trait anxiety.

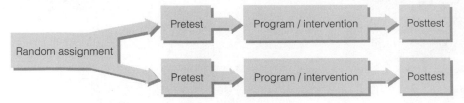

FIGURE 6.8 *Pretest/posttest control-group design*

Pretest/Posttest Control-Group Design

The difference between the **pretest/posttest control-group design** and the previous one is that the comparison group and experimental groups are randomly assigned. When this occurs, the comparison group is referred to as a *control group* (see Figure 6.8). In our example, random assignment to either the control or experimental group might be made from a high school class. As a result of a randomly assigned control group, the internal validity threats of history, maturation, mortality, selection, regression to the mean testing, and instrumentation are virtually eliminated.

As we mentioned previously, those designs with control groups are known as experimental designs and are stronger than quasi-experimental designs in their ability to determine the cause of a particular outcome. Consequently, to avoid criticism such as "These are interesting findings, *but* it is possible that something else was influencing the results due to problems with your research design," use experimental designs with randomly assigned control groups. You will be surprised how often it is feasible to implement these designs, and the conclusions you will be able to draw from the findings are well worth the effort.

E X A M P L E

A Pretest/Posttest Control-Group Design

Goodman (1990) evaluated the impact of a model telephone network program for caregivers of Alzheimer's disease victims. The study looked at the caregiver's use of informal supports, perceived social supports, mental health, burden, and information about Alzheimer's disease. Participants were randomly assigned to the program or to an informational lecture series accessed over the telephone. In addition, the researchers combined a matching element along with the random assignment. The caregivers were matched initially for age (under 65, 65 or over), gender, and relationship to victim (adult child, spouse, sibling). Then one of each pair was assigned randomly to the network or lecture component.

FIGURE 6.9 *Posttest-only control-group design*

There remains only one potential external validity problem with the pretest/posttest control-group design. This involves the possible reactive effect of the pretest.

Despite the strength of this design, there are some problems in its implementation. Some of the problems are similar to those encountered in setting up nonrandomly assigned comparison groups, including nonavailability of a list or pool of clients from which random assignment can occur, contamination problems, and ethical issues.

First, as with random sampling, for random assignment to occur there has to be a list of the pool from which each of the groups will be drawn. This could be a problem if we were interested in the effect of the birth control classes on teenagers who had already experienced a pregnancy. Obtaining a list of these individuals to assign them to two groups is likely to be difficult. Consequently, the establishment of a control group often is not feasible, particularly in program evaluation.

Second, contamination problems can still occur, either between the groups or in terms of the consistency of the types of interventions received by each group.

Third, ethical issues are intensified with the use of a control group. Obtaining the consent of subjects is doubly problematic if you cannot even inform them prior to their involvement in the evaluation whether they will be in the experimental or the control group. The potential for reactivity effects exists if the subjects are informed whether they are in the control or experimental group. Other ethical problems associated with control groups, including a "denial of treatment" issue, will be discussed toward the end of this chapter.

Posttest-Only Control-Group Design

One way of eliminating the threat to external validity posed by the previous design is to simply eliminate the pretest. In the **posttest-only control-group design,** the two groups are again randomly assigned and consequently should be equivalent, and there should be no need for the pretests (Figure 6.9). However, some researchers are reluctant to eliminate what is essentially a safety measure to ensure the equivalency of the groups.

EXAMPLE

A Posttest-Only Control-Group Design

Cuenot (1982) assessed the effectiveness of a one-time alcohol abuse preventive presentation to 7th graders using a posttest-only control-group design. Scores of the alcohol questionnaire of 179 7th graders who were exposed to the educational program were compared to the scores of 153 7th graders who were not. Students who attended the program more readily identified the existence of peer and parental drinking behavior. However, they did not communicate any differences regarding personal drinking behavior and values.

The Solomon Four-Group Design

The **Solomon four-group design** is a combination of the above two designs and, as a result, is extremely valid (see Figure 6.10). However, it is rarely used in social work research. It is usually difficult to find enough subjects to randomly assign between two groups, and the cost of the design exceeds the budgets of most social work program evaluations.

EXAMPLE

A Solomon Four-Group Design

Sawyer and Beck (1991) studied the effects of two types of educational videotapes on the perceived susceptibility of university freshmen to HIV (AIDS virus). The research design consisted of two experimental conditions with pretests and posttests and two control groups—one with a pretest and a posttest and one with a posttest only. The addition of the pretest to one of the control groups makes this design different from the four-group design illustrated in Figure 6.10.

The results indicated a significant increase in perceived susceptibility to HIV in the students who viewed the more affective, rather than the more cognitive videotape, particularly in those students who were not yet sexually active.

Table 6.1 summarizes each of the group designs and their threats to internal and external validity discussed in this chapter.

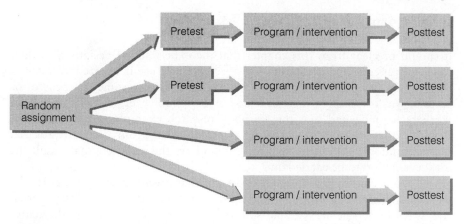

FIGURE 6.10 *Solomon four-group design*

TABLE 6.1 *Group research designs—threats to internal and external validity*

Type of design	Threats to internal validity	Threats to external validity
One-group posttest-only	Selection, history, mortality	Selection–treatment interaction, history–treatment interaction
One-group pretest/posttest	History, maturation, testing, instrumentation, regression to mean, interaction of selection and other threats	History–treatment interaction, reactive effects
Static-group comparison	Selection and mortality	Selection–treatment interaction
Time series	History	History–treatment interaction, reactive effects
Pretest/posttest comparison	Selection and maturation	Selection–treatment interaction, maturation–treatment interaction, reactive effects
Pretest/posttest control-group	None	Reactive effects
Posttest-only control-group	None	None
Solomon four-group	None	None

The Agency and Group Design

It should be clear from this chapter that the experimental designs with their randomly assigned control groups are preferable to use if we are interested in establishing whether a program or intervention, and not some other factor or factors, was responsible for a specific outcome. However, as generalist social workers we may find that the textbook research examples are not feasible. Don't be discouraged if you can't use a Solomon four-group design or, for that matter, random assignment; we often do not have the resources that enable the ideal evaluation to be carried out.

Our challenge is to develop designs that are *feasible,* and that is why we have included in this chapter some practical ideas on, for example, alternative ways of setting up comparison groups. Not only are these alternative strategies compatible with agency practice, but if the comparison groups received services or treatments (including simply part of the intervention being provided to the experimental group), many of these strategies become even more feasible and attractive to agencies. This becomes a particularly useful approach with crisis-oriented or court-ordered services. Some argue that since the goal of applied research is to improve on present services, the best test of a new intervention may be a comparison with a traditional form of practice (Basham, 1986; Jacobson, 1985).

Another strategy that may result in the greater participation of agencies involves the use of unbalanced designs with fewer subjects assigned to the comparison or control group. Consequently, clients referred to the agency are more likely to receive services (Schilling, et al., 1988).

More important than striving for the perfect design is to acknowledge your design's drawbacks and address them in the reporting of the evaluation. Finally, recognize that although many of the earlier designs discussed in this chapter may have internal and external validity problems, they have other contributions to make. For example, the posttest-only design can result in an extremely useful descriptive or formative evaluation of a program. By conducting research in this practical, knowledgeable, and responsible way, knowledge building in social work can progress with a solid agency-based foundation.

Ethical Issues in Group Design

There are two major ethical issues related to group design, both of them associated with control or comparison groups. First, there is the issue of whether establishing a comparison/control group involves denying services to clients. Second, there is the question of whether informed consent of the subjects should be gained so that a comparison group can be established.

Assignment to the Comparison/Control Group

This research strategy could be viewed as a denial of services, justified in the name of science, and is an ethical dilemma that can have implications for the administration of the evaluation. The personnel may see the creation of comparison/control groups as a way of manipulating clients and could consequently influence the evaluation. For example, in a situation where the comparison group is receiving a variation of the intervention to be evaluated, the staff—if they disagree with the creation of the comparison group—may not adhere to the guidelines governing this variation in an attempt to bring legitimate services to the subjects in the comparison group. In addition, clients simply may not be referred to the project.

However, two counterarguments can be posed. First, the decision about who receives services in an agency is often arbitrary and political. Program services may run on demand, and the deprivation of services is not uncommon. Second, by suggesting that denial of treatment is occurring, we are assuming that the intervention being evaluated is effective. Often, though, we have no empirical basis for assuming that this is the case. In fact, if we had, there would be little reason for carrying out the research in the first place. However, as in practice, often the situation is not this clear-cut. Usually there is some evidence—perhaps a combination of practice wisdom and research findings—indicating that the treatment is helpful to some extent. The purpose of the evaluation is thus to determine how helpful it is. Consequently, our concern that we are violating subjects' rights by possibly denying them beneficial treatment involves other factors such as our own judgments and values about how detrimental the denial could be. This is another example of the important role that values play in the scientific process.

Decisions relating to the establishment of control/comparison groups are probably governed by the seriousness of the problem. Under most circumstances it would be hard to justify establishing groups of emotionally disturbed children involved in self-destructive behaviors. In addition, the use of waiting lists and cohort groups, baseline comparison groups, and assignment to other types of interventions or programs can help ameliorate some of the potential ill effects of being assigned to the comparison or control group.

Informed Consent

Informed consent involves informing potential subjects fully of their role and the consequences of their participation in the research and seeking their permission. We discussed informed consent in Chapter 5 as it related to sampling. Informed consent also impacts group design.

First, it is an issue because of the difficulty of forming comparison groups. In seeking a comparison group, we may be reluctant to fully inform potential participants that they will not be receiving a service. In an attempt to ensure their participation, we may justify to ourselves that consent is not necessary if they are not receiving the service. This is less of a problem with control groups where participants can be told they may or may not be receiving the service (because of random assignment to the control and experimental groups). However, *consent must be gained at all times for any participation*—whether in the experimental group or the comparison/control group.

As discussed in the previous section, the effects of being in the control group can be improved somewhat by adopting alternative strategies—waiting lists, alternative programs, and so forth. These strategies can also help with the consent issue. In other words, the researcher will not be so tempted to avoid seeking informed consent (in anticipation of the potential subject refusing to participate) because ultimately the client will receive some type of intervention.

The second issue relating to informed consent is the possibility that informing the subjects of the details of the evaluation will jeopardize the validity of the findings. For example, if the experimental group knows they are the experimental group and the control/comparison group knows that they are the control/comparison group, this can set up expectations that can affect outcome. The experimental group may expect to change and—regardless of the actual impact of the intervention itself—may show improvement. We talked about this threat to validity earlier in the chapter as a reactive effect. With this threat, it is tempting to avoid giving subjects all the details of their participation.

However, informed consent should still be obtained. One way of dealing with the reactive problem is to inform the subjects that they will either be placed in a control/comparison or experimental group but they will not be told which one in order to protect the validity of the findings. Of course, this is only possible if the control/comparison group is receiving at least some type of intervention, whether it is a variation of the one being evaluated or another intervention completely. If this is not feasible, possible reactive effects need to be acknowledged rather than not informing the subjects.

Human Diversity Issues in Group Design

When developing a program evaluation and making decisions about the design of the research, the major issue relating to human diversity is ensuring that certain groups are not being exploited for the purpose of establishing comparison groups. Sometimes this can occur unintentionally. In social science research there is the tendency to assign to comparison groups (this is not an issue for control groups when subjects are randomly assigned) those in disadvantaged groups such as the poor, minorities, women, and others.

Parlee (1981) argues that the choice of particular comparison groups in psychology research (and this argument can be extended to social science research in general) demonstrates the scientist's "implicit theoretical framework." She suggests that many of these frameworks are biased against women, and this becomes a real problem when we engage matching. "Knowing" what variables to include entails biases that can favor certain groups over others. The choice of the comparison group defines the perspective that will dominate the research and this in turn will influence the findings.

Parlee cites the example of a study where a matched comparison group of women was sought for a 20-year-old men-only study of aging. One alternative was to match the women according to intelligence, education, and occupation. Another might argue for matching according to physiological similarities, for example, including the men's sisters. The former represented the social scientists' perspective while the latter reflected that of biomedical scientists. Clearly, these provide two different perspectives on the causality underlying aging and will probably result in very different conclusions being drawn from the study.

It is critical to recognize this potential bias in comparison group selection. To counterbalance this problem, we should involve people of diversity in the conceptualization of the research, particularly if this is a program evaluation that impacts on diverse populations. In this way, alternative viewpoints and perspectives can be fully incorporated into the group design.

Summary

Group design studies the effect of a variable(s) on another variable(s), for instance, examining the impact of an intervention on a particular group of clients. Internal validity is the extent to which the changes in the dependent variable are a result of the independent variable. External validity refers to the generalizability of the research findings to a wider population. Various research designs involve threats to internal and external validity to different extents. Research designs may have to be modified in agency settings. A design's drawbacks should be acknowledged in the reporting of the evaluation.

Ethical issues relating to group design include potentially denying services to clients when establishing comparison or control groups and ensuring that informed consent is obtained from the clients. Human diversity issues involve not exploiting certain groups for use as comparison groups.

Study/Exercise Questions

1 The family service agency in which you are employed is planning to conduct an evaluation of its services. As the leader of a support group of parents of developmentally disabled children, you are asked to design an evaluation of this particular service. What design could you develop that would be feasible and that would maximize the validity of your findings?

2 Review an issue of *Social Work Research and Abstracts* and select an article that used one of the research designs described in this chapter.

a What are the threats to internal and external validity?

b Were these threats explicitly discussed?

c Propose an alternative design that would be feasible.

Further Reading

Cook, T. Q., & Stanley, J. (1963). *Experimental and quasi-experimental designs for research*. Chicago: Rand McNally.

> A classic discussion of different research designs.

Fairweather, G. W., & Davidson, W. S. (1986). *An introduction to community experimentation: Theory, methods and practice*. New York: McGraw-Hill.

> Specifically written for those involved with the evaluation of community programs.

References

Basham, R. B. (1986). Scientific and practical advantages of comparative design in psychotherapy outcome research. *Journal of Consulting and Clinical Psychology, 54*, 880–894.

Cuenot, R. G. (1982). Evaluation of effectiveness of a one-time alcohol abuse preventive education assembly. *Psychological Report, 51*, 440–442.

Dobrin, A. (1989). Ethical judgments of male and female social workers. *Social Work, 34*, 451–455.

Goodman, C. (1990). Evaluation of a model self-help telephone program: Impact on natural networks. *Social Work, 35*, 556–562.

Holland, A. L. (1980). *Communicative activities in daily living: A test of functional communication for aphasic adults*. Austin, TX: Pro-Ed.

Jacobson, N. S. (1985). Family therapy outcome research: Potential pitfalls and prospects. *Journal of Marital and Family Therapy, 11*, 149–158.

Kiecolt, G., Janice, K., Dyer, C., & Shuttleworth, E. C. (1988). Upsetting social interactions and distress among Alzheimer's disease family care-givers: A replication and extension. *American Journal of Community Psychology, 16*, 825–837.

Lurigio, A. J., & Lewis, D. A. (1989). Worlds that fail: A longitudinal study of urban mental patients. *Journal of Social Issues, 45*, 79–90.

Marx, J. Q. (1988). An outdoor adventure counseling program for adolescents. *Social Work, 33*, 517–520.

Parlee, M. B. (1981). Appropriate control groups in feminist research. *Psychology of Women Quarterly, 5*, 637–644.

Sawyer, R. G., & Beck, K. H. (1991). Effects of videotapes on perceived susceptibility to HIV/AIDS among university freshmen. *Health Values, 15*, 31–40.

Schilling, R. F., Schinke, S. P., Kirkham, M. A., Meltzer, N. J., & Norelius, K. L. (1988). Social work research in social service agencies: Issues and guidelines. *Journal of Social Service Research, 11*(4), 75–87.

Whitman, B. Y., Graves, B., & Accardo, P. J. (1989). Training in parenting skills for adults with mental retardation. *Social Work, 34,* 431–434.

Workman, J. F., Bloland, P. A., Grafton, C. L., & Kester, D. L. (1987). Changes in self-concept, locus of control, and anxiety among female college students as related to assertion training. *Educational Research Quarterly, 11,* 21–28.

Single-System Design

7

Group designs are obviously appropriate for some program evaluations and needs assessments, but how do we design research for the evaluation of our own practice when there is only one client system? When evaluating the effectiveness of interventions in our own practice, we can use **single-system designs.** There is one subject in these studies; in generalist practice, this subject or single system can be of various sizes—individual, group, agency, or community.

When conducting a single-system study in the evaluation of our own practice, the first few steps of the research process are very similar to those taken when carrying out a needs assessment or program evaluation. The research question is developed, variables are operationalized, data are collected, and the sample is selected—in single-system studies, one case. However, the research design stage is significantly different when we only have one client system in our sample. In this chapter, we will describe the characteristics of single-system design as opposed to group design. We will also see that the analysis of the data requires some different techniques; however, because this chapter focuses on the design stage of single-system studies, we will wait to consider the statistical techniques used with single-system studies until Chapter 10. Similarly, the data collection methods of particular use in single-system studies (for example, goal attainment scaling) have already been described in Chapter 4. See Table 7.1 for some comparisons between single-system studies and group studies (such as needs assessments and program evaluations).

Although we use different techniques in establishing single-system designs, we are still concerned with the issue of causality. Some single-system designs can result in stronger statements about causality than others, just as with group designs. However, the strategies used by single-system designs to reach their conclusions differ from those we adopt in group designs. Most significantly, single-system studies do not use comparison groups per se, but use other methods for controlling alternative explanations.

TABLE 7.1 *Research steps of single-system studies and group studies*

Research step	Similarities and differences between single-system studies and group studies
Deciding on the question	Similar—derives directly from practice and/or the agency
Developing the question	Similar—must define and operationalize the variables
Collecting the data	Similar—can use observation, interviews, questionnaires, secondary data, journals/logs
Sampling	Similar—but only one element sampled in single-system studies
Design	Different—must use different types of design; single-system studies use no comparison groups
Organizing data	Similar—depends on whether data qualitative or quantitative
Quantitative analysis descriptive and inferential	Different—different techniques required
Writing the report	Similar

The type of design is affected by the type of research question and the extent to which causality is sought. As with group designs, single-system designs vary from exploratory or descriptive to explanatory.

This chapter will include:

▶ History of single-system studies
▶ Types of single-system designs, along with their strengths and weaknesses
▶ Advantages and disadvantages of single-system designs
▶ The agency and single-system design
▶ Ethical issues in single-system design
▶ Human diversity issues in single-system design

History of Single-System Studies

As we mentioned in Chapter 1, there were several studies in the 1960s and early 1970s that suggested that social work practice was not as effective as many had expected (Fischer, 1973). In part, these studies were a response to the increasing demand for accountability by social programs; it was no longer enough to be well intentioned and to want to help people.

On closer examination, the research studies themselves were found to have major methodological problems, raising questions about whether the findings from the studies should be viewed seriously and as an accurate reflection of the state of social work practice. First, the research studies often had no type of comparison group, which led to questions about the internal and external validity of the results. Second, because group designs pool both the results from successful and unsuccessful programs in order to determine average results, they were not able to determine what actually worked with whom, and with what kinds of problems. Consequently, the results were often of little use to the practitioner. Third, the group designs generally relied on only two measures—one before the intervention and one after the intervention. There was no way of knowing what happens between these two measurement points. For example, a posttest may indicate that the target problem has not decreased in severity. However, it is possible that there was a time after the intervention but before the posttest when some decrease did occur. It could not be determined if and why this had occurred because of the way many of these studies were designed.

In addition to the methodological problems that characterized these early group studies, there are other problems relating to ethical and social issues. First, it is often difficult to get the support of agency personnel in assigning clients to control or comparison groups because of the ethical issues we discussed in Chapter 6. Second, it is also often difficult to impossible for agencies to come up with the funds for a full-scale evaluation of even a moderate-sized program.

As a consequence of these problems and the continuing demand for the accountability of the social services, social workers were increasingly required to evaluate their own practice. These evaluations produced results identifying specific interventions and their effectiveness with specific clients with specific types of problems. As a result of this changing emphasis, a new technology was adopted from psychology to meet this need—a technology known as single-system or single-subject studies.

The premise of the single-system study is that individual practitioners evaluate interventions they implement; in the process, they take into consideration the specific client system and client problem, thereby producing more specific results that can directly inform their practice. This whole process ultimately benefits the client, as do all evaluations of practice, but with single-system studies, the client receives feedback from the evaluation much more directly than is the case with a large-scale program evaluation.

Types of Single-System Design

Our discussion of single-system designs will be divided into two broad categories—exploratory/descriptive and explanatory. Remember that these are broad categories and are not necessarily mutually exclusive; they are simply rough classification guides.

Exploratory/Descriptive Designs

Exploratory/descriptive designs focus on describing the *process* of the intervention (as in a formative program evaluation) rather than on explaining an outcome (as in a summative evaluation). As a student social worker, you may be asked to evaluate how you are applying an intervention and to describe your activities to your supervisor. You can use various data collection methods to accomplish this. Probably the most common is to use self-observation in conjunction with **process recordings,** which are simply written records of what transpired with a client system, either based on notes or on a transcription of a recording of an interview. (Exploratory/descriptive studies are also referred to as **case studies.**)

A detailed description of any change in the target behavior is not necessary in this design as the focus is on the application and use of the intervention. However, to describe the intervention some discussion of its impact on the client system and target behavior inevitably is included.

Let's look at two examples using the exploratory/descriptive design that focuses on the intervention. Suppose you are just beginning your employment with Child Protective Services, and your supervisor has given you the go-ahead to visit a family alone. However, you are still unsure about whether you are conducting the interview appropriately. Consequently, immediately after the home visit you sit down and record the major interactions and your perceptions, thoughts, and feelings about the interview. You later share this with your supervisor. This process can help identify the strengths and weaknesses in your interviewing skills; if you continue this type of monitoring for several cases, you may see patterns emerging. Ideally, data collection for this type of study should use either video or audio recording, but in the child protective case, recording would have been difficult, inappropriate, and possibly illegal.

In our second example, you are involved in trying to organize a community center for youths but have never tackled anything like this before. Consequently, you carefully monitor all your activities connected with this endeavor, and you share this information with a more experienced community organizer whom you met at a NASW chapter conference the previous year. In this situation, rather than having to rely on anecdotes and your memory, your process recordings give you a systematic record of what occurred. This in turn can provide potential data for a more explanatory design that you might want to attempt at a later date, in which you try to determine if this strategy really did have the anticipated outcomes.

Examples of the exploratory/descriptive design with the focus on the intervention can also be found in the social work literature. For example, Hollis (1968) conducted a series of studies that analyzed the content of social casework interviews in an attempt to understand the process, rather than the outcome, of treatment. She created a typology by which interviews could be coded. Details of this typology are provided in Chapter 8 where we discuss ways in which data can be organized.

E X A M P L E

An Exploratory/Descriptive Design with a Focus on the Intervention

A case study by Pomerantz, Pomerantz, and Colca (1990) examines the application of a specialized family program that provided time-intensive, home-based services to a family in which both parents were deinstitutionalized, disabled individuals. The interventions consisted of education in child care and home management and the case management of agencies. Through this case study, the program needs of disabled parents and their families were discussed.

Often the information gained from these types of studies can help to formulate hypotheses for future evaluations of our own practice. Consequently, we can view this type of exploratory/descriptive study as adopting an inductive mode of knowledge building, which we discussed in Chapter 1. We will discuss how to analyze the data for a case study in Chapter 11.

Explanatory Designs

Explanatory designs go beyond simply describing the intervention and examine the actual impact of the intervention on the target behavior. Thus, the purpose of explanatory single-system designs is to help determine the effectiveness of the intervention on the target behavior. Their design involves three elements that help establish causality: a baseline, clear identification of the intervention, and target behaviors that can be operationalized and repeatedly measured.

Baseline

Rather than depending on control or comparison groups in their search for causality, single-system designs rely on the target behavior being measured time and time again. In effect, the client system serves as its own control. A similar principle is in effect here as that used in time series designs discussed in the previous chapter; with group design, however, a group of client systems is being monitored whereas in the single-system study, only one client system is monitored.

The repeated measurement prior to the intervention is known as the **baseline.** The baseline lets us compare target behavior rates before and after the intervention, thus allowing us to assess the impact of the intervention on the target behavior. Figure 7.1 demonstrates how results from explanatory single-system designs are usually displayed. The X axis records the incidents of the target behavior, and the Y axis shows the time interval over which the behavior is recorded. The vertical line represents the point at which the intervention was introduced.

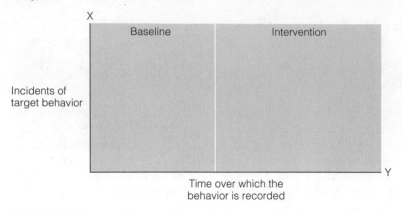

FIGURE 7.1 *Displaying the results from explanatory single-system designs*

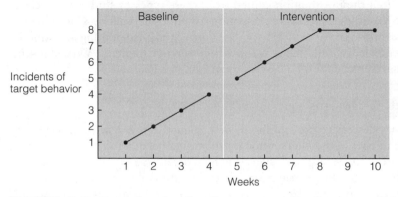

FIGURE 7.2 *Example of a baseline moving the direction of the desired outcome*

However, for the assessment to have some validity, we need a stable baseline prior to the implementation of the intervention. This consists of an observable pattern between the data points. Fluctuations may occur, but as long as they occur with some regularity this should constitute a stable baseline. An unstable baseline makes it difficult to interpret the results of the study. A problem with interpreting the findings also occurs when the baseline is stable but is moving in the direction of the desired outcome prior to the implementation of the intervention (see Figure 7.2).

Clearly Defined Intervention

Explanatory designs also require a clearly defined intervention, and the point at which it is introduced must be clearly presented. In exploratory/descriptive designs—since the focus is on process—this is not required. But if causality is a concern, it is critical to be clear about what the intervention is and when it was introduced and/or withdrawn.

TABLE 7.2 *Categories of single-system designs and their characteristics*

	Exploratory/ descriptive designs	Explanatory designs
Baseline required	No	Yes
Definition of intervention	Yes	Yes
Point at which intervention introduced/ withdrawn described	No	Yes
Target behavior operationalized	No	Yes
Repeated measures of incidents of target behavior	No	Yes

Operationalization and Repeated Measure of Target Behavior

Explanatory designs also require that the target behaviors be clearly defined. For example, rather than a target behavior being defined as "inattentiveness of a child," a clearer definition would be "number of times a question is repeated to a child before he/she answers." In addition to clear definitions, repeated data collection of the target behavior needs to be made.

The term *target behavior* has been used to refer to the behavior that is the focus of the intervention. The terms **target problem** or **target goal** can also be used.

We have already seen examples of these types of measures with a discussion of how to define and operationalize them for use in single-system designs in Chapter 4. Table 7.2 demonstrates some of the differences between exploratory/descriptive designs and explanatory designs. We will now describe the different types of explanatory single-system designs.

AB Design

The **AB design** is the simplest of the explanatory single-system designs. Data are collected on the target behavior, and this constitutes the baseline or phase A of the design. The B phase consists of the measurements of the target behavior after the intervention has been introduced. The effectiveness of the intervention is determined by comparing the A measure of the target behavior to the B measure.

Let's look at a case in which the problem is a family's low attendance at a parenting class. The goal or target behavior of the intervention is to increase attendance. The A phase would be the number of times the family attends the class prior to the intervention. The class is held twice a week, and data were already available on the family's attendance over the previous three weeks. These data can be used as a baseline.

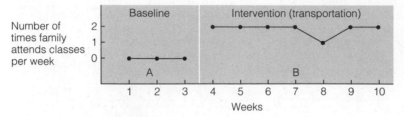

FIGURE 7.3 *Example of an AB design*

The point at which the intervention is introduced marks the beginning of the B phase. The intervention in this case might be to arrange for another family to help with transportation to the class. The frequency of the target behavior is then recorded for several weeks after intervention. An illustration of how these data might look if charted is given in Figure 7.3. The results can be analyzed by simply viewing the chart. An increase in attendance is clearly evident.

E X A M P L E

An AB Design

Slonim-Nevo and Vosler (1991) use an AB design to discuss the use of single-system designs with brief problem-solving systemic therapy.

The case involved a woman who was experiencing constant jealousy over the relationship her husband had had with his first wife. The authors developed a scale to measure the intensity of this obsession. After three weeks of baseline, an intervention was implemented using brief problem-solving therapy. An AB design was used in evaluating the impact of the intervention.

One of the advantages of the AB design is its simplicity. In addition, the design can easily be integrated into the practice process, giving important information about those interventions that appear to work with particular client systems.

However, there are some problems associated with this design. The major problem is that we do not have any control over extraneous factors or what we referred to in Chapter 6 as the history threat to internal validity. In our example, it was possible that the classes suddenly became more interesting to the family or that the mother had convinced the father, who was exhibiting the most resistance to attending, of the benefits of the class. Or the results might

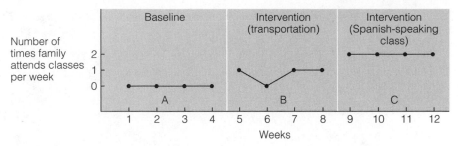

FIGURE 7.4 *ABC single-system design*

have been due to a multitude of other factors. Thus, the AB design is restricted in the information it can give us about causality.

ABC Design

The **ABC design** is also known as the **successive intervention design** because the C phase represents the introduction of another intervention. Others can also be added on as D or E phases. The ABC design is simply the AB design with the addition of another intervention. With this design, the target behavior continues to be measured after the introduction of each intervention (see Figure 7.4).

The ABC design can be convenient in that it often reflects the reality of practice. We introduce one intervention, and if it seems ineffective, we implement another intervention. The ABC design adds an empirical element to this common practice.

In the previous example, the transportation assistance did not increase attendance with another family. After further assessment it was found that the parents—although English speaking—were native Spanish speakers, and they were having difficulty following the class. Consequently, a second intervention was the organization of a Spanish-speaking class for a number of Spanish-speaking families in the community. The families' attendance was monitored following this intervention and showed an increase.

Although the ABC design nicely reflects the reality of practice, this design has the same types of problems associated with the AB design. We have no way of knowing if it was the intervention or some other factor that accounted for any change in the target behavior. This validity issue is complicated in the ABC design by not knowing whether it was the C intervention that resulted in the final outcome or a combination of B and C interventions. However, although we may not know specifically which intervention influenced the outcome, we do know about the effect of some combination of the interventions—a finding that in itself can enhance our practice and service to clients.

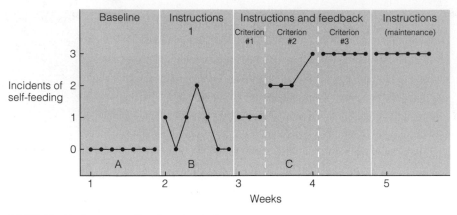

FIGURE 7.5 *Example of an ABC design*
Source: From C. Marlow et al., 1980

E X A M P L E

An ABC Design

Marlow, Green, Linsk, Briggs, and Pinkston (1980) implemented an ABC design as a means of monitoring the self-feeding behavior of a 71-year-old man.
Baseline behavior was recorded and the first intervention implemented. This
consisted of providing instructions to the client's wife and involved positive reinforcement. It was found the client did possess self-feeding skills but was not
practicing them. The second intervention included instructions plus feedback.
Feedback involved phone calls from the worker every other day and verbal reinforcement from the worker to the client's wife. It appeared that instructions
plus feedback proved more effective than simply instructions (see Figure 7.5).

This design also includes **changing criteria,** which involves setting goals
for the client that change over time. In this case, one meal a day was to be eaten
independently on three consecutive days, two meals a day for four consecutive
days, and three meals for five days. Hence, in this example the first criterion was
not met until the introduction of the second intervention—instructions and
feedback. At the end of the last intervention period, the criterion of three meals
a day for five days was being met. The changing criterion design is useful for
cases that require incremental achievements toward the final goal. This design
also included a maintenance follow-up phase that included using instructions
only. This appeared to be effective at maintaining the last criterion of three
meals being eaten independently.

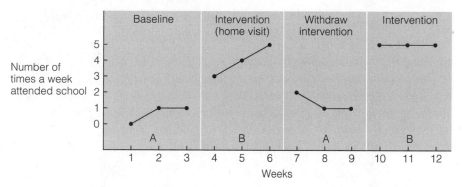

FIGURE 7.6 *ABAB—reversal single-system design*

ABAB Design

The **ABAB design** is also known as the **reversal design** or **withdrawal design;** it consists of implementing the AB design and then reversing—withdrawing the intervention and collecting baseline data again before implementing the intervention a second time.

Suppose a school social worker works constantly with the problem of absenteeism. In the past, she has made regular home visits to the families involved, and she has a sense that this is working. She decides to test the intervention, starting with one case—a 12-year-old boy. The social worker monitors his attendance at school over a three-week period and then starts the home visits which include counseling and information and referral, twice a week. She collects data on attendance for another three weeks and then stops the visits, again monitoring attendance, for another three weeks. Finally, she once again introduces the intervention. The results, displayed in Figure 7.6, indicate that the intervention appears to have some impact on the student's school attendance.

E X A M P L E

An ABAB Reversal Design

Fanslow and colleagues (1988) used an ABAB reversal design to test the effects of an intervention to reduce passive smoking. The intervention consisted of promoting self-segregation of smokers using signs and thematic prompts (ashtrays). The posting of signs and the relocation of ashtrays significantly increased the proportion of the total number of smokers restricting their activity to the designated area. The authors note that although the prompts were effective in moving smokers into the smoking area, the overall number of smokers did not differ significantly across conditions. Results from this study are displayed in Figure 7.7.

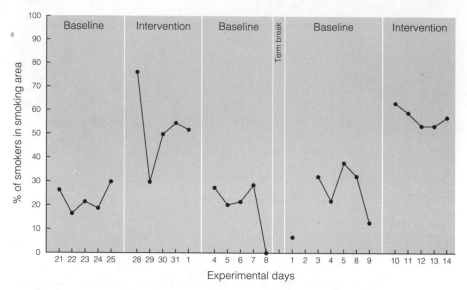

FIGURE 7.7 *Percentage of smokers in smoking area during each condition*
Source: From J. L. Fanslow et al., 1988. Used by permission.

The great advantage of this design is its ability to tell us about the impact of the intervention versus the impact of other possible factors. In other words, its ability to explain and imply causality is greater than the AB or the ABC designs.

However, this ABAB design does have a few problems. First, it cannot be applied to all target behaviors and all types of intervention. Some interventions cannot be reversed, particularly those that involve teaching a new behavior. For example, suppose we identify the target behavior as a 2nd grader's tardiness, and we assessed the problem to be the result of the mother not being assertive with the child about getting ready for school. The intervention consists of the social worker teaching the parent how to be assertive with the child. This would be a difficult intervention to reverse as the learned behavior of the mother could not be reversed.

Even if the intervention seemingly can be reversed, there might be some residues of the intervention that remain. In our previous example of lack of attendance at school, the home visits, although halted, might have resulted in some carry-over effects; in fact, this seems to have been the case with our example. This makes the interpretation of the results, as well as the precise impact of the intervention, more difficult.

A final problem with this design is an ethical one. Under some circumstances, it may not be ethical to withdraw the intervention. An example might be if we are dealing with a target behavior that causes considerable discomfort to the client system. It would be hard to justify removing an intervention that appeared to be effective. This type of decision should be mutually agreed upon by the social worker and the client system. However, a counterargument can be presented that the reversal design demonstrates to the client the direct relationship between the intervention and the desired outcome. Ultimately, this may lead to a longer-lasting change.

With any single-system study, and particularly with the reversal design, we must spell out the details and possible consequences for the clients before the intervention is instituted. This procedure is similar to the informed consent prior to engaging in a group study.

Multiple-Baseline Design

Multiple-baseline designs involve replicating the AB design by applying the same intervention to two or more target behaviors, to two or more clients, or in two or more settings at different points in time. For example, a child is exhibiting problems at school; the target problem is identified as concern by the teacher that the child is not verbally participating in class. After assessment, it becomes apparent that this behavior is associated with the child's Navajo cultural background, which discourages speaking out. Intervention consists of discussion with the teacher about cross-cultural issues, including suggesting that she use some Navajo examples in teaching. This intervention could be tested *across client systems* by using the intervention with three different Navajo children. Alternatively, it could be used *across target problems,* in which additional problems such as low grades and low socialization might be identified. These behaviors can be monitored before and after the implementation of the intervention. The intervention can also be tested *across settings,* such as looking at the change in one of the target problems in the day-care center and at home in addition to the school setting. Figure 7.8 shows how data from a multiple-baseline design might be displayed.

The multiple-baseline design offers a great deal of potential for examining the effectiveness of particular interventions and can allow us to be more confident in our belief that the intervention was responsible for any measured change. In effect, the multiple-baseline design involves the principle of comparison groups in group design—using either another client, another setting, or another target problem as a comparison. For example, if we find that the same intervention for the same target problem for the same setting was effective for two different clients, we can be more certain of the intervention's effectiveness than if we had simply looked at one client.

However, there are some limitations on the extent to which we can hold the intervention responsible for any change in the target problem even with these designs. For example, when applying the multiple-baseline design across clients, even if the change in the target problem resulted in a positive outcome

Child A

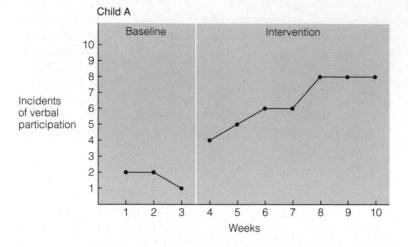

Child B

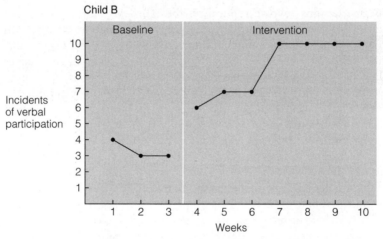

Child C

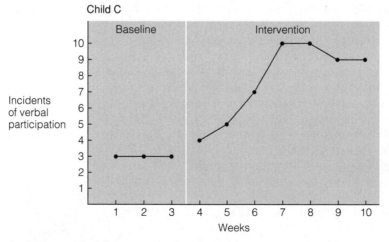

FIGURE 7.8 *Multiple-baseline design*

for both clients, there is still no guarantee that it was the intervention and the intervention alone that resulted in the specific outcome. In fact, the validity limitations are similar to those associated with many of the nonexperimental designs discussed in Chapter 6.

E X A M P L E

A Multiple-Baseline Design

Warzak and Page (1990) used a multiple-baseline design across behaviors to evaluate the acquisition of refusal skills by two developmentally disabled adolescent girls. The behaviors included eye contact, verbal refusal, specific statements regarding the unacceptability of sexual behavior, and leaving the situation. These behaviors were clearly defined and operationalized. The intervention consisted of using the behavioral techniques of rationale, modeling, rehearsal, feedback, and reinforcement. Baseline rates were low, and high frequencies of target behavior were observed as each behavior became the focus of training. The authors concluded that the girls' refusal skills were improved as a function of the training. See Figure 7.9 for the results of one of the girls. (This figure has been modified; unlike the authors' figure, it does not distinguish between those behaviors demonstrated at the beginning of the session and those at the end.)

Advantages and Disadvantages of Single-System Design

Advantages

We can identify five benefits that single-system designs offer the field of social work: ensuring the joint participation of worker and client; the provision of feedback to the client; knowledge building for practice; low cost and time commitments; and the ability to use either qualitative or quantitative methods.

Joint Participation of Worker and Client

Through incorporating single-system designs into their practice, social workers and their clients can work together to achieve a solution to the target problem. As we have seen, many single-system studies demand that the social worker and the client clearly define the target problem and agree on its nature. The moni-

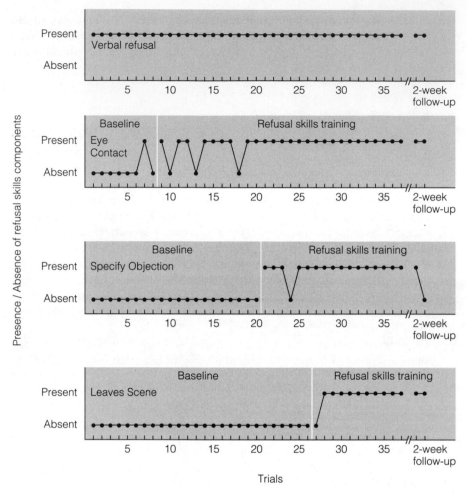

FIGURE 7.9 *Assessment of refusal skill training using a multiple-baseline design*
Source: Modified figure is from W. J. Warzak & T. J. Page, 1990. Used by permission of Pergamon Press, Inc.

toring, often by the client, ensures that the target problem has continuing relevance.

Feedback to the Client

One benefit of the guaranteed participation of both client and worker is feedback to the client during and after the implementation of the intervention. In many cases, at least with the explanatory design, the client had been provided with some tangible evidence that this intervention does or does not appear to have an impact on the behavior. This can result in longer-term effects and the clients' adopting self-help measures, avoiding further social work intervention.

Knowledge Building for Practice

After the case has been terminated, the social worker has the benefit of understanding the impact of a specific intervention with a specific target behavior and with specific types of clients. This information can then be used in their practice.

Further information can be obtained by replicating or repeating the single-system studies—testing interventions with other clients, on other target behaviors, and in other settings. Replication gives us increased internal validity (it is the intervention and not something else that is affecting the outcome) and external validity (we can generalize the results to a wider population).

In addition to replication, knowledge building through single-system studies can be achieved by integrating single-system and group approaches in evaluating intervention effectiveness (Briar & Blythe, 1985; Jayaratne, 1977). Berbenishty (1989) provides an example of how this can be done:

> The basic building blocks of the advocated methodology are single-case evaluation, intentionally designed, selected, and combined to form an assessment on the agency level. For each intervention, data on the characteristics of treatment, therapist, problem, and client are collected. These data from each single-case study are then aggregated to access the overall effectiveness of the group of cases. Further, in order to assess differential effectiveness, subgroups were identified and compared (as to their relative improvement), or certain background or treatment characteristics are correlated with outcome measures. (p. 33)

Time and Cost

Unlike group studies that often require additional funds, single-system studies can be easily incorporated into practice with no extra expense or excessive time commitment (partially because single-system designs complement practice).

Qualitative and Quantitative Methods

Single-system designs allow us to use both qualitative and quantitative data collection strategies. The same applications for qualitative and quantitative data in group studies can also be used in single-system studies. That is, qualitative data are particularly useful when you require detailed description and analysis, whereas quantitative data are more appropriate when the categories of behavior are already conceptualized and simply need to be counted.

Disadvantages

Along with benefits, there are also drawbacks to single-system designs. These include external and internal validity problems, limitations in the analysis of data, and their reputation of having limited application.

External and Internal Validity

Internal and external validity are a problem with single-system designs, even when replication occurs. Single-system studies simply are not as valid as a well-designed group study. However, as we discussed in the previous chapter, well-designed group studies are rare. More often, less satisfactory designs (in terms of causality) are used, resulting again in internal and external validity problems. Consequently, in many instances single-system studies can be thought of as no worse in terms of validity than many group designs and certainly better than no design at all.

Analysis of Results

A second potential drawback of single-system designs is that the analysis of findings is largely judgmental. Some statistical analyses can be carried out, and these will be discussed in Chapters 9 and 10. However, as Schuerman (1983) points out, all these techniques have limitations: "Some require that we make assumptions about the data that are often not reasonable. Others are quite complicated mathematically and in addition require that we have many observations in each phase" (p. 57). Nevertheless, these statistical approaches do extend the evidence beyond judgment regarding the relative effectiveness of different interventions.

Although quantitative data analysis may be somewhat limited, the techniques used in the analysis of qualitative data in single-system studies varies little from the type of analysis that is used in a group qualitative study. This type of analysis will be discussed in Chapter 11.

Limited Application

A third potential problem with single-system studies is that historically they have been used almost exclusively for testing the effectiveness of behavioral intervention techniques. In part, this was because of the emphasis in behavior theory on being able to define behaviors clearly so that any changes in the behaviors could be easily recorded. Many social workers have been deterred from using single-system studies, including generalist social workers, because they have assumed the design is only appropriate for behavioral intervention. However, as we have seen in this chapter, single-system designs can not only be used with different types of intervention, but also with different target problems and different-size client systems. Alter and Evens (1990) provide some nice examples of how single-system studies can be used with diverse client systems and target problems.

The Agency and Single-System Design

Single-system studies are designed to fit with practice. Consequently, they have the potential for being very compatible with agency-based work. Unfortunately, they have not been used as extensively as we might expect. This is probably because practitioners do not fully understand how to implement single-system studies and consider them barriers rather than complements and enhancers of practice. In part, this is because single-system studies simply have not been routinely taught in social work programs. After reading this book and trying out some of these designs in your practice, it will become evident that single-system studies not only enhance practice but are an integral part of good generalist social work practice.

Ethical Issues in Single-System Design

Ethical issues specific to single-system design are of two types: the issue of the reversal design, and the notion that single-system design interferes with practice.

Reversal Design Issues

As we discussed in the reversal design section, one could argue that withdrawing an apparently effective intervention can be perceived as being unethical. The counterargument is that the withdrawal of the intervention will allow us to determine that the intervention is responsible for any change in the target problem. This not only enhances the worker's knowledge of the effectiveness of the intervention but also demonstrates its effectiveness to the client, which may result in the intervention having a longer effect; parent training is a good example.

Interference with Practice

The second issue—the idea that single-system designs interfere with practice—has been raised consistently over the years. Some have also questioned the feasibility of combining research and practice (Thomas, 1975). One response to this position is that single-system studies can enhance practice and help direct and inform social workers in their day-to-day contact with client systems. For example, in determining the data collection method, other insights and further exploration with the clients regarding the target problem may occur. In addition, the client's involvement in the research, particularly in the data collection, can result in the client being engaged in the change process to a greater extent. This constitutes not so much an interference as an enhancement of practice.

Berlin (1983) provides an excellent example of a single-system evaluation that demonstrates how "it is possible to keep the obligations of practice central, systematically assess the extent of change in the client's problem, and become a more sensitive, knowledgeable, credible practitioner in the process" (p. 251).

In conclusion, because of the client's intimate involvement in single-system designs, the possibility of ethical violations are far less likely than in group designs.

Human Diversity Issues in Single-System Design

Throughout the process of developing single-system designs—whether it be the determination of the target problem, data collection, or the development and implementation of the intervention—we need to pay attention to human diversity issues. In many respects, human difference issues in this type of research are similar to those encountered in practice (due to the similarities in conducting single-system studies and in conducting practice). When formulating the target problem, we need to consider and involve the perspective of the client, and the data collection method must be sensitive to the particular characteristics and needs of the client.

We also need to carry out more single-system designs on diverse clients, recognizing that what may be effective for one type of client is not necessarily effective for another. In fact, single-system designs provide an excellent opportunity for exploring the richness of human diversity.

Summary

Single-system designs are used for evaluating the effectiveness of interventions in our own practice. The designs are exploratory/descriptive or explanatory. Exploratory/descriptive designs focus on the process of the intervention. Explanatory designs examine the impact of the intervention on the target behavior.

The different types of explanatory single-system design include the AB design, the ABC design, the ABAB design (reversal), and the multiple-baseline design.

Single-system designs complement and enhance practice. Because of the intimate involvement of the client with the single-system design, possible ethical violations are less likely than with group design. The human diversity issues in this type of research are similar to those involved in practice. Single-system designs can illustrate the great diversity of human beings.

Study/Exercise Questions

1 You are working with a family with an adolescent who is not attending school regularly. You want to evaluate your intervention with the adolescent and will collect data on her school attendance. What would be the advantages and disadvantages of the following designs for this evaluation?

 a AB design

 b ABC design

 c ABAB design

 What would be the ethical issues in this case?

2 You would like to incorporate some single-system studies into your practice as a generalist social worker in a hospital, but your supervisor objects, saying it would be too time consuming. Support your request and address her concerns.

3 Find an article in a social work journal that reports the use of a single-system design.

 a What design was used?

 b What other design could have been used?

 c How could the practitioner in this case have used the results to enhance his or her practice?

4 You have been facilitating a support group for teenage parents. The goal is for the group to continue without a facilitator. You will be monitoring attendance at the group as an indicator of its effectiveness. What design could you use?

Further Reading

Alter, C., & Evens, W. (1990). *Evaluating your practice: A guide to self-assessment.* New York: Springer.

 Useful to the generalist social worker because the authors apply single-system technology to different-sized systems, from communities to individuals.

Barlow, D. H., & Hersen, M. (1984). *Single case experimental designs: Strategies for studying behavioral change.* New York: Pergamon Press.

> A more technical book on single-system studies. A good reference book.

Bloom, M., & Fischer, J. (1982). *Evaluating practice: Guidelines for the accountable professional.* Englewood Cliffs, NJ: Prentice-Hall.

> A thorough guide to single-system designs; emphasizes how the roles of researcher and practitioner can be combined.

References

Alter, C., & Evens, W. (1990). *Evaluating your practice: A guide to self-assessment.* New York: Springer.

Berbenishty, R. (1989). Combining the single-system and group approaches to evaluate treatment effectiveness on the agency level. *Journal of Social Service Research, 12,* 31–48.

Berlin, S. (1983). Single-case evaluation: Another version. *Social Work Research and Abstracts, 19,* 3–11.

Briar, S., & Blythe, B. (1985). Agency support for evaluating the outcomes of social work services. *Administration in Social Work, 9,* 25–36.

Fanslow, J. L., Leland, L. S., Jr., Craig, T., Hahn, H., Polonowita, R., & Teavae, S. (1988). Reducing passive smoking by promoting self-segregation of smokers using signs and thematic prompts. *Journal of Organizational Behavior Management, 9,* 23–34.

Fischer, J. (1973). Is casework effective? A Review. *Social Work, 18,* 5–20.

Hollis, F. (1968). *A typology of casework treatment.* New York: Family Service Association of America.

Jayaratne, S. (1977). Single-subject and group designs in treatment evaluation. *Social Work Research and Abstracts, 13,* 35–42.

Marlow, C., Green, G., Linsk, N., Briggs, H., & Pinkston, E. (1980). *The development of a home-based family support system for the mentally impaired elderly.* A paper presented at the Conference for Applied Behavior Analysis. Dearborn, Michigan.

Pomerantz, P., Pomerantz, D. J., & Colca, L. A. (1990). A case study: Service delivery and parents with disabilities. *Child Welfare, LXIX,* 65–73.

Schuerman, J. R. (1983). *Research and evaluation in the human services.* New York: Free Press.

Slonim-Nevo, V., & Vosler, N. (1991). The use of single-system design with systemic brief problem-solving therapy. *Families in Society: The Journal of Contemporary Human Services, 72,* 38–44.

Thomas, E. J. (1975). Use of research methods in interpersonal practice. In N. A. Polansky (Ed.), *Social work research: Methods for the helping professions.* Chicago: University of Chicago Press.

Warzak, W. J., & Page, T. J. (1990). Teaching refusal skills to sexually active adolescents. *Journal of Behavior Therapy and Experimental Psychology, 12,* 133–139.

Organizing the Data

We may get so caught up in designing the project and in planning how we are going to collect the data that once we have the data in hand, we may wonder how to manage all the information. All three types of research we have been discussing in this book—evaluating our own practice, program evaluations, and needs assessment—have the potential to overwhelm us with data.

In this chapter we are concerned with organizing the data once they have been collected. This stage bridges the gap between data collection and data analysis. In generalist practice, we can make the analogy to collating and organizing the data prior to attempting an assessment.

The ways in which the data are analyzed depend to a great extent on whether the data are qualitative or quantitative. As we discussed in Chapter 4, quantitative methods use standardized measures that fit diverse behaviors into predetermined categories. These categories can then be analyzed using primarily statistical techniques. Quantitative analysis measures the reactions of many people—giving broad, generalizable findings. Qualitative methods, on the other hand, produce a mass of detailed data, usually on a limited number of people; these data provide more in-depth information than that provided by quantitative methods.

The different methods—because of the different types of data collected and the means by which they are analyzed—demand that we adopt different strategies when we come to organizing the data. Consequently, this chapter pseparately discusses those issues relating to the organization of quantitative and qualitative data.

This chapter includes the following topics:

▶ Organizing quantitative data—coding and basic programming
▶ Organizing qualitative data

- The agency and organizing the data
- Ethical issues in organizing the data
- Human diversity issues in organizing the data

Organizing Quantitative Data

You work for a public agency that provides assistance to foster care families. Your supervisor has just asked you to develop a questionnaire to mail to all foster families in the area served by the agency to identify unmet needs of foster families.

There are 300 foster families that you serve in your area. You send out a 2-page questionnaire to all 300 families and receive 150 back. These questionnaires contain a considerable amount of valuable data for your agency. However, these data are in raw form and as such are not very useful to you. Imagine trying to tally answers to 30 questions for 150 questionnaires by hand—very time consuming and tedious. This mass of quantitative data can be analyzed using statistical procedures, which can be further facilitated through the use of the computer.

You need to be thinking about how the data will be organized as early in the research process as possible. This is especially important when you use a questionnaire to collect data because how the questions are structured can influence the way in which the data can ultimately be organized. Organizing quantitative data involves coding the data and basic programming in preparation for analysis.

Coding the Data

Referring to the foster family questionnaire, the first step to transferring the information from the questionnaire to the computer is to code it. **Coding** involves organizing the collected information so that it can be entered into the computer. This is accomplished in three steps: (1) converting the responses to numerical codes; (2) assigning names to the variables; and (3) creating a code book.

Converting the Responses to Numerical Codes

One of the questions in the foster care questionnaire is "How many times in the last month were you contacted by a worker in the agency?" The response to this type of question is very straightforward; it simply entails entering the number reported into the computer. Note that this response is at the ratio level of measurement and reflects the absolute magnitude of the value (see Chapter 3). The level of measurement determines the type of statistical analysis that we can perform. With ratio data, we have a great deal of latitude in that responses can be manipulated in a variety of ways—added, subtracted, multiplied, and divided. They represent real numbers and are not strictly codes.

However, when we look at other types of questions and their responses, we see that often the number that is assigned to the response is a code, and there is a certain amount of arbitrariness in its assignment.

Another question may be "How would you gauge your overall level of satisfaction with the services our agency provides? (Circle the most applicable response.)"

Very satisfied	*Satisfied*	*Somewhat satisfied*	*Not satisfied*

Here, this information can be entered more easily if we assign numeral codes to each of the possible responses, for example:

Very satisfied	1
Satisfied	2
Somewhat satisfied	3
Not satisfied	4

Note that the level of measurement of this variable is ordinal. The numbers are ranked, but the distance between the numbers is not necessarily equal. There is an element of arbitrariness in the assignment of numbers to the responses. Thus, our use of these numbers in statistical analysis will be more limited than it was for those in the previous question. Also note that this satisfaction question constitutes one variable with four different possible responses—coded 1 to 4.

Another question is "Specifically, which service areas could be expanded to meet any of your needs more to your satisfaction? Please check all that apply."

_____   *Individual counseling*

_____   *Family counseling*

_____   *Training—preparation for foster child*

_____   *Other, please specify:* _____

For this question, more than one response could be checked. The easiest way to deal with this type of question is to divide it into three subquestions or three variables, rather than one. The three would consist of individual counseling, family counseling, and training. A number would be assigned (a 1 or 2) according to whether the respondent checked or did not check each item. Note that here we are dealing with variables that are at the nominal level of measurement. The numbers have been assigned arbitrarily to the responses, and they are not ranked in any way.

		Numerical Code
Individual counseling	*Checked (yes)*	1
	Not checked (no)	2
Family counseling	*Checked (yes)*	1
	Not checked (no)	2
Training	*Checked (yes)*	1
	Not checked (no)	2

Another characteristic of this question that demands special attention is dealing with the "other" item. One solution is to categorize the response to this subquestion or variable into a finite (countable) group (for example, individual services, group services, information and referral, and so on) and then assign numbers to each. Alternatively, the data can be fitted into existing categories. We need to be careful not to lose the meaning intended by the respondent. An alternative strategy is to treat this item as qualitative data. After all, this is essentially a qualitative mode of collecting data in that it is attempting to seek information from the subject's perspective rather than imposing previously constructed categories to understand the behaviors.

Whatever type of question you are confronted with in the coding process, two basic guidelines need to be followed: The coding categories should be mutually exclusive and exhaustive. By *mutually exclusive,* we mean that a given response can be coded in one way only for each variable. That is why in the last example the question needed to be treated as several variables to accommodate the fact that several yes responses were possible for each question.

The codes should also be *exhaustive;* in other words, all the data need to be coded in some way. Coding is a tedious task in research. Do not omit coding some responses because you think you will not need them in the analysis. If this is the case, the questions should not have been asked. Also, it is very difficult to perform coding later and to add to the data set once the data analysis has begun. So, although it can be tiresome, coding must be done with care. Any mistakes would lead to a misrepresentation of the results.

Assigning Names to the Variables

It is too cumbersome to enter the entire question into the computer. Also, the computer cannot read questions in this way. Consequently, the variables themselves need to be coded or named so that they can be understood by the computer. This means translating the questions into words that are of a certain length—for example, no more than seven characters. Usually, the first character has to be a letter; it cannot be a numeral. It is useful to pick a variable name that relates to the question. For example, for the question "How would you gauge your overall level of satisfaction with the services our agency provides?" a possible variable name could be SATISFY. For the services question that contained three variables, these could be named SERVICE1, SERVICE2, and SERVICE3.

Developing a Code Book

This is useful once you have decided how all the responses will be coded and how each variable will be named. The code book is used to record how the various responses from the questionnaire were coded. Part of a code book would include those questions and respective codes that we have already discussed. The code book provides a reference for other researchers who would need to know what the codes originally referred to. Sometimes, particularly on smaller projects, there may not be a need for a code book because the codes can be included on the questionnaire. When designing the questionnaire, bear this in mind; it can save work later.

The next step is to enter the information into the computer. In order to do this, we need to discuss statistical packages.

Basic Programming Using a Statistical Package

Statistical software packages can be used to make data analysis a simple and efficient task. Data are collected and then organized to be entered into the computer and analyzed by the statistical packages, producing statistical results.

There are many statistical programming packages available for computers today. Most universities with large computer systems, referred to as **mainframes,** have the two main packages used for data analysis in the social sciences: **Statistical Analysis Systems (SAS)** and **Statistical Package for the Social Sciences (SPSS).** However, social agencies normally do not have access to mainframe computers. You will be more likely to encounter statistical packages that can be used with personal computers, such as SPSS/PC+, SAS-PC, and BMDP-PC. Although well worth the initial cost in terms of ultimately benefiting the agency, for many agencies the cost of these packages is beyond their budgets, and a cheaper option is to purchase **Shareware.** These are software packages—for example, KWIKSTAT and EXPRESSGRAPH—that are less expensive but that can still perform most of the statistical procedures of the more commercial packages.

Many of the programming principles are similar regardless of which particular package you are using. For our examples here and in Chapters 9 and 10, we will be referring to SPSS/PC+ programming conventions. If you are using other statistical software packages, refer to the manuals that accompany them.

Figure 8.1 shows what an SPSS/PC+ file looks like using our foster care questionnaire example. The first line of this file describes the title of the program. The next line, DATA LIST, lets the computer know where and how to look at the data you have collected and coded from each questionnaire. The codes are arranged in rows. Each code also has its specific column assignment within each row. This type of format is referred to as **fixed format** and is the most commonly used format for statistical data. Below this is a column of the variable names next to a column of numbers indicating the specific column assignment for each variable. The first variable name is ID, the identification number for each questionnaire. As 150 questionnaires were returned, we need three columns to represent the ID numbers 001 to 150. The next variable SATISFY needs only one column since the codes vary only from 1 to 4. The same applies to SERVICE1 through SERVICE3—their codes are either 1 or 2.

The next part of the file, the variable label list, allows you to label your variables so that when you have the computer generate the results, descriptions of the variables will be displayed. After each variable, the corresponding definition is described within apostrophes ('——').

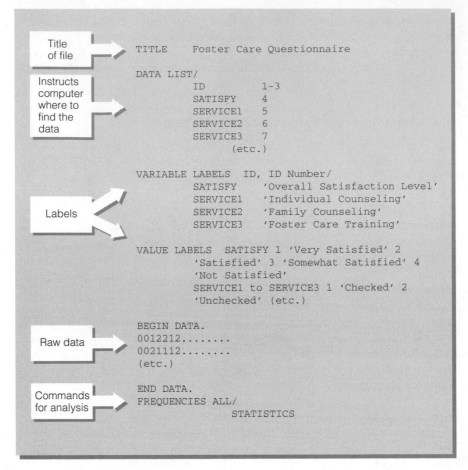

FIGURE 8.1 *SPSS/PC+ file using foster care questionnaire*

The next part of the file is similar to the previous section. Here you have the opportunity to describe the meanings of the values of the variables. Each variable is listed with its associated numerical value. After each value, the corresponding meaning is described within apostrophes ('——'). For the SERVICE variables, the word *to* can be used; it is recognized by SPSS to mean that the variables SERVICE1, SERVICE2, and SERVICE3 all have the same value labels because they all have the same coded numerical values (1 for yes and 2 for no) and all are listed one after the other in the DATA LIST section (that is, SERVICE1 is in column 5, SERVICE2 is in column 6, and SERVICE3 is in column 7).

The next section of the file is for the actual data. Remember that each row of numbers corresponds to the coded numbers on one questionnaire. For example, the first row of numbers can be deciphered as:

column	1	2	3	4	5	6	7	8	9	10	11
value	0	0	1	2	2	1	2	.	.	.	.
variable	I	I	I	S	S	S	S				
	D	D	D	A	E	E	E				
				T	R	R	R				
				I	V	V	V				
				S	I	I	I				
				F	C	C	C				
				Y	E	E	E				
					1	2	3				

Each line of data is referred to as a **record.** The number of columns in each line is the **record length.** The record length for many statistical software packages, including SPSS/PC+ is 80. It may be necessary to use several records or lines for each case or subject.

After the data section, the actual programming starts. Commands are used to make the computer tally up the frequencies of how each respondent answered each question and then calculate the totals. Typical SPSS/PC+ commands here include FREQUENCIES (for the frequency distributions of each variable) and CROSSTABS (for cross-tabulations of two particular variables). These data analysis strategies will be discussed in the next two chapters.

After the data have been entered and the SPSS/PC+ program has been completed, the data is analyzed by submitting it to the computer. Once the job has been submitted and run, you will receive **output.** This will appear on the screen or you can produce hard copy (printout), which contains the results of the statistical analysis.

To gain familiarity and confidence with computers and software packages, check out university computer centers. They usually provide workshops on personal computers and instruction in the use of specific software packages. They can also teach you how to use the mainframe computer. If you plan on doing statistical analysis using a computer, these workshops, which are usually free to students, can be very helpful.

Organizing Qualitative Data

Organizing qualitative data can be even more overwhelming than organizing quantitative data simply because of the different nature of this type of information. Quantitative data by definition are pieces of information that fit into certain categories that in most cases have been previously assigned. Consequently, organizing the data is a matter of ensuring that the data are correctly assigned to the categories and are in a form that can be read by the computer. On the other hand, qualitative data, once collected, are usually completely uncategorized in order to capture as much in-depth information as possible; analysis becomes a much more complex process.

We will discuss five different elements involved in the organization of qualitative data: note keeping, organizing files, coding the notes, using the computer, and identifying gaps in the data.

Note Keeping

As we discussed in Chapter 4, the primary mode of collecting qualitative data is through observation or interviewing, and much of this involves note keeping. Sometimes, particularly in the case of participant observation or informal interviewing, these notes are haphazard. Consequently, one of the first steps is to organize and rewrite these field notes as soon as possible after you have taken them. Rewriting the notes will help jog your memory, and the result will be more detailed, comprehensive notes than you could have produced in the field.

Bernard (1988), an anthropologist, suggests five basic rules in the mechanics of note taking and managing field notes:

1   Don't put your notes in one long commentary; use plenty of paper and keep many shorter notes.

2   Separate your note taking into physically separate sets of writing.

   a   Field jottings—notes actually taken in the field. These provide the basis of field notes.

   b   Field notes—write up from your jottings.

   c   Field diary—a personal record of your experience in the field. It chronicles how you feel and how you perceive your relations with others in the field.

   d   Field log—a running account of how you plan to spend your time, how you actually spend it, and how much money you spend.

3   Take field jottings all the time; don't rely on your memory.

4   Don't be afraid of offending people when you are taking field jottings. (Bernard makes an interesting point regarding this: Being a participant observer does not mean that you *become* a fully accepted member of the group, but rather you *experience* the life of your informants to the extent possible.)

   Ask permission to take notes and usually it will be given. You can also offer to share your notes with those being interviewed.

5   Set aside some time each day to write up your field notes.

When collecting qualitative data, social workers often **transcribe** interviews. This means writing down verbatim a recording of the interview. Transcriptions are extremely time consuming. It takes six to eight hours to transcribe a one-hour interview. Unless transcriptions are absolutely critical to your research, avoid doing them and use codes for interview material. Even when you are carrying out a process recording of a case (a type of single-system study discussed in Chapter 7), coding can be as helpful as full transcriptions and far more compatible with practice.

Of course, there may be occasions when the transcription is necessary and central to the study. For example, Marlow (1983) transcribed from a videotape a behavior therapy interview to look at the relationship between nonverbal and verbal behaviors. The transcription included very small behaviors—for example, intonation and slight movements of the hands and facial features. In the type of research in which you will be engaged as generalist social workers, however, you will be unlikely to undertake something of this nature.

Organizing Files

Your rewritten field notes will form your basic or master file. Always keep backup copies of these notes as a precautionary measure.

As you proceed with the data collection, you will need different types of files or sets of notes. Generally, as a minimum you will need five types of files: descriptive files, methodological files, biographical files, bibliographical files, and analytical files.

The *descriptive file* includes information on the topic being studied. In the case of a program evaluation, this file would include information on the program itself, its history, development, and so forth and will initially contain most of your notes. The *methodological file* or set of notes deals with the techniques of collecting data; it gives you the opportunity to record what you think has improved or damaged your interviewing and observation techniques.

The *biographical file* includes information on individuals interviewed or included in the study—for example, clients, the director, and so on. The *bibliographical file* contains references for material you have read related to the study; it is very similar to the type of file you might keep when completing a research term paper.

Finally, the *analytical file* provides the beginnings of the analysis proper. It contains notes on the kinds of patterns you see emerging from the data. For example, when interviewing the clients from a family service agency, you may have detected the relationship between their perceived benefits of the program and the specific type of problem they brought to the agency. Consequently, you may start a file labeled "Benefit-Problem." Your analytical set of notes will initially be the smallest file.

Do not forget to cross-reference your files. Some materials in "Benefit-Problem" pertaining to a particular client may need to be cross-referenced with a specific biographical client file. A note in each will suffice. This preparation and organization will help the analysis later on.

Coding the Notes

In addition to cross-referencing the five main types of notes, additional coding will help when you come to the analysis stage. As you write up the field notes, use codes for categorizing the notes. These codes can be recorded at the top of each page of notes or in the margin and can be either numbers or letters. Don't forget, though, to keep a code book just as you would for quantitative data.

Obviously, these codes will vary in their precision and form depending on the purpose of the study. In a program evaluation, the codes may refer to the different channels of authority within the organization, the different types of clients served, or any other aspect of the program that is of concern in the evaluation. In a single-system study where you may be monitoring the application of an intervention or carrying out a process recording, codes can be used to categorize the content of the interview or meeting.

This level of coding is referred to as content analysis, which we first mentioned in Chapter 4. We will elaborate on the process of content analysis in Chapter 11.

Using the Computer

Use of the computer is not confined to quantitative data. We recommend recording field notes with a word processor. Word processing packages such as Wordstar, DisplayWrite, WordPerfect, and MacWrite allow you to easily move the text around. The different types of files can also be maintained and cross-referenced with minimal effort.

In addition, new software packages are being developed specifically for analyzing qualitative data, such as ETHNOGRAPH (Seidel & Clark, 1984). This program requires coding the data into categories, which then allows the researcher to assemble certain units according to their code for examination.

If a computer is not available when you initially write up your field notes, you can still use the computer in the analysis without entering all your field notes. One way of doing this, described in detail by Bernard (1988), is to number each page of your field notes and the codes for each page. This information is then entered into the computer. This allows you to easily access where in your notes there is reference to a particular item, identified by the code.

Before you start collecting the data, it is a good idea to decide what role the computer is going to play in your project and what software you will be using. Then you will be able to organize your field notes and codes accordingly.

Identifying Gaps in the Data

Throughout the organization of the data, we need to keep notes regarding gaps or missing information. This is not so necessary in a quantitative study when decisions pertaining to data collection are made early in the study. However, with a qualitative study, we often do not know what data need to be collected until well into the project when new insights and ideas relating to the study become apparent.

We have now discussed the factors involved in organizing qualitative data. In Chapter 11 we will study the actual analysis of qualitative data.

The Agency and Organizing the Data

The central message of this section is to make optimal use of computers if you have them available in your agency. They can save an enormous amount of time, and for larger projects, are indispensable.

If your agency does not have computer access, lobby for it. Fairly inexpensive personal computers can be purchased, as can Shareware software. Not only can computers organize and analyze data, but they can be used for many aspects of practice and research, including literature reviews, writing reports, clinical assessment, electronic bulletin boards, and computer networking. (See Appendix B for the computer-related content discussed in this text.)

Ethical Issues in Organizing the Data

Two ethical issues are involved in data organization, one for each of the methods—quantitative and qualitative. For the quantitative data, ethical issues are minimized because most of the decisions about how to handle the data have been made prior to this stage. The major problem is how to deal with the "other" responses. We mentioned before that we can create categories for these responses, or they can be fitted into existing categories. In adopting this approach, we need to be careful that we preserve the integrity of the data and that we do not try to put the data into categories that are inappropriate or that simply reflect our preferences.

Ethical issues relating to the organization of qualitative data are more pervasive. At each stage we must be careful that our biases do not overtly interfere. For example, when compiling field notes from your field jottings, ensure that the field notes reflect as closely as possible your observations in the field and are not molded to fit your existing or developing hypothesis. When coding the notes, be aware of the same issue. If you doubt your objectivity, you may want to consult with someone who can examine part of your notes or your coding scheme and give you some feedback. What you are doing here is conducting a reliability check. This in itself can serve the purpose of ensuring that the research is being conducted in an ethical manner.

Human Diversity Issues in Organizing the Data

The primary human diversity issue springs from the ethical issues related to quantitative data discussed above. Namely, when ambiguous data are categorized, such as responses to "other" questions, attention needs to be paid to ensuring that the categorization reflects the various human diversity issues that may be involved in the responses.

Human diversity issues arise in different stages in the organization of qualitative data. Field notes need to reflect any human diversity elements, although this depends on whom we are getting our information from. The coding also needs to tap this dimension. And we may want to pay particular attention to whether or not human diversity issues have been addressed when trying to determine if gaps exist in the data. For example, in collecting data on clients' perceptions of the services they are receiving from a family service agency, it may be important to ask clients about how significant the ethnicity of their social worker is to them, or about whether or not they feel that their social worker and/or agency is sensitive to cultural differences.

Summary

Organizing quantitative data involves coding the data and using statistical programming software packages. Organizing qualitative data involves note keeping, organizing the files, coding the notes, using the computer, and identifying gaps in the data. Using a computer, for analysis of data and for word processing and referencing, is an integral part of organizing data.

Ethical and human diversity issues include ensuring that the integrity of the data is preserved and that we do not try to interpret the data to fit our own hypothesis.

Study/Exercise Questions

1 The agency in which you are employed has no computers available to the social workers. As a means of lobbying for computers, draw up a list of the ways in which the computer could be used for research and practice in the agency.

2 Construct a questionnaire of about five items to find out students' attitudes on combining research with practice. Administer the questionnaire to five students in the class.

   a Create a code book.

   b Write an SPSS/PC+ program following the format on page 180.

3 Interview five students in the research class about their attitudes on combining research with practice. How would you organize these data?

Further Reading

Butterfield, W. (Ed.). (1983). Computers for social work practitioners. *Practice Digest* (NASW), 6.

A discussion of the possible applications of computer technology in practice.

Hall, L. D., & Marshall, K. P. (1992). *Computing for social research*. Belmont, CA: Wadsworth.

Hedderson, J. (1991). *SPSS/PC+ made simple*. Belmont, CA: Wadsworth.

An excellent introduction to SPSS/PC+.

Schwartz, M. (Ed.). (1984). *Using computers in clinical practice*. New York: Haworth Press.

The use of computers in different practice situations; some are applicable to generalist practice.

References

Bernard, H. R. (1988). *Research methods in cultural anthropology*. Newbury Park, CA: Sage Publications.

Marlow, C. R. (1983). *The organization of interaction in a behavior therapy interview*. Unpublished Ph.D. dissertation. University of Chicago.

Seidel, J. V., & Clark, J. A. (1984). The ethnography: A computer program for the analysis of qualitative data. *Qualitative Sociology, 7*, 110–125.

Analysis of Quantitative Data: Descriptive Statistics

9

This chapter and Chapter 10 discuss how quantitative data can be analyzed. As we discussed in Chapter 4, these are data that can be counted, that is, quantified. The analysis stage of the research process makes some sense out of the information that has been collected. This is a comparable stage to assessment in practice.

There are two ways in which we can derive meaning out of the quantitative data. One is through the use of **descriptive statistics,** which summarize the characteristics of the sample or the relationship among the variables. During this process, we want to get as full a picture as possible; there are a number of different statistical techniques that allow us to do this. We can also use **inferential statistics.** These are techniques for determining if we can make generalizations or inferences about the population using the data from our sample. This chapter discusses descriptive statistics while the next chapter discusses inferential statistics.

Except when you have conducted a small needs assessment or have evaluated your own practice, you may not be directly responsible for analyzing quantitative data. Consequently, the focus of the two chapters is not on statistical formulas and the computation of statistics, but rather on understanding which statistics are useful for which purpose. This approach is particularly appropriate now that computers can do statistical computations in fractions of seconds. We will also see that some statistics are simply not appropriate and become meaningless when used with certain types of data. The approach to statistical understanding adopted here prepares you to become an informed and observant consumer of research, a critical role of the generalist social worker as discussed in Chapter 1. And as we will discover in Chapter 13, part of using findings for practice involves understanding and interpreting the statistical analysis of the data in various studies. This chapter discusses:

- ❯ Frequency distributions
- ❯ Measures of central tendency
- ❯ Measures of variability or dispersion
- ❯ Measures of association
- ❯ Descriptive statistics and single-system studies
- ❯ The agency and descriptive statistics
- ❯ Ethical issues in descriptive statistics
- ❯ Human diversity issues in descriptive statistics

Frequency Distributions

Each variable is measured and has a value for each case included in the study. In Chapter 8, we saw how each one of these can be entered into the computer. One of the first things we need to do in our statistical analysis is to get an idea about how these values are distributed for each variable.

For example, you have collected data on the need for a day care center on the local university campus. Let's assume that 25 students with preschool children were interviewed. Each of these students represents one **observation** or case; these are equivalent to the units of analysis. The variables included the number of preschool children, ethnicity, expressed need for day care on campus, and miles from campus. The ethnic groups are represented by codes: 1 equals white non-Hispanic, 2 equals Hispanic, and 3 equals African American. Expressed need for day care on campus is coded on a 4-point scale; 4 equals greatest need and 1 equals least need. The number of preschool children in a family and miles from campus are represented by the actual number of children and miles respectively. We could present the data as in Table 9.1.

By simply reviewing this table, it is difficult to understand what the data really look like. Consequently, we use a **frequency distribution,** which is a description of the number of times the values of a variable occur in the sample.

We can construct several frequency distributions for the previous example: one for the variable ethnicity (see Table 9.2), one for expressed need for day care (see Table 9.3), and one for number of preschool children (see Table 9.4). One can also be constructed for miles from campus (see Table 9.5), however, rather than list each distance separately, we can categorize the values to make the data more readable. When we do this, we try to use categories that make some intuitive or theoretical sense to us, and we also need to ensure that the categories are of the same size. For example, we might use categories such as "less than 5 miles," "5–9 miles," "10–14 miles," and "15 miles and over." However, by grouping data points into categories in this way, we inevitably lose some information.

A sample of a frequency distribution table that resulted from SPSS/ PC+ analysis—using the FREQUENCIES command—is presented in Figure

TABLE 9.1 *Data on four variables by each observation*

Observation number	Number of children	Ethnicity	Need for day care	Miles from campus
1	2	1	3	2
2	1	1	4	1
3	1	3	4	10
4	1	1	4	23
5	1	2	3	4
6	1	1	3	2
7	2	2	4	1
8	2	1	3	1
9	1	2	2	6
10	3	1	4	40
11	2	1	3	2
12	1	2	1	1
13	1	1	2	3
14	2	1	4	7
15	2	1	4	8
16	1	3	4	9
17	1	1	3	15
18	2	1	4	12
19	1	2	1	23
20	2	1	1	1
21	2	1	4	2
22	1	2	4	1
23	2	1	4	3
24	1	1	4	1
25	2	1	3	6

TABLE 9.2 *Frequency distribution of ethnicity*

Label	Value	Frequency	%
Non-Hispanic white	1	17	68
Hispanic	2	6	24
African American	3	2	8
	Total	25	100

TABLE 9.3 *Frequency distribution of need for day care*

Label	Value	Frequency	%
No need	1	3	12
A little need	2	2	8
Some need	3	7	28
Great need	4	13	52
	Total	25	100

TABLE 9.4 *Frequency distribution of number of preschool children in the household*

Value	Frequency	%
1	13	52
2	11	44
3	1	4
Total	25	100

TABLE 9.5 *Frequency distribution of miles from campus*

Value	Frequency	%
Less than 5	14	56
5–9 miles	5	20
10–14 miles	2	8
15 miles and over	4	16
Total	25	100

```
AGEGR      AGE AT GRADUATION

VALUE LABEL              VALUE        FREQUENCY        PERCENT

                          20             1              1.0
                          21            16             16.2
                          22            23             23.2
                          23            15             15.3
                          24            10             10.1
                          25             5              5.1
                          26             1              1.0
                          27             1              1.0
                          28             1              1.0
                          29             1              1.0
                          30             1              1.0
                          31             2              2.0
                          32             6              6.1
                          33             1              1.0
                          35             1              1.0
                          37             2              2.0
                          40             1              1.0
                          41             1              1.0
                          44             1              1.0
                          45             1              1.0
                          46             1              1.0
                          48             2              2.0
                          49             1              1.0
                          50             1              1.0
                          51             1              1.0
                          62             1              1.0
                           .             1              1.0
                                       ____            _____
                        Total           99            100.0
```

FIGURE 9.1 *Frequency distribution: Output from SPSS/PC+ program*

9.1. This table is from a study of the types of positions that persons who graduated with B.S.W. degrees held after they graduated. This is another example in which the data could have been grouped, this time according to the age of the graduates, making the frequency distribution easier to read.

Note that there is one respondent who did not respond to the question on age. This is represented by the dot at the bottom of the value column. These incomplete data are referred to as **missing values.**

Sometimes frequency distributions can be displayed as graphs or charts. We discuss how to do this in Chapter 12. An example of a frequency distribution from a published article is displayed in Table 9.6. This presents some of the results from a study carried out by Anastas, Gibeau, and Larson

TABLE 9.6 *Work and caregiving conflict (n = 419)*

Conflict and Work Adjustments Among Working Caregivers		
Measure	%	*n*
Conflict score		
No conflict (0)	53	223
Conflict (1)	39	164
Considered quitting (2)	8	32
Work adjustments because of caregiving		
Used vacation time	64	269
Changed work schedule	33	138
Used personal leave	32	132
Missed work meetings	18	77
Missed outside conferences	14	57
Missed overtime	13	54
Called in sick	8	35
Refused a more responsible position	7	30
Unable to seek a new job	6	27
Left a job	5	21
Declined a job offer	4	15
Taken a leave of absence	3	14

Source: From J. W. Anastas et al., 1990, *Social Work*, vol. 35(5), © 1990 NASW, Inc. Used by permission.

(1990) concerning the problems experienced by working families in their provision of elder care. Note that both the raw number (*n*) and the percentage (%) are presented.

Measures of Central Tendency

Another dimension to our data is finding out where the middle of the distribution lies, or the average value. There are three different types of averages, each determined in a slightly different way. These three types are the mode, median, and the mean.

Mode

The **mode** is the value possessed by the greatest number of observations. In Table 9.2, "non-Hispanic white" is the mode for ethnicity because this category or value occurred most often. In Table 9.3, "great need" is the mode for expressed need for day care and in Table 9.5, "less than 5 miles" for distance from campus. The mode can be used regardless of the level of measurement. It can be used for ethnicity (a nominal level of measurement), expressed need for day care (an ordinal level of measurement), and for miles from campus (a ratio level of measurement). However, other measures of central tendency and other statistics discussed in this chapter (measures of variability and measures of association) are restricted in terms of the levels of measurement that they can use.

Median

The median, another type of average, can only be used with ordinal, interval, and ratio level data. The **median** refers to the value where 50% of the observations lie above the value and 50% of the observations lie below the value. That is, it is the value that divides the distribution in half.

The median cannot be used for nominal levels of measurement because it only has meaning with ranked data. We cannot rank nominal data and consequently cannot determine whether cases lie above or below a particular value. We often assign numbers to nominal level data, but these numbers do not have any inherent meaning. We cannot rank, say, the values of ethnicity in any order from highest to lowest and thus cannot determine the middle or median value.

The median is complicated to calculate, but with computers, this is no longer a problem. The median is a popular measure of central tendency primarily because it is not influenced by the extreme values that can be a problem with the mean (see below). In addition, the median is more stable than the mode, although less stable than the mean. Salaries are often described using the median.

Mean

The mean, which is the third type of measure of central tendency, is even more restrictive in the level of measurement that can be used and can only be computed from interval and ratio levels of measurement. The **mean** is a result of summing the values of the observations and then dividing by the total number of observations. The mean miles from campus for our participants in the needs assessment (Table 9.1) is 7.36 miles (184/25 = 7.36). If data are grouped in the way that we grouped miles from campus in Table 9.5, the mean cannot be computed this way, as these categories mask much of the data. The mean can be used with ordinal, interval, and ratio levels of measurement.

The major strength of the mean is that it takes into consideration each value for each observation. However, extreme values, either high or low, can distort the mean, particularly if the sample size is relatively small. Let's look at the example of miles from campus again but substitute one high value (60 miles) for a middle-range value (6 miles). The mean now becomes 9.52 (238/25 = 9.52), a 2-mile difference in the mean as the result of one observation. However, the mean is the most stable measure of central tendency and in addition provides the prerequisite for the computation of other statistics.

In summary, to determine which measure of central tendency to apply, we need to consider how we are going to use the information. For example,

TABLE 9.7 *Means and standard deviations on parent child-rearing attitudes*

	Center day care and family education		Family education		Control	
	M	SD	M	SD	M	SD
	(*n* = 14)		(*n* = 21)		(*n* = 22)	
Progressive scale score on combined form (36 months)	30.3	6.1	29.2	5.7	28.5	4.9
Authoritarian scale score on combined form (36 months)	22.6	5.7	23.9	4.6	23.3	5.3
Modernity score on combined form (36 months)	59.7	8.4	57.3	5.6	57.2	6.7

Source: From B. H. Wasik et al., 1990. © 1990 The Society for Research in Child Development, Inc. Used by permission.

E X A M P L E

A Study Using the Mean

Wasik, Ramey, Bryant, and Sparling (1990) assessed the relative impact of two interventions. One was family education and a center-based family educational day care program and the other a less intensive intervention group consisting of home-based family education only on child-rearing attitudes. Table 9.7 shows the means and standard deviations (which we will discuss in the next section) of the three groups—intensive intervention, less intensive intervention, and no intervention—on child-rearing attitudes.

means are appropriate when you are interested in totals. If you know the national average is 2.3 children per family, then you can guess that a town of 100 families should have about 230 children. If you know that the mode is one child per family, then any family you choose at random will probably have one child. The reason the average household income is often reported as the median rather than the mean is that we are interested in an individual comparison of our own financial situation to other normal-range incomes. The mean is inflated by the few unusual persons who make millions. However, mean income is more useful in comparing gross national products (GNP's) among countries.

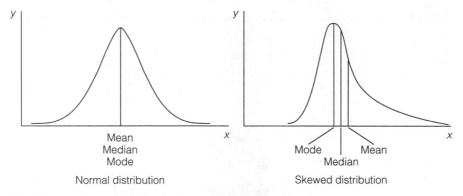

FIGURE 9.2 *Normal and skewed distributions*

Visual Distribution of Data

There is a **normal distribution** of data, sometimes referred to as the bell-shaped curve. The properties of a normal distribution are

▶ The mean, median, and mode have the same score value.

▶ It is symmetrical—the right half of the distribution is the mirror image of the left half.

▶ Most of the scores are concentrated near the center.

If distributions have most of the scores concentrated at one end of the distribution rather than at the middle this is referred to as a **skewed distribution** (see Figure 9.2).

When we talk about inferential statistics in the next chapter, we need to know whether a distribution is normal or skewed because that helps us select an appropriate statistical test.

Measures of Variability or Dispersion

Another dimension of our population or sample is the extent to which the scores vary or are dispersed in the distribution. In Figure 9.3 we see three distributions depicted. They have the same measure of central tendency; however, they differ in the extent to which they are spread out, or in their variability.

As with measures of central tendency, there are different ways to measure variability, with each being more appropriate in some situations than in others. Two types of measures of variability are discussed: the range and the standard deviation.

Range

The **range** is the easiest of the measures of variability to compute and to understand: It is simply the distance between the largest or maximum value and the

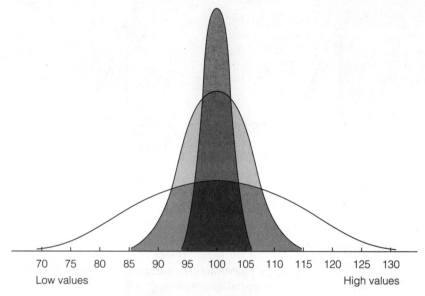

70   75   80   85   90   95   100   105   110   115   120   125   130

Low values   High values

FIGURE 9.3 *Three distributions with the same measure of central tendency but different variabilities or dispersions*

smallest or minimum value. This is computed by subtracting the lowest value from the highest value. The range can only be used with interval and ratio levels of data because of the assumption of equal intervals.

The problem with the range is its extreme instability. Remember that different samples drawn from the same population may have very different ranges. Consequently, the range does not give us a very reliable view of what the variability is in the population. The range for the age variable in Figure 9.1 is 42 (62 minus 20). However, if we change either the highest or lowest score to an extreme value, the range would be dramatically affected.

Table 9.8 presents data from a study by Martinez-Brawley and Blundall (1989). They studied farm families' preferences toward personal social services. The table presents the demographic characteristics of the farm households and includes both the median and range on a number of variables—age of heads of households, age of parents, and so forth.

Standard Deviation

The standard deviation is a measure that averages the distance from the mean of each value. The **standard deviation** involves

1   Calculating the mean
2   Measuring the distance of each score from the mean
3   Squaring these distances (to eliminate negative values)
4   Dividing by the *n*, thus resulting in a mean of the differences from mean
5   Taking the square root of the result

TABLE 9.8 *Demographic characteristics of the farm households*

Characteristic	Pennsylvania (n = 22)		Iowa (n = 20)		Combined (n = 42)	
	Median	Range	Median	Range	Median	Range
Age of heads of household[1]	41	20 to 69	48	20 to 79	45	20 to 79
Age of parents	49	20 to 69	50	30 to 79	49	20 to 79
Families' income[2]	20,100	<9,999 >40,000	22,667	<9,999 >40,000	21,062	<9,999 >40,000
Household size	2.5	2 to 7	2.5	1 to 7	2.5	1 to 7
Acreage[3]	165	30 to 500	300	120 to 1200	180	30 to 1200
Length of residence on farm	22.5 years	1 year– 60 years	19.5 years	2 months– 70 years	21.5 years	2 months– 70 years

[1]Includes children older than age 21 working the farm, living in the same house, and acting as heads of households. In Pennsylvania, there were 22 households containing 24 families.

[2]Income median was computed from group data. Modal income for Pennsylvania and Iowa was $10,000 to $17,999.

[3]Includes rented, owned, or custom.

Source: From E. Martinez-Brawley & J. Blundall, 1989, *Social Work*, Vol. 34(6), © 1989 NASW, Inc. Used by permission.

Because the standard deviation uses the mean and is similar to the mean in many respects, it can only be used with interval and ratio level data. The standard deviation is the most stable of the measures of variability, although it too, because of its use of the mean, can be affected by extreme scores.

Refer back to Table 9.7 for an example (from the Wasik et al. 1990 study on the impact of different programs on child-rearing attitudes) that includes the standard deviations of outcome measures.

Using the computer to calculate the standard deviation involves using the SPSS/PC+ command FREQUENCIES in conjunction with STATISTICS. This produces the frequency distribution and a number of statistics including the standard deviation. Figure 9.4 gives an example of what this output would look like.

Measures of Association

Up to this point we have only been looking at **univariate measures;** that is, we have been looking at one variable at a time and trying to develop a picture of how that variable is distributed in a sample. However, we often want to measure the relationship between two or more variables; this is referred to as either **bivariate** or **multivariate measure,** respectively.

There may also be an interest in the relationship between two or more variables when carrying out a program evaluation. For example, we may want

```
CHILD1    NUMBER OF CHILDREN LIVING IN HOME


                                                      VALID
VALUE LABEL    VALUE    FREQUENCY    PERCENT    PERCENT

                 0          70         42.7        44.6
                 1          32         19.5        20.4
                 2          36         22.0        22.9
                 3          16          9.8        10.2
                 4           3          1.8         1.9
                 .           7          4.3      MISSING

              TOTAL        164        100.0       100.0

       MEAN  1.045   MAXIMUM  4.000   MINIMUM  .000

       VALID CASES   157      MISSING CASES   7
```

FIGURE 9.4 *Output from SPSS/PC+ (FREQUENCIES and STATISTICS commands) for the variable CHILD1*

to study the effect of a special program for high school students on their self-esteem. We need to look at the relationship between the independent variable (the special program) on the dependent variable (self-esteem). Bivariate statistics are needed to do this.

Similarly, although not always to the same extent, in needs assessments sometimes we are interested in examining the relationship among variables. For example, in investigating a community's need for a Y, we want to know not only how many people express this need but also the characteristics of these individuals—the ages of their children and so forth. Here the two variables are expressed need and ages of children.

Computerized statistical analysis has made our job a great deal easier. **Multivariate analyses,** involving examining the relationship between more than two variables, used to be extremely time consuming to compute; as a consequence, very little multivariate analysis appears in the older literature. Today, we do not have that problem, however we still need to know when to use these types of analyses and what they can and cannot tell us.

Two types of measures of association are discussed in this section: cross-tabulation and correlation.

Cross-Tabulation

Cross-tabulation is probably the most widely used bivariate statistic. This is because it is simple to use and extremely versatile. Cross-tabulations are also known as **contingency tables.** (They can be easily generated by the CROSSTABS command on SPSS/PC+.) Cross-tabulations may be used with any level of mea-

CHORE	Count Row Pct Col Pct Total Pct	FLEX		Row Total
		YES	NO	
Low Participation 1		75 83.3 65.8 53.6	15 16.7 57.7 10.7	90 64.3
Medium Participation 2		15 83.3 13.2 10.7	3 16.7 11.5 2.1	18 12.9
High Participation 3		24 75.0 21.1 17.1	8 25.0 30.8 5.7	32 22.8
Column Total		114 81.4	26 18.6	140 100.0

FIGURE 9.5 *Cross-tabulation of two variables: FLEX and CHORE*

surement. However, if interval and ratio (and sometimes ordinal) levels of measurement are used, they must be collapsed into a smaller number of categories (the meaning of "smaller" is discussed below).

An example of a cross-tabulation is shown in Figure 9.5. This is output from the CROSSTABS command of SPSS/PC+ from a study that examined the workplace service needs of women employees. This particular contingency table looks at the relationship between how the women perceived their husband's participation in household chores (CHORE) and their need for flexible work hours (FLEX).

Generally, the dependent variable (in this case, need for flexible work hours) is displayed in the columns, and the independent variable (husband's participation in chores) is displayed in the rows. The row totals plus percentages and column totals plus percentages are written at the end of each row and column respectively. CHORE has three values (low, medium, and high participation), and FLEX has two values (yes, a need; no, no need); consequently, we have what is called a 3 by 2 (3 values by 2 values) contingency table with 6 cells or boxes. If the variables had more values, the table would be larger. We need to be careful that the table is not too large; we also cannot let the number of cases on any of the cells get too low (five or less) because then there are problems in interpreting the results. (We will talk about these problems in Chapter 10.) Sometimes several values need to be combined to reduce the number of values and so reduce the size of the table. As a result the number of cases in each cell increases.

Let's continue reading the table. The top number in each cell refers to the number of cases. In the top left-hand cell in Figure 9.5, the number of cases is 75. The second number refers to the row percentages, that is, for the percentage of women who stated their husbands were low participants in household chores, 83.3% requested flexible work hours. The third number in the cell is the column percentage: in our example, 65.8%. This represents the percentage of women who requested flexible work hours—53.6% reported low participation of their husbands in household chores. The bottom number in the cell refers to the total percentage. In other words, the number of cases is the percent of the total number of cases. The total number of cases can be found in the lower right-hand corner. In Figure 9.5, this number is 140 and represents 100% of the cases, which is recorded below the 140. We can go through and read each of the cells in this manner. To the extreme right are the row totals and percentages, and at the bottom of the table, the column totals and percentages. Note that there are labels on the table to help guide your interpretation.

The availability of percentages allows us to compare groups of unequal size. A sense of the association can be gained by comparing these percentages. For example, a slightly lower proportion of those reporting high participation of their husbands in household chores requested flexible work hours (75%) than those who reported medium and low participation (83.3% for both). Is this difference big enough to signify a relationship between the variables or is it simply due to change? We address this question in the next chapter when inferential statistics are discussed.

Correlation

Correlation is another common way of looking at the relationship between variables. However, this can only be used with interval and ratio level data. We conducted a study that investigated the impact of a program directed at increasing the self-esteem of the adolescent participants. It was hypothesized that the number of sessions the adolescents attended would have an impact on their level of self-esteem measured on an equal interval scale. Ten adolescents were tested on their level of self-esteem before and after the program (see Table 9.9).

These data can then be plotted on a chart called a **scattergram** (Figure 9.6). The horizontal axis (X) represents the client's length of time in the program, and the vertical axis (Y) represents the difference in the client's level of self-esteem before and after participation in the program.

In Figure 9.6, the line connecting the dots is perfectly straight. In this case, there is a **perfect correlation** between the two variables where, as one variable increases or decreases, the other does so at the same rate. This very rarely occurs; usually we find that the dots do not perfectly follow the line but are scattered around it. The direction of the relationship can vary. Figure 9.6 demonstrates a **positive correlation** between the number of sessions attended and the level of self-esteem. As the number of sessions attended increased, so did the level of self-esteem. However, a **negative correlation** can also occur. This is

TABLE 9.9 *Self-esteem scores and number of weeks in the program (n = 10)*

Client ID	Self-esteem score	Number of weeks in program
1	8	1
2	10	2
3	12	3
4	14	4
5	16	5
6	18	6
7	20	7
8	22	8
9	24	9
10	26	10

depicted in Figure 9.7. Here the high values of one of the variables, self-esteem, are associated with the low values of the other variable, number of sessions attended.

The extent to which the data points are scattered gives us an indication as to the strength of the relationship between the two variables. There is a for-

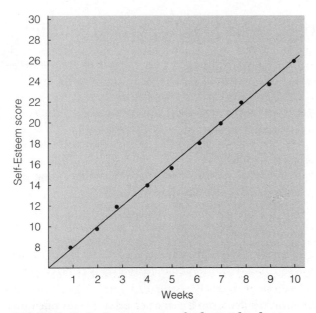

FIGURE 9.6 *Scattergram of relationship between self-esteem score and time in program (a perfect positive correlation)*

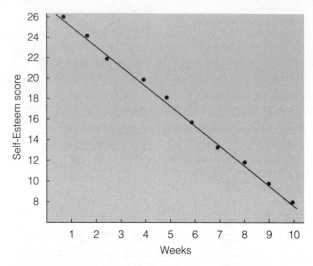

FIGURE 9.7 *Scattergram of relationship between self-esteem score and time in program (a perfect negative correlation)*

mula to precisely measure the strength of this relationship; again, this involves inferential statistics and will be discussed in the next chapter.

  The line passing through the dots is used to predict certain values. This involves **regression analysis,** which will be discussed briefly in Chapter 10.

Descriptive Statistics and Single-System Studies

When discussing descriptive statistics, we must remember that they are not necessarily limited in their application to group studies; they can also be used in single-system studies.

  Many of the measures of central tendency and of variability could be used with single-system designs; for example, mean measures during the baseline and intervention could be calculated. However, this does involve losing much data through aggregation—something that single-system studies are in fact designed to avoid. Consequently, the most effective way of describing the results of a single-system studies is to visually display the results.

We can think of the data charts as possessing certain properties (Bloom & Fischer, 1982):

▶ *Level*   This refers to the magnitude of data. Differences in levels can occur between the baseline and the intervention. A change in level is referred to as a **discontinuity** (see Figure 9.8).

▶ *Stability*   This is clear predictability from a prior period to a later one and occurs if the data can be easily represented by a mean line. Data lines can

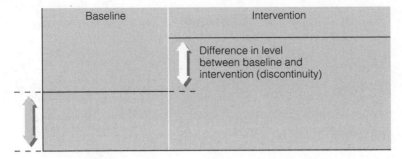

FIGURE 9.8 *Levels of data*

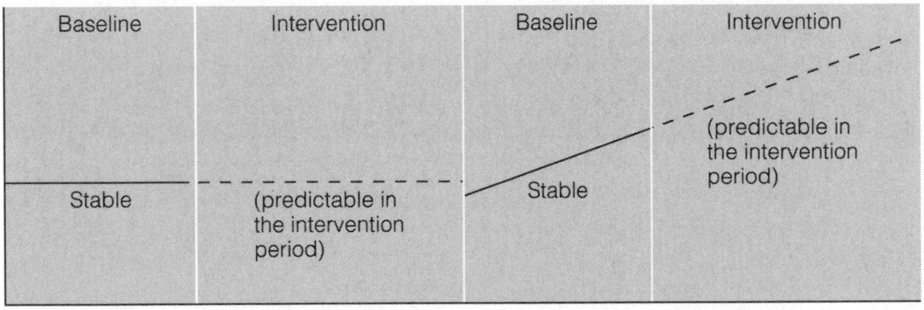

FIGURE 9.9 *Stability of data between baseline and intervention*

still be stable even if they change in magnitude. See Figure 9.9 for two examples of stability of data between baseline and intervention periods.

▶ *Trends*   This refers to the directionality of the data—whether the pattern is increasing or decreasing. Trends are referred to as **slopes** when they occur within a given phase and **drifts** when they occur across phases. See Figure 9.10 for variations of trends.

▶ *Improvement or deterioration*   This refers to specific comparisons between the baseline and intervention periods. Of course, a determination of what is improvement and what is deterioration depends on whether greater or lesser magnitudes of the behavior are desired. Figure 9.11 illustrates this idea.

Other factors that need to be considered when describing findings from the charts include:

▶ *The timing of the effects.* Sometimes they occur immediately after the baseline and sometimes they are delayed (Figure 9.12).

▶ *The stability of the effects.* The effect of the intervention may wear off. If this appears to happen, the implementation of a different intervention is indicated (Figure 9.13).

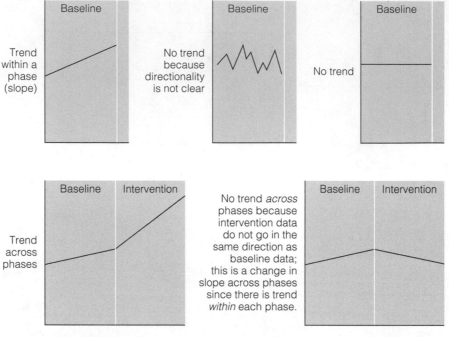

FIGURE 9.10 *Trends within and across phases*

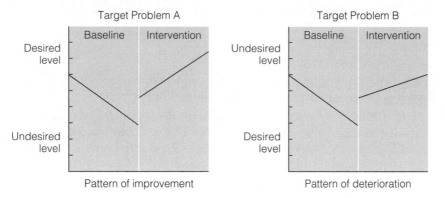

FIGURE 9.11 *Patterns of improvement and deterioration*

▶ *Variability in the data.* This often happens but needs to be treated cautiously, particularly when it occurs during the baseline period. In both examples in Figure 9.14, it is difficult to interpret the effects due to the variability in the baseline data.

In the next chapter we will discuss how data from single-system studies can be analyzed using specifically designed statistical techniques. These techniques then give us an indication of the statistical significance of the data. This is particularly useful when the data are variable, as in Figure 9.14.

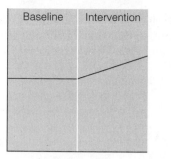 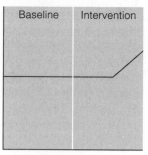

FIGURE 9.12 *Immediate and delayed effects*

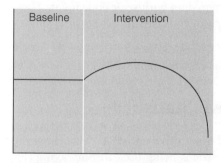

FIGURE 9.13 *Unstable effects*

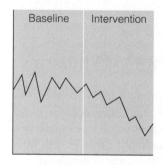 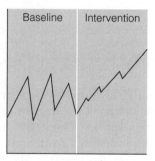

FIGURE 9.14 *Variability in data*

When displaying results, we need to ensure that we accurately graph the data. Computer packages specifically designed to handle data from single-system designs are very helpful. One is the Computer Assisted Practice Evaluation (CAPE) (Bronson & Blythe, 1987), which is based on the Lotus 1-2-3 program. This program plots the data on a graph and does the statistical tests that the user specifies. Another computer option is the Computer Assisted Social Services (CASS), which combines the ability to do single-system data analysis with the Multi-Problem Screening Inventory (Hudson, 1990) discussed in Chapter 4. This package produces graphs that plot the results of the scales.

Great advances are being made in the development of computer aids for single-system data. These strides are encouraging in that they facilitate the analysis of data from single-system studies and prompt social workers to evaluate their own practice.

The Agency and Descriptive Statistics

Descriptive statistics can be easily generated in agency settings for needs assessments and program evaluations. Obviously, using a computer enhances the generation of such statistics.

Discuss your analysis of single-system data with your colleagues. They can help validate your conclusions. In addition, you can show them how single-system designs can enhance their practice.

Ethical Issues in Descriptive Statistics

One of the major ethical issues in the use of descriptive statistics is ensuring that the correct—that is, the appropriate—statistic is being used in portraying the data. We must avoid presenting the data in a distorted manner to fit with any preconceived ideas.

Human Diversity Issues in Descriptive Statistics

In categorizing values—for the purpose of constructing frequency distribution tables or for cross-tabulations—care must be taken that differences between groups of individuals are respected. Often, the number of subjects in some minority groups is small, and there is a temptation to collapse these groups into one. However, in doing so we may lose critical information about human diversity. Consequently, it is important to devise a means to retain this information. One strategy would be to add a descriptive/qualitative note on the separate groups.

Summary

Descriptive statistics summarize the characteristics of a sample. Frequency distributions are descriptions of the number of times the values of a variable occur in a sample. The measures of central tendency are mode, median, and mean. Data can be distributed in a normal or bell-shaped curve or in a skewed pattern. The measures of variability are range and standard deviation. The measures of association are cross-tabulation and correlation. One of the most effective ways to use descriptive statistics with single-system studies is to visually present the results, although statistical analyses can also be conducted.

Study/Exercise Questions

1 Look for articles in social work journals that use
   a The mean/median or mode
   b The standard deviation
   c Correlation
   d Cross-tabulations
2 One of the Study/Exercise Questions in Chapter 8 asked you to develop a questionnaire for measuring student attitudes on combining research and practice, to administer the questionnaire, and to construct a code book. Construct a frequency distribution table for two of the variables included in this questionnaire.
3 Find an article in a social work journal that uses a single-system design. Are the data visually presented from this study? Are the results clear as a result of this visual presentation?

Further Reading

Besag, F. P., & Besag, P. I. (1985). *Statistics for the helping professions*. Beverly Hills, CA: Sage Publications.

> A good consumers' guide to statistics.

Blalock, H. M. (1979). *Social statistics*. New York: McGraw-Hill.

> A good sourcebook for delving into the intricacies of statistical analysis.

Graft, J. L. (1990). *Statistics and data analysis for social workers* (2nd ed.). Itasca, IL: Peacock Publishers.

> An easy-to-read introduction for social workers; includes most of what you will need.

Weinbach, R. W., & Grinnell, R., Jr. (1989). *Statistics for social workers*. New York: Longman.

> Basic statistics for social workers; very readable.

References

Anastas, J. W., Gibeau, J. L., & Larson, P. J. (1990). Working families and eldercare: A rational perspective in an aging America. *Social Work, 35,* 405–411.

Bloom, M., & Fischer, J. (1982). *Evaluating practice: Guidelines for the accountable professional.* Englewood Cliffs, NJ: Prentice-Hall.

Bronson, D. E., & Blythe, B. J. (1987). Computer support for single case evaluation of practice. *Social Work Research and Abstracts, 23,* 10–13.

Hudson, W. (1990). *Computer assisted social services.* Tempe, AZ: Walmyr Publishing.

Martinez-Brawley, E., & Blundall, J. (1989). Farm families' preferences toward the personal social services. *Social Work, 34*(6), 513–522.

Schuerman, J. R. (1981). *Research and evaluation in the Human Services.* New York: Free Press.

Wasik, B. H., Ramey, C. T., Bryant, D. M., & Sparling, J. J. (1990). A longitudinal study of two early intervention strategies: Project CARE. *Child Development, 61*(6), 1682–1696.

10

Analysis of Quantitative Data: Inferential Statistics

Now that you have an understanding of how to describe quantitative results, when you are evaluating a program or your own practice you might ask, "How important is a difference in outcome between those who received the intervention and those who did not? And can we generalize these findings to a wider population?" These questions can be answered with inferential statistics. *Inferential statistics* allow us to determine if an observed relationship is due to chance or if it reflects a relationship between factors, and they allow us to generalize the findings to the wider population.

In Chapter 9 we were concerned with describing the profile of our sample or population, which is central to a needs assessment. In this chapter we take quantitative analysis one step farther and begin to think about the testing of the hypotheses. This stage of analysis is critical in the evaluation of a program or our practice. Hypotheses, as we discussed in Chapter 2, are specific ways of structuring and stating our research questions. In the case of a program evaluation, our hypothesis might be, "If pregnant adolescents complete the prenatal classes provided by program A, then they will be less likely to give birth to low birth-weight babies than those adolescents who do not complete the program."

We need to know whether this type of hypothesis can be supported by data. Descriptive statistics could be used to present the characteristics of the sample—for example, their ages, marital status, other children, and other demographic information. The entire sample could be described as one group or the comparison and program group could be described separately. Similarly, the results could be described for each of the groups in the sample. However, descriptive statistics are unable to go farther than this; inferential statistics are needed for additional analysis.

As generalist social workers, we are not necessarily involved in the direct analysis of data. Thus, the emphasis of this chapter, as in the last, is not on the computation of the statistics but rather on understanding which statistics are useful for which purpose.

This chapter will discuss:

▶ Sources of error and the role of inferential statistics
▶ Types of hypotheses
▶ Significance levels
▶ Statistical power
▶ Types of statistical tests
▶ Inferential statistics and single-system studies
▶ The agency and inferential statistics
▶ Ethical issues in inferential statistics
▶ Human diversity issues in inferential statistics

Sources of Error and the Role of Inferential Statistics

Throughout the research process, there is a possibility for error in our conclusions. Errors can come from three different sources, and each source of error can be assessed by specific strategies.

First, there may be some measurement error that affects the data collection; this can be assessed by checking the reliability and/or validity of the data. Second, other variables might be responsible for the relationship, and they need to be controlled. This can usually be handled by the type of research design or, as we discussed in the last chapter, they can be controlled statistically. The third source of error is chance. Chance has to do with sampling variability, which we discussed in Chapter 5, and is the difference that may occur due to probability between even a randomly drawn sample and a population. The role of these chance factors can be assessed through the use of inferential statistics, which uses probability theory. (The specific statistical tests involved are described later in this chapter.) These three sources of error and the strategies for their assessment are illustrated in Figure 10.1.

Types of Hypotheses

An hypothesis suggests that two or more variables are associated in some way. There are two types of hypotheses. First, the **two-tailed** or **nondirectional hypothesis** simply states that there is an association between two or more variables but predicts nothing about whether this is a negative or positive association.

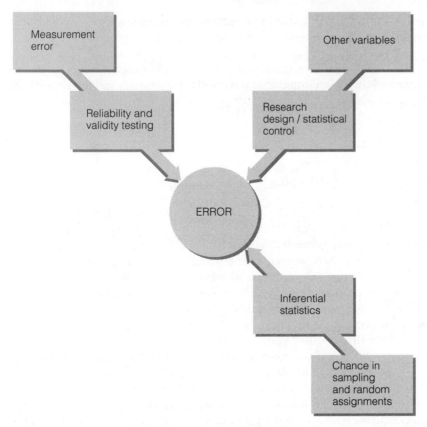

FIGURE 10.1 *Sources and corrections for error*

One such example would be the hypothesis that gender has an impact on the likelihood of hospitalization for depression. A **one-tailed** or **directional hypothesis** specifies not only that there *is* an association between the variables but also the nature or direction of the relationship or association, whether it is positive or negative. For example, women are more likely than men to be hospitalized for depression. The state of our prior knowledge will in part determine whether we develop one-tailed or two-tailed hypotheses. Remember that when we are developing hypotheses we need to draw on existing knowledge, not just on impulse or initial impressions.

A type of hypothesis that is central in inferential statistics is the null hypothesis, which is derived from either the one-tailed or two-tailed hypothesis. The **null hypothesis** states there is no association between the variables. Using our previous example of a one-tailed hypothesis, we would phrase the null hypothesis as women are not more likely than men to be hospitalized for depression. Statistical analysis then accepts or rejects this null hypothesis. If the null hypothesis is not rejected, then we conclude that no relationship appears to exist between the variables. On the other hand, if the null hypothesis is rejected, this means that there does appear to be a relationship between the variables that is not a result of chance.

This may seem unnecessarily complicated. However, the concept of the null hypothesis is important because it reminds us that statistical tests are set up to determine to what extent a relationship is due to chance, rather than whether or not the hypothesis is true.

Significance Levels

As we mentioned at the beginning of this chapter, when we begin looking at our data, we cannot make a clear conclusion based on the findings. For example, in our question relating to gender and hospitalization for depression, the results may disclose that 55% of women were hospitalized versus 45% of men. We do not know by looking at these results whether this 10% difference between the men and women is simply due to chance. The statistical test used with the null hypothesis can help us determine if this is the case.

A finding is **statistically significant** if the probability of it occurring due to chance (if the null hypothesis were true) falls at or below a certain cutoff point. This cutoff point has been established by statistical convention to be .05. In other words, if an observed relationship should occur due to chance no more than 5 times out of 100, the null hypothesis is rejected. In this case it is very unlikely that the relationship is due to chance, and we acknowledge that the variables tested are having an impact on the outcome. Sometimes the significance level is set at lower levels (for example, .01) or under special circumstances, higher levels (.10). However, the important thing to remember is that the significance level is set prior to the statistical testing.

The observed level of significance is signified by $p < .05$ (or $p < .01$), and any level below .05 (or .01) would be regarded as statistically significant. Establishing statistical significance at the .05 level or less does not mean we have proven a relationship exists between variables. It simply means that there is only a 5% probability that the relationship is a result of chance occurrence. Avoid stating that a hypothesis has been "proved." A more accurate statement is that the hypothesis "is statistically significant at the .05 level."

Statistical Power

Sometimes we can make decision errors in either accepting or rejecting the null hypothesis. These two errors are referred to as Type I and Type II errors. **Type I error** is the rejection of the null hypothesis and the conclusion that a relationship exists between the variables when no relationship does in fact exist. The

	True	False
Accept	Correct decision	Type II error
Reject	Type I error	Correct decision

FIGURE 10.2 *Type I and Type II errors*

probability of this occurring is determined by the significance level. **Type II error** is the failure to reject the null hypothesis and so failing to identify the relationship between the variables (see Figure 10.2). Obviously these errors can present some serious problems.

The ability of a statistical test to correctly reject a null hypothesis is referred to as the **power** of the test. Generally, the power of the test is increased as the size of the sample increases. Also certain types of tests have greater power than others. (A full discussion of power is not possible here, but this aspect of inferential statistics can be found in many statistics texts.)

Types of Statistical Tests

In this section we describe the most common statistical tests you encounter in the social work literature and those you will need to use in the analysis of your data. Four tests will be discussed: *t*-tests, analysis of variance (ANOVA), correlational analysis, and chi-square analysis.

Each test is only appropriate under certain conditions. When selecting a test, we need to consider four factors: first, the structure of the null hypothesis; second, certain tests can only be used with certain levels of measurement; third, the size of the sample; fourth, the distribution of the responses—whether or not this distribution is normal. A summary table of the tests and their conditions for use is presented in Table 10.1.

T-Test

Condition of Use

The *t*-test is used when:

▶ We are interested in testing a null hypothesis to find whether or not the means in two populations are the same. Note here that we are interested in

TABLE 10.1 *Types of statistical tests and some conditions for use*

	T-test	ANOVA	Correlation coefficient	Chi–square
Comparing means of two populations	Yes	No	No	No
Comparing means of more than two populations	No	Yes	No	No
All variables at interval/ratio level of measurement	No	No	Yes	No
One variable only at interval/ratio level of measurement	Yes	Yes	No	No
All variables at ordinal/nominal level of measurement	No	No	No	Yes

the means of the *population;* in other words, if we find a difference between the means in the sample, can these results then be generalized to the population.

▶ Related to the above, the dependent variable is at least at the interval level of measurement (although some argue that the ordinal level of measurement is acceptable), and the other variable (usually the independent variable) is at the nominal level of measurement.

▶ The sample size can be small if the responses are approximately normally distributed.

The *t*-test is often used in social work research because the above conditions are often those with which we are confronted.

Many program evaluation designs include comparison groups. Each group that is compared represents a value at the nominal level of measurement. Also, in program evaluations the outcome or dependent variable (for example, the number of months an individual has held a job) is measured at the interval or ratio level. The null hypothesis in such a program evaluation would be that the intervention had no effect; in other words, the two groups had similar outcomes. However, just on the basis of probability, the outcomes are likely to be different. The *t*-test tells us whether this difference could be due to chance.

Note that all the statistical tests discussed in this chapter result in a specific statistic, often denoted by a letter of the alphabet. In the case of the *t*-test the statistic is referred to as the *t*-statistic. This is used to determine a probability level. If we were computing the statistic by hand, we would look up the value of the *t*-statistic in probability tables, which you can find in many statistics texts. If the computer is calculating the results for us, the output would include both the statistic (in this case, *t*) and an associated probability value ($p = .03$). To carry out a *t*-test, use the SPSS/PC+ command MEANS.

E X A M P L E

The Use of T-Tests in the Literature

The use of a *t*-test is provided in a study by Jamison and Virts (1990). They investigated the influence of family support on chronic pain. Two groups of chronic pain patients were compared—those who described their family as being supportive (233 patients) and those who stated they had family conflicts (275 patients). The outcome, or dependent variables, included demographic, medical, behavioral, and psychological factors (all at the ratio or interval level of measurement). A *t*-test analysis comparing the supportive and nonsupportive groups disclosed that several of the independent variables—sleep disturbances ($t = 3.73$), depression ($t = 6.54$), and irritability ($t = 8.21$)—were found to be significant at the $p < .05$ level.

Analysis of Variance (ANOVA)

Conditions of Use

The analysis of variance statistical test (ANOVA) is used when:

▶ We are interested in testing a null hypothesis to find whether or not the means in more than two populations are the same.

▶ Related to the above, the dependent variable is at least the interval level of measurement, and the other variable, usually the independent variable, is measured at the nominal level.

▶ The sample size can be small if the responses are approximately normally distributed.

Sound familiar? The *t*-test is in fact a special case of ANOVA, and the conditions of the use of ANOVA are consequently very similar to those of the *t*-test, except that ANOVA is used to compare more than two groups. The ANOVA results in an *F*-test statistic.

ANOVA is useful if, for example, we are comparing the outcomes of three or more programs in different parts of the state and the outcome is being measured at the interval level or above. One SPSS/PC+ command for ANOVA is MEANS.

E X A M P L E

The Use of ANOVA in the Literature

Hopper and McCarlnielsen (1991) carried out an interesting study that investigated factors that contributed to people's recycling behavior. The study also evaluated the impact of different recycling program strategies, including block leaders, prompts, and information. The randomly selected sample of 240 households were randomly assigned to the five different recycling programs. Outcomes variables included a recycling score, a social norm score, and an awareness of consequences score. Whether or not the households actually participated in recycling was also recorded.

The data showed that recruited block leaders had the greatest impact on the recycling score, prompts had a somewhat smaller effect, and information had the least impact. The data indicated that only the recruited block leader group resulted in statistically significant increases in both the social norm and personal norm scores. None of the groups showed significant increases in awareness of consequences.

Correlational Analysis

Conditions of Use

The correlation coefficient gives us an indication of the strength of the correlation between two variables. It is used when:

- We are interested in testing the null hypothesis to find whether two variables in a population have no linear relation.
- Both variables are at least at the interval level of measurement.
- A normal distribution of responses is not required.

We talked about correlation in Chapter 9, and the use of the scattergram to look at the relationship between two variables. The correlation coefficient examines the strength and direction of the relationship between two variables and can tell us whether the relationship is statistically significant. The correlation coefficient statistic is represented by an r. The coefficient is in the range of -1.0 to $+1.0$. The -1.0 represents a perfect negative correlation, and $+1.0$ represents a perfect positive correlation. The SPSSPC+ command is CORRELATION.

We need to remember that the r statistic is simply looking at the strength and relationship between two variables; under no circumstances is it to be used to imply causation. Level of self-esteem and performance on an aptitude test for social work might be highly correlated but this does not mean that one causes the other. The other conditions of causality need to be met (see Chapter 2).

E X A M P L E

Correlational Analysis

Polansky (1985) studied loneliness among 306 rural and urban women. The mothers in the families were administered loneliness scales that measured the dependent variable of loneliness. Independent variables included friendliness in the neighborhood, helpfulness in the neighborhood, affective support, instrumental support, and marital satisfaction; each of these variables was measured with a scale. One aspect of the analysis involved a correlational analysis that examined the relationship between the independent variables and responses to the loneliness scales.

The relationships between several of the independent variables and scores on the loneliness scale were found to be statistically significant at the 0.5 level; these tended to be negatively associated. For example, low marital satisfaction and a perception of little friendliness in the community resulted in a high score on the loneliness scale.

One of the main strengths of the *r* statistic is with prediction. We mentioned in Chapter 9 that if a relatively straight line exists between the data points, we can use regression analysis. The usual purpose for regression analysis is to estimate how much change in the dependent variable is produced by a given change in an independent variable or several independent variables. Regression produces coefficients that indicate the direction and amount of change in the dependent variable to be expected from a unit change in the independent variable.

E X A M P L E

Regression Analysis

Hamilton and Zimmerman (1985) used regression to further describe the relationship in their study between the dependent variable (weight loss success) and the nine independent variables. The authors concluded that:

> *wife's income is the single best predictor and in combination with control of checks provides the best model for predicting weight loss success. It would appear that having no income combined with being in charge of checks is the best model for predicting lack of success in sustaining weight loss while success is best predicted by having an income and not having sole control of the checks. (p. 62)*

Chi-Square Analysis

Conditions of Use

Chi-square is one of the most widely used statistical tests in social work research, in part because it is a test that can be used with the ordinal or nominal levels of measurement.

The chi-square is used when:

▶ We are interested in testing the null hypothesis to find whether there is no relationship between two variables.

▶ The variables are both measured at the nominal or ordinal level.

▶ A normal distribution of responses is not required.

In the last chapter, we discussed cross-tabulation, which is a way of describing the relationship between two values measured at the nominal or ordinal level. With cross-tabulation, we are eyeballing or estimating the relationship. The chi-square statistic can be applied to cross-tabulation to give us a more accurate reflection of the significance of the relationship between two variables.

Chi-square assesses the extent to which the frequencies in our cross-tabulation, called the **observed frequencies,** differ from what we might expect to observe if the data in the cross-tabulation were a result of chance. These chance frequencies are called the **expected frequencies.** The chi-square statistic is represented by χ^2. The SPSS/PC+ command is CROSSTABS.

Exercise caution when using chi-square. If the sample is too small or if one or more of the cells has an expected value of less than 5, chi-square should not be used.

E X A M P L E

Chi-Square

Andujo (1988) examined the development of positive ethnic identities in Hispanic adoptees who were raised in Hispanic families and those who were raised in non-Hispanic families. Data were collected from the 60 families (30 transethnic and 30 same-ethnic) through interviews. The adoptees were administered the Tennessee Self-Concept Scale, the Twenty Statements Test, the Mexican-American Value Attitude Scale, and a 60-item interview schedule. The results from the Mexican-American Value Attitude Scale for the two family types are displayed in Table 10.2. Significant differences were found between the scores of the transethnic and same-ethnic families.

TABLE 10.2 *Transethnic and same-ethnic adoptees attitude scale scores*

| | Type of adoption | | | |
| | Transethnic family ($n = 30$) | | Same-Ethnic family ($n = 30$) | |
Score	n	%	n	%
Low	0	0	19	63
Medium	7	23	9	30
High	23	77	2	7
Total	30	100	30	100

$\chi^2(2, n = 30) = 37.00, p < .0001$; correction for continuity performed.

Source: From E. Andujo, 1988, *Social Work,* Vol. 33(6), © NASW, Inc. Used by permission.

Inferential Statistics and Single-System Studies

In Chapter 9 we discussed how results from single-system studies can lend themselves to the use of descriptive statistics, and how this could be facilitated through the use of various software packages. It is also possible to use certain statistical techniques with the results from single-system studies that give us some indication as to the effectiveness of our interventions.

Before describing some of these techniques, we need to make a distinction among three types of significance, which can be encountered in the analysis of group data but which often are more relevant in single-system studies. The three types of significance are practical or clinical, visual, and statistical. **Practical** or **clinical significance** is attained when the specified goal of the intervention has been reached. For example, the goal of an intervention may be to increase a child's school attendance from 50% to 90%. Anything below this may not be of practical significance; however, this figure may be much higher or lower than what is needed for statistical significance.

Hersen and Barlow (1976), who wrote a comprehensive text of single-system studies, state that "applied interventions strive for change that ordinarily surpasses statistical significance" (p. 267). By the way, this distinction between practical and statistical significance is also relevant to the analysis of group data, not just single-system data.

In Chapter 9 we talked about the importance of the visual presentation of the data from single-system studies. If the results look significant, this is known as **visual significance.** As with practical significance, there can be some discrepancy between visual significance and statistical significance. Occasionally there may be visual significance, but this does not always represent statistical significance because we may be looking for a visual trend and the trend may be very slight.

Some have argued that statistical analysis cannot be conducted on data from single-system studies (Campbell & Stanley, 1966) because of the completely different nature of single-system and group data. Another potential problem with using inferential analysis with single-system data is that often we find that outcome scores are related to one another. This is referred to as **autocorrelation** and occurs when scores are related so that if we know what happened in the past, we can predict what will happen in the future. This can result in misleading findings and can complicate any statistical analysis.

However, in recent years attempts have been made to accommodate to these potential problems involved in analyzing single-system data. For example, Bloom and Fischer (1982) describe methods to manage autocorrelation and discuss some procedures that can be used based on inferential statistics. Some have suggested that in light of the differences between single and group data procedures for analysis should be used as rules of thumb rather than as statistical absolutes; they can instead be viewed more as supportive evidence (Jayaratne & Levy, 1979).

We will describe the three following analytical procedures: celeration line approach, standard deviation approach, and relative frequency approach.

Celeration Line Approach

This approach for analysis of single-system data was developed by Gingerich and Feyerherm (1979). It involves connecting the midpoints of the two values of baseline data with a line and projecting this line into the intervention period. The line may either accelerate or decelerate depending upon its direction, hence the term **celeration line.** If a certain proportion of the data are on the desired side of the celeration line, then an estimate can be made of the statistical significance using tables developed by Bloom (1975). Details of this method can be found in Gingerich and Feyerherm (1979), Behling and Merves (1984), or Bloom and Fischer (1982).

The celeration line approach has the advantage of not being influenced by autocorrelation, but it is subject to a number of limiting conditions. These include the fact that the number of observations in the baseline and intervention phases should be approximately the same number. Second, celeration lines cannot be used when the baseline is bounded, that is, when the line reaches either the maximum or the minimum; in these cases, the line obviously cannot be extended into the intervention phase. See Figure 10.3 for a visual representation of the celeration line.

Standard Deviation Approach

This approach is based on the standard deviation, which measures the dispersion of scores around the mean (see Chapter 9). With this approach for analyzing data of single-system studies, if the possible intervention mean is more than

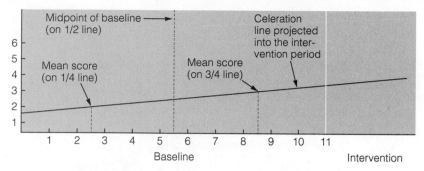

FIGURE 10.3 *Celeration line approach*

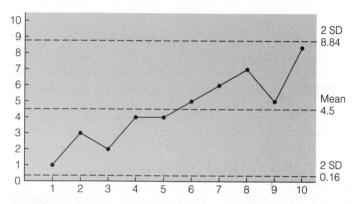

FIGURE 10.4 *Standard deviation approach*

two standard deviations from the baseline mean then there is a statistically significant change. Figure 10.4 illustrates this procedure. See Bloom and Fischer (1982) for details of how to compute this approach.

This is a simple procedure that can be used for almost any number of data points. However, this approach cannot be used with data that is autocorrelated unless the adjustments mentioned earlier are made (see Bloom & Fischer, 1982).

Relative Frequency Approach

This approach assumes that typical behavior is represented by the middle two-thirds of the baseline behavior. The proportion of scores that falls outside this range during the intervention period is calculated, and the proportion is located on a probability table. The value from the probability table is the estimate of statistical significance of the change. See Bloom and Fischer (1982) for details on the computations involved in this approach. The relative frequency procedure is illustrated in Figure 10.5.

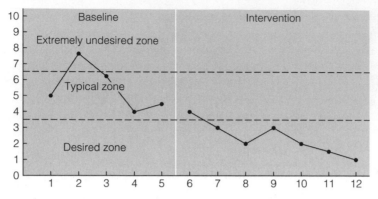

FIGURE 10.5 *Relative frequency approach*

As with the celeration approach, the number of observations in the baseline and intervention period should be approximately the same; also, autocorrelation can interfere with the interpretation of the results using this approach.

The Agency and Inferential Statistics

Commonly, the outcomes from agency-based research studies are not subject to much in-depth analysis, and often the report simply contains descriptive statistics. This is a result of a number of different factors: first, the need to focus on practical over statistical significance; second, the lack of statistical knowledge; and third, the lack of access to computers.

The focus on practical significance is understandable in an agency setting. Often this practical significance can be thought of as political significance. If an agency is carrying out a program evaluation, the agency may not be concerned with whether the results are statistically significant but rather with whether the goals of the program have been met. However, demonstrating statistical significance could enhance practical findings considerably, strengthening the agency's case.

Unfortunately, lack of statistical knowledge in agency settings is all too common. We hope that this overview of statistics has given you some basic knowledge that you can build on by enrolling in statistics courses or by exploring the many available statistics texts. If you still feel at a loss when confronted with the analysis of your data, seek consultation. Universities often have statistical consultants, or you can look in your community for someone with statistical know-how. If you are writing a grant/research proposal, budget in the cost of a statistical consultant. Whenever possible, bring in the consultant early in the project's planning stage. As we have seen, the type of analysis you carry out is contingent upon other aspects of the research process—the levels of measurement, design, and sample size. Thus, utilizing the consultant from the start will ultimately help the data analysis itself.

The lack of access to computers and software is another potential stumbling block to data analysis in an agency setting. However, personal computers and statistical software (such as Shareware) are becoming more affordable, and we need to lobby as generalist social workers for their inclusion in the budget.

Ethical Issues in Inferential Statistics

Two ethical issues need to be considered in the use of inferential statistics: first, the selection of the most appropriate test; and second, the presentation of statistical significance.

Selection of the Test

Selection of the most powerful test is critical. For example, if a less powerful test is used in place of a more powerful one—assuming conditions allow the use of the latter—then there is a smaller likelihood that the null hypothesis will not be rejected when, in fact, this should not have occurred. In other words, a Type II error may be committed. Essentially, this is a distortion of the results and can be regarded as unethical.

We must be careful to avoid only selecting tests that support our hypotheses. Watch for this not only in your own research but when you are reading articles.

Statistical Significance

Several authors have commented on how important it is to recognize that statistical significance is not a concrete entity or property of a particular set of data (MacRae, 1988). The presence of statistical significance may or may not indicate strong relationships and depends on a number of factors, many of which we have already discussed including sample size, type of question being asked, and the influence of other factors. Consequently, we need to be careful in how we present results and in how we draw conclusions when referring to statistical significance. Weinbach (1989) states, "If practitioners are to make intelligent and informed discussions regarding whether a finding is meaningful for them, they must know more than just whether a relationship between variables is statistically significant" (p. 35). He stresses the importance of responsible reporting of results. This would include a statement of the sample size and whether this size falls within the usual-size range for which the test is best suited, which would help the reader assess the appropriateness of the use of the particular test. The strength of the relationship should be presented as clearly as possible—as a percentage difference or an actual correlation. Weinbach concludes: "The ethical researcher who invites replication and feels comfortable in the use of statistical testing should not object to any of these requirements" (p. 35).

Human Diversity Issues in Inferential Statistics

Human diversity issues in inferential statistics relate to our interpretation and understanding of statistical findings, however clearly and responsibly they are reported. Occasionally findings can seduce us into believing that something really is related to something else. We must be careful that these results are used responsibly and that they have acknowledged their potential bias against certain groups. As we have discussed throughout this book, the sources of these biases can exist at each stage of the research process.

Summary

One possible source of error in research is chance. The role of chance factors can be assessed with inferential statistics and the use of probability theory. Hypotheses can be two tailed, one tailed, or null. A finding is statistically significant when the null hypothesis is rejected and its probability of occurring falls at or below a certain cutoff point. The ability of a statistical test to correctly reject a null hypothesis is the power of the test.

Four statistical tests are *t*-tests, ANOVA, correlational analysis, and chi-square. Techniques for analyzing the results from single-system studies include the celeration line approach, the standard deviation approach, and the relative frequency approach.

Ethical issues involved in inferential statistics are the selection of the most appropriate test and the notion of statistical significance. We must also ensure that the findings are used responsibly and that they acknowledge potential bias against certain groups.

Study/Exercise Questions

1 Look in social work journals and find two articles reporting on program evaluations that used inferential statistics.

   a What hypotheses were being tested?

   b What inferential statistics were used?

   c Did they seem to be appropriate tests?

   d What was the statistical significance of the findings?

2 Under what circumstances would you need to undertake the statistical analysis of findings from a single-system study?

Further Reading

See Chapter 9 for further reading on statistical analysis.

Bloom, M., & Fischer, J. (1982). *Evaluating practice: Guidelines for the accountable professional*. Englewood Cliffs, NJ: Prentice-Hall.

> One of the more detailed accounts of how to analyze data from single-system studies.

References

Andujo, E. (1988). Ethnic identity of transethnically adopted Hispanic adolescents. *Social Work, 33*, 531–535.

Behling, J. H., & Merves, E. S. (1984). *The practice of clinical research: The single case method*. New York: University Press of America.

Bloom, M. (1975). *The paradox of helping: Introduction to the philosophy of scientific practice*. New York: Wiley.

Bloom, M., & Fischer, J. (1982). *Evaluating practice: Guidelines for the accountable professional*. Englewood Cliffs, NJ: Prentice-Hall.

Campbell, D. T., & Stanley, J. C. (1966). *Experimental and quasi-experimental designs for research*. Chicago: Rand McNally.

Gingerich, W., & Feyerherm, W. (1979). The celeration line technique for assisting client change. *Journal of Social Service Research, 3*, 99–113.

Hamilton, N., & Zimmerman, R. (1985). Weight control: The interaction of marital power and weight loss success. *Journal of Social Service Research, 8* (3), 51–64.

Hersen, M., & Barlow, D. H. (1976). *Single-case experimental designs*. New York: Pergamon Press.

Hopper, J. R., & McCarlnielson, J. (1991). Recycling as altruistic behavior: Normative and behavioral strategies to expand participation in a community recycling program. *Environment and Behavior, 23*, 195–220.

Jamison, R. N., & Virts, K. L. (1990). The influence of family support on chronic pain. *Behavior Research and Therapy, 28*, 283–287.

Jayaratne, S., & Levy, R. (1979). *Empirical clinical practice*. New York: Columbia University Press.

MacRae, A. W. (1988). Measurement scales and statistics: What can significance tests tell us about the world? *British Journal of Psychology, 79*, 161–171.

Polansky, N. A. (1985). Determinants of loneliness among neglectful and other low-income mothers. *Journal of Social Service Research, 8*, 1–15.

Weinbach, R. W. (1989). When is statistical significance meaningful? A practice perspective. *Journal of Sociology and Social Welfare, 16*(1), 31–37.

Analysis of Qualitative Data

11

No matter how you collect qualitative data—through interviews, open-ended questionnaires, or personal logs—the amount and apparent lack of order of qualitative data can be overwhelming. This chapter describes the ways in which these types of qualitative data can be analyzed.

Analyzing qualitative data requires different techniques than analyzing quantitative data. This chapter includes the following topics:

▶ Approaches to analyzing qualitative data
▶ The agency and qualitative analysis
▶ Ethical issues in qualitative analysis
▶ Human diversity issues in qualitative analysis

We see in this chapter that the distinction among data collection, data organization, and data analysis is much more difficult to make when the data are qualitative. In addition, the methods of analysis are much less structured than with quantitative data. Many of the decisions are left to the discretion of the researcher.

Approaches to Analyzing Qualitative Data

The primary mission in the analysis of qualitative data is to look for *patterns* in the data, noting similarities and differences. We identify the patterns by using various techniques, which we discuss later in this chapter. It is also important to keep the data *in context* to avoid the temptation to present emerging data patterns as independent conclusions that will stand on their own. Data must

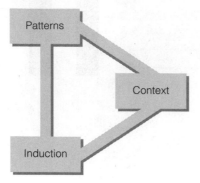

FIGURE 11.1 *Key concepts in qualitative data analysis*

always be presented in context by referring to the specific situations, time periods, and persons in which the identified pattern occurred. Finally, qualitative data analysis *tends* to be inductive rather than deductive. Careful observation leads to the description of connections and patterns in the data that can in turn enable us to form hypotheses and ultimately develop them into theoretical constructs and theories (see Figure 11.1).

Qualitative analysis is much less structured than quantitative analysis and allows the researcher to creatively pursue characteristics of the data in a less restricted manner. We will discuss five dimensions to use as guidelines for the analysis of qualitative data. The researcher may choose to use all of the dimensions or just one or two. Generally, the steps are repeated, forming cycles of analysis, with each cycle reducing the data until the results reach a manageable and usable form. These dimensions are presenting the data as a descriptive account, constructing categories in preparation for further analysis, techniques for carrying out logical analysis, proposing hypotheses, and techniques for validating the data (see Figure 11.2).

Descriptive Accounts

The basis of qualitative analysis often consists of a description. This narrative includes all the materials you have collected: observations, interviews, data from case records, or impressions of others. These descriptive accounts are also referred to as **case studies.**

Patton (1987) suggests three steps for constructing a case study. First, the raw case data are assembled. These data consist of all the information collected for the case study. The second step is constructing a case record; the case data are organized, classified, and edited into an accessible package. The third step is writing the case study narrative. This can be done either chronologically or thematically (or both). This narrative should be a "holistic portrayal" of a person or program.

The descriptive account or case study can take the form of any of the types of research we have considered in this book—a single-system study for

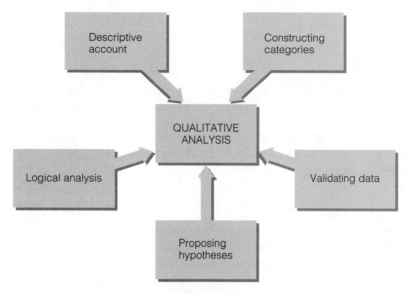

FIGURE 11.2 *Dimensions of qualitative analysis*

the evaluation of practice, a description of the problem for a needs assessment, or a description of a program for a formative program evaluation.

E X A M P L E

A Case Study for Evaluation of Practice

Sefansky (1990) describes a case study that involves work with the family of a young survivor of a plane crash. She discusses the use of crisis intervention and family-centered social work practice with this case. She also describes the effects of the media on the staff and the institution and her personal reactions and involvement with the family.

E X A M P L E

A Case Study for Needs Assessment

Sklar and Hartley (1990) studied the bereavement of persons who have experienced the death of a close friend. Their findings indicated that these "survivor friends" experienced similar bereavement patterns as those who have suffered the loss of family members. The authors argue that the experience and needs of this bereavement group need to be addressed.

E X A M P L E

A Case Study for Program Evaluation

Miller and Whittaker (1988) describe four family support programs in an attempt to guide the development of family support agencies. They use a chart to compare the programs according to agency base, population served, intervention approach, social support, duration of contact, and outcome measures.

The authors conclude that the four program examples give some important guidelines for developing support services to families needing protective services. First, there must be a blending of informal and formal services that resolves the traditional conflicts between public and private agencies. Second, prevention and early intervention planning need more emphasis. Third, assessment and intervention planning require more careful attention. Fourth, new roles should be developed for child welfare workers such as "broker," "advocate," and "network system consultant." Finally, programs need to work more closely with communities through joint funding efforts.

Constructing Categories

As mentioned earlier, qualitative research analysis generally uses an inductive rather than a deductive approach. Patterns, themes, and categories emerge from the data rather than being developed prior to collection. There are two main strategies for identifying categories once the data have been collected: indigenous and researcher-constructed categories. These two strategies have been developed quite extensively in anthropology.

Indigenous Categories

Indigenous categories, which use the **emic** approach, involve identifying the categories used by those being observed, or adopting the natives' point of view. In many ways, this approach is very compatible to the practice skills of building rapport and developing empathy so that the worker can see the world from the client's point of view.

Indigenous categories are constructed from data collected using the frame elicitation technique. **Frame elicitation** involves framing questions in such a way that you find out from your subjects what *they* include in a particular topic or category. An approach that works well for needs assessments is to ask a question such as "What kinds of _____ are there?" For example, if you are interested in finding out the needs of the physically challenged in your community, you can ask a question like "What kinds of services for the hearing impaired are needed?" This results in categories of responses that have not been imposed by the researcher, but rather, elicited from the respondents. Framing a question in the format of "Is _____ the same as (or part of) _____?" can help identify overlaps between respondents. Using our example, the question would be: "Is afterschool care the same as respite care?" These questions elicit data with which you can construct a taxonomy of the respondent's perception of services needed by the physically challenged.

There are a number of issues to be aware of when constructing taxonomics or categories in this way. First, interinformant variation is common; that is, different informants may use different words to refer to the same category of things. Second, category labels may be fairly complex, consisting of a phrase or two rather than simply a word or two. Third, there are categories for which informants have no label at all. Fourth, the categories overlap.

However, once these issues have been considered, indigenous categories can be useful to the generalist social worker; you can be assured that the case is being presented from the client's perspective and that it is not being interpreted inappropriately by the researcher.

E X A M P L E

Using Indigenous Categories

Sorensen and Snow (1991), in their analysis of children's disclosure of sexual abuse, retrospectively studied children from 3 to 17 years of age using clinical notes, conversations, audio- and videotapes, and reports. Common elements emerged from these data, and the authors identified four variables of the disclosure process: *denial,* the child's initial statement to any individual that he or she had not been sexually abused; *disclosure,* the child's acknowledgement of having experienced a specific sexually abusive activity (this was broken down into tentative or active disclosure); *recant,* the child's retraction of a previous allegation of abuse; *reaffirm,* the child's reassertion of the validity of a previous statement of sexual abuse that had been recanted.

Researcher-Constructed Categories

Researcher-constructed categories, which use the **etic** approach, are derived from patterns that are identified in the data. These categories may be relatively meaningless to the people under study, but the categories do provide a good overall picture of the phenomenon being investigated. Studies that use researcher-constructed categories are considered qualitative as long as the study incorporates the other key concepts of qualitative studies: namely, the data are considered in context allowing for the observation and detection of patterns (see page 231).

E X A M P L E

Using Researcher-Constructed Categories

Biller and Rice (1990) studied people who had survived multiple losses of persons with acquired immune deficiency syndrome. They used a three-stage model of grief that had already been developed. This model included the phases of avoidance, confrontation, and reestablishment. The researchers used information gathered by interview from seven respondents—five gay males and two lesbian females—and noted how these data fitted into the predeveloped phases.

Researcher-constructed categories dominate content analysis. Content analysis involves coding written and oral communications and then making inferences based on the incidence of these codes. We first mentioned this approach in Chapter 4 when we were discussing the use of secondary data and then again in Chapter 8 when we discussed organizing this type of data. Content analysis can be performed on transcribed recorded interviews, process recordings on a case, published articles in newspapers or journals, and so forth.

Alter and Evens (1990) suggest six steps for content analysis:

1 Select the constructs of interest and define them clearly.
2 Select a unit of analysis (word, sentence, phrase, theme, and so on) to be coded.
3 Define the categories. They should be mutually exclusive and should be fairly narrow.
4 Test this classification scheme on a document.
5 Revise if reliability is low and test again until an acceptance level of reliability is achieved.
6 Code the text of interest and do a category count.

As mentioned in Chapter 8, this approach to analyzing data can be facilitated through the use of computer word processing programs or a more specific software package; an example of a software package developed specifically for qualitative data analysis is ETHNOGRAPH.

Allen-Meares (1984) discusses the important role content analysis can have in social work research. An early example of content analysis is provided by Hollis (1972), who used a coding "typology." She was interested in describing and understanding the communications that take place in social casework interviews. Interviews were transcribed and coded line by line using the following codes:

U = unclassified
A = sustainment
B = direct influence

C = exploration, description, ventilation
D = person–situation reflection
E = pattern–dynamic reflection
F = developmental reflection

Interviews could then be understood depending upon the frequency of the different types of communication. These codes were developed specifically for casework practice; thus, different categories would need to be developed to do content analysis on generalist practice interviews.

E X A M P L E

A Content Analysis

A content analysis was carried out by Abelman (1989) who compared black and white families as portrayed in religious and secular TV programming. Content categories included the family configuration type, whether the family was black or white, and family interactions. Abelman's overall findings disclosed that for both black and white families there was virtually an absence of relatives portrayed outside of the traditional nuclear family—for example, no stepparents, uncles, aunts, and so on. Elders were also noticeably absent, and black families were underrepresented.

Although content analysis is often used in social work research, it is associated with a number of problems. First, there may be an issue with the validity of the codes, which is involved with any researcher-constructed category. Second, the coding of the text can be unreliable if it is only done by one coder. Intercoder reliability should be established, which often means training the coder. Third, the coding almost inevitably involves lifting concepts out of context, which essentially negates much of the value of qualitative research.

Logical Analysis

Logical analysis involves looking at the relationships between the variables and concepts. This is similar to the quantitative processes of correlation and cross-tabulation that we described in Chapter 9 in which we extend the one-dimensional picture of the data. Qualitative analysis has a similar process called **cross-classification** to look at these relationships. Patton (1987) describes cross-classification as

> *creating potential categories by crossing one dimension or typology with another, and then working back and forth between the data and one's logical constructions, filling in the resulting matrix. This logical system will create a new typology, all parts of which may or may not actually be represented by the data. (p. 155)*

An important aspect of examining the data this way is to display the data in a table or matrix.

E X A M P L E

Cross-Classification

Patton (1987) uses a hypothetical example of cross-classification in evaluating a juvenile justice program.

> *Suppose we have been evaluating a juvenile justice program which places delinquent youths in foster homes. We have visited several foster homes; observed what the home environments are like; and interviewed the juveniles, the foster home parents, and the probation officers. A regularly recurring theme in the interviews is the importance of the process of "letting kids learn to make their own decisions." A regularly recurring outcomes theme is "keeping the kids straight" (reduce recidivism). The blank cell in a matrix created by crossing the program process ("kids making their own decisions") with the program outcome ("keeping kids straight") creates a data analysis question: What actual decisions do juveniles make that are supposed to lead to reduced recidivism? We then carefully review our field notes and interview quotations looking for data that help us understand how people in the program have answered this question based on their actual behaviors and practices. By describing what decisions juveniles actually make in the program the decision makers to whom our findings are reported can make their own judgments about the strength or weakness of this linkage between this program process and the desired outcome. (p. 156)*

Proposing Hypotheses

Qualitative analysis is primarily concerned with developing hypotheses, rather than testing them. However, part of qualitative analysis does involve speculation about causality and linkages. One way of representing and presenting this causality is to construct **causal flowcharts.** These are visual representations of ideas that emerge from studying the data, seeing patterns, and seeing possible causes for phenomena. We have been using causal flowcharts in this text to illustrate some of the research methods. Often causal flowcharts consist of a set of boxes connected by arrows. The boxes contain descriptions of states (attitudes, perceptions, ages, and so on), and the arrows tell how one state leads to another. For example,

A leads to or causes B.

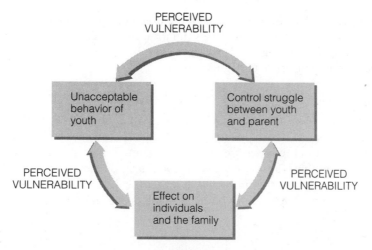

FIGURE 11.3 *Main elements of the Parent–Adolescent conflict process*
Source: From R. K. Tomlinson, 1991. Used by permission of Human Services Press.

E X A M P L E

A Causal Flowchart Analysis

Tomlinson (1991) carried out a qualitative research study about concerned parents of acting out teenagers. Tomlinson provides a profile of the characteristics of the parents that includes a multidimensional view of parent competence, an analysis of the main components of the parent–adolescent conflict, and a theory that perceived vulnerability provides a context in which the conflict flourishes. Tomlinson depicts these elements in a causal flowchart (see Figure 11.3).

The development of hypotheses and causal statements should be firmly rooted in the data and not be imposed on or overly influenced by the theoretical biases of the researcher. If a researcher uses a category previously defined theoretically, the qualitative nature of the research can be ensured by the nature of the data collection methods and the manner in which those data are used to either support or refute the categories. The context of the data must be taken into full consideration. The researcher should try to avoid the linear thinking associated with quantitative analysis. One of the strengths of qualitative analysis is the potential for understanding contextual interrelationships among factors and their circular and interdependent natures.

Validation

Just as we need to validate quantitative findings, so do we also need to validate the findings of qualitative research. Quantitative analysis validation is achieved both through the research design and through the use of certain statistical tests as we discussed in Chapter 10. Qualitative validation requires rather different processes, including considering rival or alternative hypotheses, considering negative cases, and the process of triangulation.

Rival Hypotheses

After a hypothesis has been developed and proposed, **rival hypotheses** need to be explored and comparisons made between these two perspectives. Rival hypotheses can emerge from the literature or from the data. The rival hypotheses and our proposed hypothesis are both tested by looking at the data and considering which hypothesis appears to most closely reflect the data. This may result not only in the rejection of hypotheses but also in the proposal of a number of explanations.

E X A M P L E

Multiple Explanations

Lewis (1990), in his study of shopping malls, was interested in explaining why the elderly and teenagers view and use the mall as the locus of community. He suggests five different reasons. First, teens and elders both represent social groupings for whom our society provides little social space and the mall can provide this space. Second, the elders and teens tend to be faceless persons to adult American society, and this facelessness allows them to be generally overlooked in the malls. Third, the mall is centrally located, easy to get to, safe, and climate controlled. Fourth, there are two reasons why the mall personnel encourage teens and elders to use the mall. Both groups can enhance the public relations of the malls. The elderly "can be used to advantage to further the mall's illusion of community by publicizing their support of community programs such as that of walking for health. For the teens, many of them work in the fast food stores and do leave money in the video arcade and record stores" (p. 135). A final explanation is that these two communities, elders and teens, seem to police themselves quite well.

Negative Cases

When we are looking for patterns in the data, the patterns emerge by looking at what occurs *most often*. However, there are almost always exceptions or **negative cases** that do not fit the patterns, and these need to be examined and explained. When you encounter a case that does not fit your theory, ask yourself whether it is the result of (1) normal social variation, (2) your lack of knowledge about the range of appropriate behavior, or (3) a genuinely unusual case. Force yourself to think creatively on this issue. As Bernard (1988) states, "If the cases won't fit, don't be too quick to throw them out. It is always easier to throw out cases than it is to reexamine one's ideas, and the easy way out is hardly ever the right way in research" (p. 321).

Triangulation

Triangulation involves the use of different research approaches to study the same research question. One way to use triangulation is to collect different kinds of data, such as interviews and observations, which may include both qualitative and quantitative data. Another approach is to have different people collect the data, or use different theories to interpret the data. Finally, data from different services can be compared, such as examining consistent and inconsistent information from different informants.

Using triangulation may result in what appears to be conflicting information. This does not automatically mean that the proposed hypotheses are invalidated. Instead, it may simply mean that new and different information has been gained, and it adds another dimension to our understanding of the phenomenon.

E X A M P L E

Triangulation

Patton (1987) cites an example of triangulation and the use of both qualitative and quantitative methods by Shapiro (1973), who found that the results of qualitative and quantitative methods conflicted in her study of elementary school classrooms. Shapiro concluded that some of the conflicts between the different types of data were a result of measuring quite different things. She had initially anticipated that the results would reinforce each other but found through the use of triangulation that this was not the case. Resolving the conflicts, however, led to a greatly enriched final analysis.

The Agency and Qualitative Analysis

Qualitative data and its subsequent analysis can be invaluable to the generalist social worker. By its nature, it is very compatible with practice. We interview as part of our practice, and we keep logs as part of our practice. Both are important sources of qualitative data.

However, one preconception about qualitative analysis is that it is not as complex as quantitative analysis and that it does not require such sophisticated skills. Part of the goal of doing qualitative research in an agency setting is dispelling this notion—both to enhance the credibility of qualitative studies and to earn the time and support necessary to conduct qualitative data analysis, thereby producing reports that can make a meaningful contribution to the agency.

Ethical Issues in Qualitative Analysis

There are ethical issues in the analysis of qualitative data that you don't encounter in the analysis of quantitative data. Quantitative analysis is protected by the nature of statistical analysis and the rules that govern whether or not findings are statistically significant. Without this kind of objective guide, the interpretation and analysis of qualitative data depend a great deal more on judgment; consequently, there is increased possibility that ethical standards might be violated.

Personal, intellectual, and professional biases are more likely to interfere with qualitative data analysis, despite the existence of validation controls. For example, we discussed earlier the use of negative cases as a method of validation. Sometimes it can be tempting to ignore these, implying that there is more agreement than actually exists among the findings and, consequently, appearing to strengthen the proposed hypothesis or argument.

There may be a fine line between knowing whether an ethical standard has been violated intentionally or whether the researcher simply missed a particular avenue of inquiry. For example, a negative case may not have been examined because the researcher did not see it that way but had, in fact, interpreted it as one that supported the developing hypothesis.

On the other hand, qualitative analysis can sometimes expose distortions in previous research. Consequently, qualitative studies can make an important ethical contribution to our knowledge. Srinivasan and Davis (1991) conducted research on the organization of shelters for battered women. They stated that these shelters have tended to be idealized as collectivist organizations that empower both residents and staff. Their qualitative research at one shelter indicated that despite an "implicit philosophy of empowerment," a shelter is an organization like any other: An egalitarian, collectivist structure existed for the relationships among staff members, and a hierarchical structure existed for the relationships between the staff and the residents. The authors concluded by recommending that feminist social workers must continuously assess how ideology affects the organizational environment in which services are delivered.

Human Diversity Issues in Qualitative Analysis

As with ethical issues, there can be more opportunities to violate human diversity issues in the analysis of qualitative data than in the analysis of quantitative data. Data can be analyzed and hypotheses generated that directly reflect the biases of the researcher, which may reflect negatively on certain groups. Although this can happen in quantitative research, it is more likely in qualitative research and additional precautions need to be taken. Researchers conducting qualitative analysis should constantly use self-examination to determine whether they are perpetuating stereotypical or negative images of the subjects in their studies. The purpose of validation procedure is partly to ensure that this does not occur.

As with ethical issues, qualitative analysis can actually be an asset in ensuring that human diversity issues are recognized. The qualitative approach can provide a richer and more diverse picture of phenomena. Davis (1987) explored the attitudes of service providers toward abused women and abusing men, using both quantitative (which she labeled "masculine" research) and qualitative ("feminine" research) methods. The quantitative approach, using questionnaires that contained vignettes that the respondents rated, revealed widespread victim blaming among the respondents (which included police, social workers, nurses, physicians, judges, and so on). The qualitative approach revealed that when given the opportunity to explore the problem at length, service providers avoided making judgments and worked toward understanding and explaining the men's and women's behaviors. Thus, the results from the qualitative study seemed to reflect more realistically the complexity of the situation and avoided stereotyping and blaming the victim.

Overcoming biases can be a difficult task, even through the use of careful qualitative strategies. Sometimes, it is very hard for us to identify these biases in our thinking, and even the definition of a bias can be problematic. As social workers, we know that the environment and society in which we live profoundly affects the way we think, including the way we think about different groups. This may result in our unconscious exclusion of certain groups and provides the foundation for discourse analysis. **Discourse analysis** focuses on ways in which all analyses are embedded in the researcher's biographical and historical location (Warren, 1988). A great deal of emphasis in discourse analysis has been placed on how women have been marginalized (Keller, 1985).

> *"Our laws of nature" are more than simple expressions of the results of objective inquiry or of political and social pressures; they must also be read for their personal—and by tradition, masculine—content. (p. 10)*

This perspective relates to the discussion in Chapter 1 concerning the difficulty of achieving true objectivity and the impact of values on how we carry out and interpret science.

Summary

The primary mission in qualitative data analysis is looking for patterns in the data while maintaining the context of the study. Approaches to qualitative analysis include descriptive accounts (case studies), constructing categories (indigenous categories and researcher-constructed categories—including the use of content analysis), logical analysis (cross-classification), proposing hypotheses (using causal flow charts), and techniques of validation (using rival hypotheses, negative cases, and triangulation).

Although qualitative data analysis is naturally compatible with practice, the myth persists that it is unduly time consuming, unsophisticated, and nonproductive. Researchers in agency settings have the responsibility of dispelling this myth. Due to the unstructured nature of qualitative analysis, we must ensure that personal, intellectual, and professional biases do not interfere with the process. We must also take care that diverse groups are recognized at the analysis stage.

Study/Exercise Questions

1 Conduct an interview with a fellow student, gathering information on what he or she considers to be the family's culture.

   a Use the indigenous category approach discussed in this chapter.

   b Compare your findings with others in the class.

   c Is it possible to propose a hypothesis based on these findings?

   d How would you validate your findings?

2 Carry out a content analysis on ethics and research using issues of a social work journal. Note: You will need to define *ethics* and *research* and specify the number and type of journal. What conclusions can you draw from your findings?

Further Reading

Berg, B. (1989). *Qualitative research methods for the social sciences.* Boston: Allyn & Bacon.

   A very clear introduction to qualitative methods, including a chapter on ethical issues.

Bernard, H. R. (1988). *Research methods in cultural anthropology.* Newbury Park, CA: Sage Publications.

   Although written for anthropologists, social workers also will find this book a useful and clear introduction to qualitative data collection and analysis.

Miles, M. B., & Huberman, A. M. (1984). *Qualitative data analysis: A sourcebook of new methods.* Newbury Park, CA: Sage Publications.

   An extensive, technical guide to qualitative analysis.

Patton, M. Q. (1987). *How to use qualitative methods in evaluation.* Newbury Park, CA: Sage Publications.

   A useful guide for applying qualitative methods in program evaluations, which is a perspective usually not taken by program evaluation guides.

References

Abelman, R. (1989). A comparison of black and white families as portrayed on religious and secular television programs. *Journal of Black Studies, 20,* 60–77.

Allen-Meares, P. (1984). Content analysis: It does have a place in social work research. *Journal of Social Science Research, 7,* 51–68.

Alter, C., & Evens, W. (1990). *Evaluating your practice.* New York: Springer.

Bernard, H. R. (1988). *Research methods in cultural anthropology.* Newbury Park, CA: Sage Publications.

Biller, R., & Rice, S. (1990). Experiencing multiple loss of persons with AIDS: Grief and bereavement issues. *Health and Social Work, 15,* 283–290.

Davis, L. V. (1987). Views of wife abuse: Does the research method make a difference? *Affilia, 2,* 53–66.

Hollis, F. (1972). *Casework: A psychosocial therapy.* New York: Random House.

Keller, G. F. (1985). *Reflections on gender and science.* New Haven, CT: Yale University Press.

Lewis, G. H. (1990). Community through exclusion and illusion: The location of social worlds in an American shopping mall. *Journal of Popular Culture, 24,* 121–136.

Miller, J. L., & Whittaker, J. K. (1988). Social services and social support: Blended programs for families at risk of child maltreatment. *Child Welfare, LXVII,* 161–174.

Patton, M. Q. (1987). *How to use qualitative methods in evaluation.* Newbury Park, CA: Sage Publications.

Sefansky, S. (1990). Pediatric critical care social work: Interventions with a special plane crash survivor. *Health and Social Work, 15,* 215–220.

Shapiro, E. (1973). Educational evaluation: Rethinking the criteria of competence. *School Review* (November), 523–547.

Sklar, F., & Hartley, S. F. (1990). Close friends as survivors: Bereavement patterns in a "hidden" population. *Omega, 21,* 103–112.

Sorensen, T., & Snow, B. (1991). How children tell: The process of disclosure in child sexual abuse. *Child Welfare, LXX,* 4–15.

Srinivasan, M., & Davis, L. V. (1991). A shelter: An organization like any other? *Affilia, 6,* 38–57.

Tomlinson, R. K. (1991). Unacceptable adolescent behavior and parent-adolescent conflict. *Child and Adolescent Social Work, 8,* 33–55.

Warren, C. (1988). *Gender issues in field research.* Newbury Park, CA: Sage Publications.

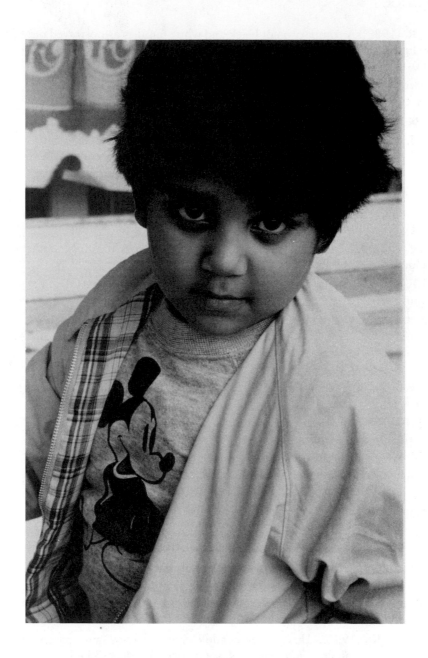

Research Writing $\quad$ **12**

You've analyzed the research results, and in front of you are several computer printouts or, in the case of qualitative data, masses of notes and coded material. Inevitably, there comes a point when you need to write up your research results. Writing the research report is necessary both for yourself—particularly when you are evaluating your own practice—and for others. In fact, for needs assessments and program evaluations, the writing of the report is a critical research stage; as a generalist social worker, you may be more involved in this stage than any other. In addition, you may be asked to assist with developing research proposals, often as part of larger grant proposals.

Writing about research is the focus of this chapter. The two basic types of research writing—proposal writing and reporting research results—are analogous to similar steps in practice: first, the writing of an assessment and intervention plan; and second, the reporting of the results of the intervention.

This chapter discusses:

- ▶ General principles of research writing
- ▶ The research proposal
- ▶ The research report
- ▶ Disseminating the report
- ▶ The agency and research writing
- ▶ Ethical issues in research writing
- ▶ Human diversity issues in research writing

General Principles of Research Writing

In conjunction with research writing, remember that whenever possible your writing should be carried out using the computer. There are many excellent software programs available for writing. Using a word processing program will facilitate your research writing efforts.

Four general principles of research writing are addressed here: knowing your audience; using appropriate citations and references; the structure of the report or proposal; and finally, the process of writing.

Knowing Your Audience

One of the basic principles of writing, research or otherwise, is to identify your audience. This will directly impact the content and style of the written product. For example, in writing a research proposal for a needs assessment to establish a date rape prevention program on a university campus, clarify from the outset to whom the proposal is directed—the university administration, a local chapter of NASW, or some other audience. Obviously, audiences are very different. The university administration might need considerable information about the phenomenon of date rape and a discussion of its potential impact on the recruitment of students, whereas the NASW chapter might require more emphasis on the social and psychological costs of the problem, such as date rape's impact on women's self-esteem.

Your audience not only influences the content of your proposal or report but also the style you adopt. If writing for the university administration, your writing style would be more formal than if you were writing a report for a group of parents in the community.

Referencing Sources of Information

When you are writing any type of report that refers to work by other authors, whether quoting them directly or through indirect reference, it is critical that you appropriately cite your sources of information. Although you can use a number of different referencing styles, the one most widely used in social work literature is the American Psychological Association (APA) referencing method. This is the style used in this book.

The *Publication Manual of the American Psychological Association* (1983) is the guidebook for the APA style. This book contains a great deal of information; therefore, we will summarize some of the more important and common rules.

Quotations from a Source
He stated, "That is why a new theory, however special its range of application, is seldom or never just an increment to what is already known" (Kuhn, 1970, p. 7).

Referencing Citations in the Text

Kuhn (1970) discussed the role of paradigms in the development of scientific thought.

These citations in the text, whether direct quotes or ideas, are then listed in a bibliography. The sources are listed alphabetically by author, using the following format:

Journal articles

1. One author

Paivio, A. (1975). Perceptual comparisons through the mind's eye. *Memory and Cognition, 3,* 635–647.

2. Two authors, journal paginated by issue

Becker, L. J., & Seligman, C. (1981). Welcome to the energy crisis. *Journal of Social Issues, 37*(2), 1–7.

Books

Bernstein, T. M. (1965). *The careful writer: A modern guide to English usage.* New York: Atheneum.

Articles or chapters in edited books

Gurman, A. S., & Kniskern, D. P. (1981). Family therapy outcome research: Knowns and unknowns. In A. S. Gurman & D. P. Kniskern (Eds.), *Handbook of family therapy* (pp. 742–775). New York: Brunner/Mazel.

Reports

National Institute of Mental Health. (1982). *Television and behavior: Ten years of scientific progress and implications for the eighties* (DHHS Publication No. ADM 82-1195). Washington, D.C.: U.S. Government Printing Office.

The Structure of the Proposal/Report

This section outlines some general principles relating to the structure of the report. (The specifics of the content of both the proposal and the report are discussed in the following section.) Again, the APA manual is useful since it contains not only details about referencing sources but also describes each component of the report/proposal.

In general, these conventions should be followed:

▶ *Title* Use a clear and concise title.

▶ *Authorship and sponsorship* This should be inclusive. Don't forget anyone!

▶ *Abstract* This is to prepare the reader by providing an overview of the contents of the report/proposal.

▶ *Appendices* Sometimes the report may include material that is relevant but too bulky to include in the text of the proposal/report. These materials are then included as appendices. Common materials to place in the appendices are the data collection instruments and statistical tables that do not relate directly to the findings.

▶ *Bibliography and referencing* These were discussed in the previous section.

Remember that your report/proposal should maintain a consistent style. For instance, if you use the APA style for references, you should also use this manual for instructions in how to structure titles and abstracts.

The Process of Writing

Research reports and proposals should be written as clearly and as concisely as possible. This is not the place for flamboyant writing. Remember that you want others, possibly from very diverse backgrounds, to read and understand the results of your research. Long and convoluted reports may not only cloud comprehension of the findings but may also discourage some from even trying to read them. Be as straightforward in your writing as possible. The following suggestions can help you achieve this clarity:

▶ Keep a research log to facilitate the process of the report/proposal writing as well as the process and development of the research itself. A **research log** is an informal although systematic record of ideas and progress relating to the research. Once the research is completed, it may be difficult to remember exactly why one research strategy was adopted over another or what doubts there were about a particular approach. The research log can help jog the memory.

▶ Prepare an outline. (We will discuss the details of this in the next section.) You may not end up following this exactly, but that's okay. The idea is to at least have a rough idea in your mind and on paper of how the report/proposal is structured. This helps avoid a written product that wanders from one topic to another.

▶ Write a first draft, then revise and revise and revise, if necessary. Do not expect your first draft to be anything like the final one.

▶ Ask colleagues, faculty, and/or students to read early drafts and give their comments. Do not be afraid of criticism at this point. Generally, the more input you receive the higher the quality of the written product. Have your readers comment on structure, content, style, grammar, and spelling.

▶ Have someone proof the final copy—primarily for grammar and spelling.

The Research Proposal

A **research proposal** is a paper proposing the undertaking of a specific type of research. This is often necessary to obtain permission and funds to conduct the study.

The writing of the proposal can also directly assist the researcher in his or her conceptualization of the research. By systematically thinking through each step of the research process, which is what is required in the research proposal, the researcher can gain new insights and clarifications regarding the research itself.

There are some variations as to the format required for a research proposal depending upon the specific conditions under which the proposal is being written. These include the following:

▶ The funding agency may provide application forms that specify the information that is being requested.

▶ The funding agency may request a letter of intent, which requires the researcher to briefly describe the proposal. The funding source, based on this letter, may or may not ask the researcher to submit a full-fledged proposal.

▶ Sometimes, funding agencies send out Requests for Proposals (RFP's) that specify what they are interested in funding and how the proposals should be submitted (see Figure 12.1).

Taking the above conditions into consideration, there is generally a standard outline that is used for writing research proposals. The different components include:

▶ Statement of the research topic
▶ Theoretical framework
▶ Research questions and hypotheses
▶ Data collection, including operationalization of the variables in the research questions
▶ Sampling strategy
▶ Research design, including a description of the comparison groups (if any) and when the data will be collected
▶ Data analysis
▶ Presentation of the results
▶ Administration and budget
▶ Credentials of the researcher and other relevant personnel

Some have commented that these outlines tend to have a quantitative or positivistic bias (Lincoln & Guba, 1985). Although it could be argued that the outline could also accommodate, for example, a qualitative/exploratory

U.S. Department of Labor   Office of the Assistant Secretary
                                      for Administration and Management
                                      Washington, D.C. 20210

RFP L/A 92-15

MAY - 8 1992

Ladies and Gentlemen:

You are invited to submit a proposal to conduct basic research to
elicit information on new and emerging issues in the current labor
force status of women and provide report to the U.S. Department of
Labor Women's Bureau. Your proposal should be prepared in accordance
with the requirements of this solicitation document, consisting of
the following checked sections:

                            PART I

/X/	SECTION	DESCRIPTION
/ /	A	Solicitation/Contract Form
/X/	B	Supplies or Services and Prices/Costs
/X/	C	Description/Specifications/Work Statement
/ /	D	Packaging and Marking
/X/	E	Inspection and Acceptance
/X/	F	Deliveries or Performance
/X/	G	Contract Administration Data
/X/	H	Special Contract Requirements

               PART II - CONTRACT CLAUSES

| /X/ | I | Contract Clauses |

   PART III - LIST OF DOCUMENTS, EXHIBITS AND OTHER ATTACHMENTS

| / / | J | List of Attachments |

             PART IV - REPRESENTATIONS AND INSTRUCTIONS

/X/	K	Representations, Certifications and Other Statements of Offerors
/X/	L	Instructions, Conditions and Notices to Offeror
/X/	M	Evaluation Factors for Award

You are requested to submit written questions concerning any areas
which in your opinion require clarification in sufficient time for
answers to be researched and responses to be mailed simultaneously to
all prospective offerors at least five days prior to the closing date
for receipt of proposals. Also see the clause in Section L
"Submission of Questions".

Your proposal must be received by the U.S. Department of Labor,
National Capital Service Center, Office of Procurement Services, Room
S-5220, Frances Perkins Building, 200 Constitution Avenue, N.W.,

Washington, D.C. 20210, not later than the close of business (4:45
P.M., Washington, D.C. time) on __JUN 12 1992__. You are requested to
review the clause entitled "Late Proposal Provisions" set forth in
Section L. The proposal must be signed by an official authorized to
bind the offeror, and it shall contain a statement to the effect that
the proposal is firm for a period of at least one hundred eighty
(180) days from the date specified above for the receipt of offers.

This solicitations does not commit the Government to pay any costs
incurred in the submission of proposals or to contract for the
articles or services. It is also brought to your attention that the
Contracting Officer is the only individual who can legally commit
the Government to the expenditure of public funds in connection with
this procurement.

Requests for any information concerning this solicitation are to be
referred only to the Contract Negotiator, Jeff Saylor, who may be
reached at telephone number (202) 523-9355.

        Sincerely,

        FREDERICK H. TRAKOWSKI
        Chief, Division of Contract
        Negotiations and ADP Procurement
        Office of Procurement Services
        National Capital Service Center

        Attachments

FIGURE 12.1 *Request for Proposal*

study, many funding agencies are, in reality, still primarily interested in more traditional approaches. However, as we discussed in Chapter 1, researchers are increasingly adopting less traditional methods of inquiry, which will eventually influence the format and expectations of RFP's.

Each step of the outline has been explained sequentially in this book. However, we should clarify a few items. First, the "theoretical framework," in the case of a program evaluation, would report why the program is being evaluated and would include findings from the evaluations of similar programs. For a needs assessment, this section would include a description of prior research that has reported on the extent of the social problem to be investigated. Some of this information could be found in the social work literature, but it may also be found in various government document depositions or in agencies' archives. This is unlike the theoretical framework for a less applied study—for instance, looking at the impact on a child's self-image of one parent being physically challenged (a possible thesis topic). Here the framework would include a discussion of the various theories that have suggested a relationship may occur, in addition to reporting similar research and their findings. This information could be found in the social work and social science literature in university libraries. As a rule, the theoretical framework is developed by referring to the existing literature and reporting the relevant findings.

In the "data collection" section, you are generally only required to state the method you will be using to collect data. For example, if the data collection requires the development of an instrument—such as an interview schedule or a questionnaire—typically this does not need to be completed for the proposal, but you will need to state what types of variables you will be including. If you plan to use scales or other instruments that have already been developed, then you would include these in an appendix to the proposal.

The "data analysis" section clearly cannot be discussed in any detail in the proposal except to indicate which statistical tests or other forms of analysis will be used.

The "presentation of results" section should include a discussion of how and to whom the results will be presented.

The "budget" section should itemize all expenses, including supplies, personnel costs, mailing costs, computer costs, and so forth (see Figure 12.2).

Finally, you usually need to both summarize your credentials as they relate to the project and/or include a curriculum vitae.

The Research Report

As with the research proposal, the organization of the research report depends in part upon the demands of the agency or the funding source. However, in general this outline is followed:

Personnel Costs

Students: _____ hrs. @ $ ___ /hr. = $ _____
    +Fringe benefits: .5% of student costs = $ _____
                        TOTAL student costs = $ _____
Other personnel (identify): _____

        _____ hrs. @ $ ___ /hr. = $ _____
    +Fringe benefits: 21% of personnel costs = $ _____
                        TOTAL other costs = $ _____

                        TOTAL PERSONNEL COSTS = $ _____

Supplies (identify and give unit cost if known; use separate sheet if necessary)

_____ @ $ _____ each = _____
_____ @ $ _____ each = _____
_____ @ $ _____ each = _____
_____ @ $ _____ each = _____
_____ @ $ _____ each = _____

                        TOTAL SUPPLY COSTS = $ _____

Other Costs

Telephone: $ _____
Postage: _____ units @ $ _____ /unit
Copier costs: _____ copies @ $ _____ copy
Other (identify): _____
                _____
                _____

                        TOTAL OTHER COSTS = $ _____

Travel

Travel from _____ to _____
Mileage: _____ miles @ $.25 _____ mile = _____
Per diem: _____ days @ $ _____ day = _____

                        TOTAL TRAVEL COSTS = $ _____

                        TOTAL PROJECT COSTS = $ _____

TOTAL AMOUNT REQUESTED FOR RESEARCH MINIGRANT $ _____

NOTE: The above is provided as a guide to assist in developing your research
       minigrant budget. The categories listed are suggestions of costs you
       may wish to include in your request. Please use this form, taking care
       that the detail clearly identifies your needs and breaks out any source
       of cost sharing.

                                                        Rev. 1/91

FIGURE 12.2 *Research minigrant budget detail*

- Statement of the research topic
- Theoretical framework
- Research questions and hypotheses
- Data collection method(s)
- Sampling strategy
- Research design
- Results
- Discussion
- Limitations
- Recommendations for future research
- Implications for practice

These sections apply whether you are reporting on a single system, needs assessment, or program evaluation study and regardless of whether the study employs a primarily quantitative or qualitative approach.

Obviously, this outline is very similar to the proposal; in fact, if you have a well-structured and well-informed proposal, the research report will be much easier to complete.

Some differences do exist between the proposal and the report; the report includes four additional sections: the results of the study, a discussion of the findings, the limitations of the study, and suggestions for future research.

Results Section

Regardless of your audience and the type of research, the focus of your report will be on the results. How the results or findings are reported depends on whether the study has adopted a qualitative or quantitative approach, and reference will be made to this throughout the following sections. Reporting findings often involves the use of tables, graphs, and charts. These visual representations are particularly useful for presenting quantitative data. In the following section, we will describe some forms these can take.

Tables

Statistical tables are the most common form of reporting quantitative findings and are essentially types of frequency distributions. Several principles need to guide the presentation of the data. First, clearly display the data and do not clutter the table with unnecessary details. Second, make the table as complete as possible, usually including both raw numbers and percentages (percentages facilitate comparison). Third, provide a summary of the statistical tests at the bottom of the table when appropriate. Finally, clearly label the table, including footnotes where appropriate. Table 12.1 indicates the distribution according to

TABLE 12.1 *Persons who performed unpaid volunteer work at some time during the year ended May 1989, by race or Hispanic origin and selected characteristics*

Characteristic	White		Black		Hispanic	
	Volunteer workers	**Volunteers as percent of population**	**Volunteer workers**	**Volunteers as percent of population**	**Volunteer workers**	**Volunteers as percent of population**
Total	34,823	21.9	2,505	11.9	1,289	9.4
Age						
16 to 24 years old	3,532	13.3	325	7.0	180	5.3
16 to 19	1,700	14.7	133	6.1	83	5.9
20 to 24	1,832	12.3	192	7.7	97	4.9
25 to 34 years old	7,816	21.7	676	12.7	374	9.6
35 to 44 years old	9,541	31.1	585	15.1	374	14.4
45 to 54 years old	5,207	24.5	356	13.7	180	10.9
55 to 64 years old	4,095	21.8	294	13.9	131	11.4
65 years old and over	4,632	17.7	267	10.9	50	4.7
Sex						
Men	15,273	20.0	1,082	11.5	587	8.6
Women	19,550	23.6	1,423	12.3	702	10.1
Marital status						
Never married	5,548	15.2	598	7.7	274	6.6
Married, spouse present	24,627	26.0	1,295	16.4	811	11.1
Married, spouse absent	585	15.0	151	9.2	70	8.0
Divorced	2,140	17.5	305	15.4	101	11.9
Widowed	1,923	16.4	155	9.2	33	6.0
Years of school completed by persons 25 years old and over						
0 to 11 years	2,524	8.8	379	6.9	234	4.7
12 years only	10,315	19.9	684	11.3	311	10.8
13 to 15 years	6,859	29.3	547	19.7	302	21.0
16 years or more	11,594	40.2	569	28.7	262	26.0

Numbers in thousands

Source: From *Monthly Labor Review*, February 1991

ethnicity, sex, age, and marital status of people performing unpaid volunteer work. This is a good example of a table that is clearly laid out and labeled.

Graphs

Graphs are an alternative or a supplement to tables that present the data more visually. As with tables, you must follow similar guidelines with graphs. One drawback of graphs is that they lack the detail of tables; however, their advantage is that they present a visual image of the data that makes the results

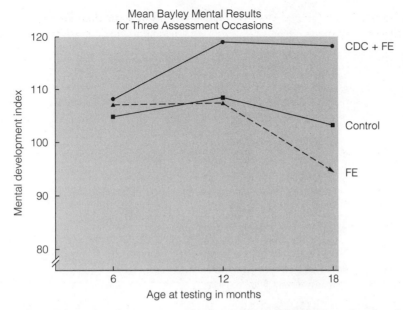

FIGURE 12.3 *The mean Bayley Mental Development Index for the 6-, 12-, and 18-month assessment occasions for the Child Development Center plus Family Education (CDC + FE), Family Education (FE), and control groups*
Source: From B. H. Wasik et al., 1990. © 1990 The Society for Research in Child Development, Inc.

apparent at a glance. They are particularly useful in presenting data from single-system studies, and we discussed some of the principles of graphing in Chapter 7.

Various types of graphs can be used. The **line graph** connects various data points with lines. Figure 12.3 represents some of the results from a longitudinal program evaluation carried out by Wasik et al. (1990). This study compared two early intervention strategies, one intensive and one less intensive, and a control group. The graph presents the results from one of the outcome measures—the Bayley Test of Infant Development (Bayley, 1969)—for the 3 groups of children at 3 points in time—6, 12, and 18 months.

Another type of graph is the **bar graph**. Bar graphs are useful visual means of displaying data at the nominal level of measurement. In a report issued by the National Commission on Children (1991), bar graphs were used extensively to display the data. Figure 12.4 is from this report and illustrates the percentage of children (ages 10–17) who wish their parents were stricter or more attentive.

Pie Charts

A final type of pictorial or visual presentation of data is the pie chart. **Pie charts** can be used when we want to show the relative contributions of each of the

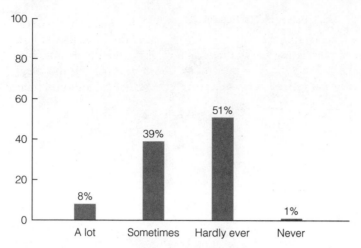

FIGURE 12.4 *Percentage of children (ages 10–17) who wish their parents were stricter or more attentive*
Source: From National Commission on Children, 1991

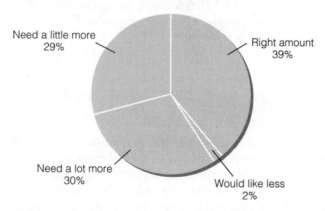

FIGURE 12.5 *Parents' assessment of the amount of time they spend with their families*
Source: From National Commission on Children, 1991

values to the whole variable and are particularly useful for displaying a budget. However, if there are too many values that need to be included, they can look cluttered and be confusing. Figure 12.5 is an example of a pie chart used in the National Commission on Children (1991) report illustrating parents' assessment of the amount of time they spend with their families.

Many computer programs can generate graphs and charts, often in different colors. However, we must remember as we construct these visual aids that our goal is to make the data more accessible and clearer to the reader.

We have discussed the visual presentation of data. The other part of presenting findings is describing them in writing. This need not be extensive and can simply consist of translating the findings as straightforwardly as possible. When describing the findings, it is important to avoid interpreting the data; simply report the information and, when necessary, the statistical tests and their results.

E X A M P L E

Reporting Results from a Quantitative Study

Whitman, Accardo, Boyert, and Kendagor (1990) studied the impact of homelessness on children's cognitive, language, and emotional development as a means of providing information that would assist in the development of programs for these children. They presented the results of the study as follows:

> The results of the screening battery for the 88 children are presented in Table 1. Because children begin formal schooling at age five, the data were looked at separately for preschool children (under age five) and school-age children (age five and over). Although the majority of the children's SIT scores were in the average range, clustering of scores at the low end of this range was marked. Language screening indicated the children were even more depressed in language development, with mean PPVT-R scores falling in the low-average and slow-learner range.
>
> More suggestive were the age and sex distributions of the scores. The SIT results for males were distributed across the full range of scores (60 to 130), but scores in the mentally retarded and borderline range (35.3 percent) were three times greater than expected. Similarly, 63 percent (27 of 43) of the boys also had PPVT-R scores in the retarded or borderline range. For girls, the contrast of scores was exaggerated yet further. While only 35 percent (16 of 46) female SIT scores were in the mentally retarded or borderline range, 71 percent (32 of 45) of the language scores showed similar delays.
>
> The average human figure drawing quotient was 84.87 for males and 93.69 for females. These scores reflected essentially the same means as the more verbally based SIT scores. When scored for emotional indicators, the H-T-P means were 1.38 (house), 1.59 (tree), 1.36 (person), and 3.98 (summed score). Few children displayed significant emotional pathology in their drawings, and none of the drawings qualified as extremely bizarre or deviant. (p. 517)

E X A M P L E

Reporting Results from a Qualitative Study

Farber (1990) reported on the significance of race and class in marital decisions among unmarried adolescent women. The data were collected through semistructured interviews. The first section of her presentation of the findings relates to how the young women view the value of marriage as an ideal:

> Nearly all of the teens, regardless of their class or race, view marriage and marital childbearing as an ideal type of family. Their attitudes are typified by this 16-year-old white middle-class mother: "When I got pregnant and I decided to bring Joshua home with me, it didn't seem nice . . . for a little boy or little girl to have one of what he should have—you know, half of what he should have. . . . I wouldn't wish that on anybody. A child was meant to have a mother and a father. . . . I can't imagine myself having only my mother. My life wouldn't be the same without my mother and my father."
>
> This young woman expresses traditional values about families being composed of two parents. Most teens expressed similar attitudes suggesting that, for them, being a single mother does not reflect changed values about how families should be formed. This ideal is also evident in their childhood memories of how they imagined their adult lives would be. The same white middle-class mother said: "I always wanted to be married and have kids when I was older. When I was done with school and things like that. I always imagined that after I was a big person, all grown up, never young, you know." A similar childhood goal was expressed by a 16-year-old black middle-class teen: "I wanted to be married and have a career before I even had a baby. That's how I wanted it to be. I wish it wasn't like this."
>
> Like the middle-class and working-class teens, the black lower-class mothers had childhood dreams of living in the ideal American family, as defined here by a 16-year-old black lower-class mother: "I thought I would be married, and I had at least two kids—a boy and a girl. I would be married to this one person I was in love with, you know, and we had our own house and stuff." The white lower-class 16-year-old mother stated: "I seen myself before I had a kid, you know, I would be married. And I would have babies, but not until I was married. I was pretty sure about that."
>
> The young mothers from all backgrounds described ideal visions that are congruent with traditional values about family formation. These childhood reflections suggest that their present judgments about the undesirability of out of wedlock childbearing are not simply responses to the stress of single motherhood. Most of these teen mothers grew up valuing a way of life from which they have deviated. They were unable to, or chose not to, act in accordance with these ideals. (p. 54)

Sometimes the qualitative and quantitative approaches are combined in a study, and the reporting of the results reflects this. The quantitative results are presented followed by, for example, a description of the qualitative findings. A discussion section then integrates these findings.

E X A M P L E

Reporting Quantitative and Qualitative Results

Vera (1990) studied the effects of divorce groups on individual adjustment. She reported the qualitative and quantitative findings in the following manner:

Analysis of Group Data

A paired-comparison t-test (p < .05) was computed from the scores obtained in the Index of Well-Being at the first and last group meetings. These scores indicated that, taken as a group, the subjects on the average show significant improvement on the Index of Well-Being. Differences between group A and group B on the Index of Well-Being were not significant. Further, no significant differences were found between subjects who completed and who did not complete the follow-up instrument.

Analysis of Qualitative Data

Qualitative data were obtained from the screening interview and from information elicited during the group meetings. Analysis of these data revealed that some factors reoccurred in the subjects' histories. These factors have been identified in the literature as interfering with the adjustment to divorce and psychosocial well-being (B. F. Fisher, 1976). Analysis of the researcher's notes suggested that factors such as the passage of time, divorce-related losses, other life events, characteristics of the divorce event, and the presence of support may have interfered with divorce recovery. The 11 cases were rank ordered according to the number of factors present (Table 1). Subjects with the largest number of factors appeared to show less improvement in divorce adjustment and psychosocial well-being than did those with fewer factors. (p. 16)

Discussion Section

Unlike a research proposal, a research report always contains some kind of discussion section. The discussion section follows and is closely linked to the results section, and it provides an explanation of the results. This section is important whether you are discussing the results of an evaluation of your own practice, a needs assessment, or a program evaluation. The findings are related to the hypotheses (if there are any) and to the theoretical premise of the study

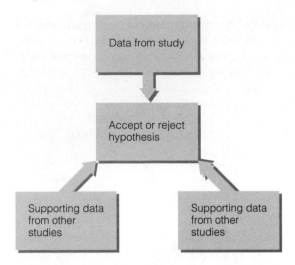

FIGURE 12.6 *Structure of the discussion section of a research report*

itself. Part of this process involves comparing your research findings to findings from comparable research in the literature and pointing out similarities and differences in the results and conclusions. In this way, we can make connections among various empirical findings, thereby providing collective support and evidence for theories (see Figure 12.6).

E X A M P L E

A Discussion Section of a Report—Quantitative Data

Rauch and Tivoli (1989) carried out a study of social workers' knowledge and utilization of genetic services. Their discussion was as follows:

> *The Ashery (1977) and the current study document that social workers do refer clients to genetic services. However, further research is needed to ascertain the proportion of clients who meet criteria for referral to genetic services, the actual proportion of these referred, and the extent to which non-referral reflects a client-informed choice or social worker failure to inform clients about services. The two studies also indicate that some practitioners are uninformed about genetic referral criteria and the availability of genetic services. The findings presented here and Black's (1984) summary of surveys of schools of social work suggest that the curricula of schools of social work provide relatively little genetic content. Black's (1980) survey of social workers in health and the findings reported here both suggest that interest in continuing education on genetics is high.*

(Example continued on next page)

The findings are not surprising. Knowledge of human genetics is growing so rapidly that most social workers cannot keep up to date. Genetic services are proliferating; an array of services that virtually was nonexistent less than 25 years ago now is in place, and its capabilities continuously are augmented. Many people—including social workers —continue to view genetic technology as esoteric and irrelevant to mainstream concerns. For these reasons, a gap between developments in genetics and social work practice is to be expected. (pp. 55–56)

In qualitative studies, the distinction between a description of the results and a discussion of the findings can be fuzzy. In part, this may be a result of our attempt to provide an insightful description of the phenomenon under study. However, we still need to make a careful distinction between the description and the interpretation.

E X A M P L E

A Discussion Section of a Report—Qualitative Data

Iannaccone and Miles (1990) studied the Mormon Church's response to change in women's roles. They collected both quantitative and qualitative data and reported the qualitative data as follows:

A qualitative examination of the statements from the articles in the analysis shows how the Church has managed to accommodate change without appearing to abandon its ideals.

The Mormon Church teaches that one of women's fundamental responsibilities is to bear and raise children. This teaching was consistently supported throughout the period of our content analysis. The "ideal" life situation for an adult woman always included marriage, several children, and a husband who earned enough money that the woman need not work. Within this basic framework, however, the articles changed significantly over time, particularly with regard to working mothers.

Whereas writing in the 1950's and 1960's invariably stressed that a wife's first responsibility is to her family and that she should not work outside of the home unless there is no other way to support them, writings in the 1970's began making exceptions to these restrictions. Articles from about 1974 permitted a "sequential" arrangement in which women first raised families and later seek careers. By the 1980's, a career after the children are grown is encouraged so strongly as to have become virtually an assumed part of the ideal woman's life. Simi-

(Example continued on next page)

larly, before the mid-1970's, mothers with young children were permitted to work only if the father was absent or disabled. After 1976, however, several authors defended employment for mothers who received their husband's approval, know their children will not be neglected, and have prayed and received personal approval from God. These concessions make it possible for wives to work without violating Church doctrine. Still, Church leaders have not abandoned their traditional ideal of the nonworking mother caring full-time for her family. Exceptions to the ideal are always justified in terms of it. Only her husband, children, and God can release a woman from her obligations to them.

These examples illustrate how an organization can sometimes exercise "flexibility in practice while maintaining purity of doctrine" (Tawney, 1926). Continuing to express a traditional value protects organizational integrity; allowing deviations from the ideal gives the individual member a means of reconciling the conflict between the religious ideals and the behaviors rewarded by society. Although on a symbolic level the conflict between Church and society persists, on a practical level members increasingly can do what they have to do without rejecting the Church. (pp. 1245–1246)

Limitations Section

By now, it should be very evident that no research is perfect. There are always flaws and limitations. Sometimes this is a result of the nature of the question that is being asked, but often—and particularly so with social work research—it is simply a function of the social and political context in which the studies take place. For example, random assignment into the experimental and control groups is not always feasible, as discussed in Chapter 6.

In reporting the limitations, go through the research process and point out the drawbacks of the method at each stage. We have already discussed some common limitations in previous chapters, but here is a summary of these problems:

▶ *The inadequacies of the sampling method*   Probability sampling is the method that allows the greatest amount of generalization. Otherwise, generalization will be limited.

▶ *The problems of generalizing from inadequate response rate*   A response rate of less than 50% limits generalizations.

▶ *The problems associated with reliability and validity of the measuring instruments*   These need to be specified.

▶ *The problems associated with internal and external validity*   Often these threats to internal validity are a result of the lack of a comparison group, particularly one that has been randomly assigned. This needs to be pointed out.

▶ *The problems associated with the interpretation of results in the absence of statistical tests*   These are limitations with single-system studies or with qualitative studies.

▶ *The problems associated with the interpretation of the statistical tests and the power of these tests.*

You will vary the extent to which you discuss limitations depending on your audience. However, you must devote at least a paragraph to addressing these issues. If you are writing up the results of a needs assessment or a program evaluation, the limitations section can be minimal. But if your audience is more knowledgeable about research, you must provide a more extensive limitations section.

E X A M P L E

A Study that Emphasizes Limitations

Toomey, First, Rife, and Belcher (1989) evaluated community care for homeless mentally ill people. They identified four types of limitations in their study; they suggest that these limitations are characteristic of studies of the homeless mentally ill:

1   *Research design and sampling*   The difficulty of establishing a sampling frame leads to problems relating to the generalizability of the findings. In addition, it is difficult to establish a control group and maintain any kind of follow-up.

2   *Instrumentation and data collection*   Even closed-ended and forced-choice responses are not necessarily valid or reliable with this population.

3   *Ethical issues*   The researchers could never be certain that informed consent had really been given.

4   *Organizational issues*   The authors described how staff at different levels had different goals for the evaluation. This led to conflicts and negatively affected the documentation needed for a thorough evaluation.

Recommendations Section

The next section of the report consists of recommendations for further study and explicitly states the questions that have arisen from the research itself. In a needs assessment report (and sometimes in program evaluation reports) this section is critical because all the research is, in fact, building up to this conclusion.

E   X   A   M   P   L   E

A Recommendations for Further Research Section

In the Toomey et al. (1989) study of the homeless mentally ill, recommendations for further research included:

> *The literature and the findings of the two studies document the need for evaluation methods powerful enough to compare treatment success at different points in the cycle of homelessness and the effectiveness of interventions among people with many different kinds of treatment needs. (p. 25)*

Implications for Practice

An implications for practice section can also be included in social work research reports. Here we need to explain the connection between the specific findings of our research and practice. Usually, this section is only included in reports that are published in the social work literature. In the reports written by generalist social workers that are typically disseminated to community, agency, or funding representatives, often this section is not included.

E   X   A   M   P   L   E

An Implications for Practice Section

Marlow (1990), in her needs assessment of employed clerical workers, concluded:

> *The major result of this study is the information that it provides on the characteristics that affect employed women's service needs. This information can contribute to policy development to support employed women, an area in which social workers increasingly are becoming involved. Such policies have received increasing support in recent years and include public policies such as the development of federal day care funding programs, and developments in the private sector, such as the growth of employee assistance programs. The findings from this study indicate that the service needs of this group of clerical workers are relatively uniform, regardless of ethnicity, countering some assumptions about the needs of Mexican-American women. This study consequently can remind social workers who are advocates for people in the workplace that information is needed from employees themselves to guide the development of programs and policies that will be truly responsive to their needs. (p. 264)*

We should note that the order and structure of these last few sections can vary. For example, implications for practice can be the final section of the report with the suggestions for further research being included in or following the discussion section.

Disseminating the Report

Disseminating or distributing the research report is an essential prerequisite to the incorporation of research with practice (see Chapter 13). The dissemination of a report can take several forms: orally presenting the results, distributing the written reports internally, and publishing the results.

Oral Presentation

You may be required to orally present your research results at a community meeting, at a meeting of the agency's board of directors, or to legislators. In the case of single-system studies, usually the results are discussed more informally with the client and others who might be involved. When presenting orally at a formal meeting, keep the following items in mind:

▶ Know how much time you have to give the report and stick to this time. Rehearsal of your presentation will help with this.

▶ Allow time for questions and discussion. Know in advance how much time will be allocated for this.

▶ Use visual aids (overheads, slides, and so on) and handouts (containing a summary of the results and perhaps some charts and scales) when appropriate.

▶ Try not to become defensive about the research if someone criticizes it during discussion or question time. Simply answer the questions as clearly and as straightforwardly as possible. You should already be aware of the limitations and have thought them through, but there may be some you have missed.

Distributing Written Reports Internally

The appearance of the report is important even if it is only to be distributed in-house. In-house can refer to anything from a small agency to a large government department. Be sure that the original report is clear and will reproduce good copies; it can be frustrating to read a report that has been poorly copied. Make sure that the report is received by everyone who is meant to receive it.

Publishing the Report

Although as social work practitioners we do not often publish our research results, we should strive to publish whenever possible as this undoubtedly allows the profession the most access to our research findings. Social work journals are making a conscious effort to solicit and publish articles written by practitioners. As a practitioner, you have important contributions to make that can be very different from academicians.

There are some ways to assess whether or not your report has publishing potential. Consider the following:

▶ Is it investigating a problem that has received little attention in the past in the research literature? Many journals will devote entire issues to research on a newly explored topic.

▶ Does it have a new slant or perspective on a problem? For example, there may have been many program evaluations on the effectiveness of parent training on reducing incidences of child abuse and neglect. However, if your agency has a program that serves a large number of Puerto Rican clients and you have been involved in evaluating the program, this might provide excellent material for publication if none has previously been published on this type of intervention with this particular client group.

▶ Is it an innovative research method or combination of methods?

E X A M P L E

A Study Using Innovative Methods

Fraser and Haapala (1988) evaluated a home-based family treatment program and paid particular attention to carefully explicating the nature of the program using both qualitative and quantitative data collection techniques. This was an innovative study in that there is a need for more "process" studies in family preservation, and as the authors state:

> *Careful measurement of independent variables is needed in order to correlate selected dimensions or types of treatment events with desirable social outcomes. Unfortunately, research designs that combine process and outcome evaluation are rare. The conduct of such studies is one of the challenges facing human services professionals, if empirically based practice is to grow into maturity. (p. 7)*

If you are considering publishing, you should know that different journals are interested in different types of articles. To get a sense of who is interested in what, refer to the *NASW Guide to Social Work Authors*. This gives information on many journals and lists their specific requirements in terms of length of article, reference style, number of copies, and so on.

The Agency and Research Writing

Very often the agency for which you are completing the research will give you specific requirements on how to write the report. Usually, an in-house report on a program evaluation or needs assessment will focus on the results section. A needs assessment may also concentrate on the implications of the findings for practice. If you are writing the report for publication and wider distribution, you may want to emphasize the methods section over the results and devote some attention to a discussion of how the results support or reject previous research. This will enable other researchers to replicate or augment your study.

As a generalist social worker employed in an agency, you will most often write reports on individual cases. These are also research reports if you have used a single-system design as part of your practice. So start now— combine research and practice and contribute to social work knowledge.

Ethical Issues in Research Writing

Three major ethical issues arise in research writing. The first issue is appropriately referencing material that is included in a report. The second issue is ensuring that the presentation of the results is as objective as possible. The third is the confidentiality of the results. We will discuss each of these issues in turn.

Referencing Appropriately

Existence of Previous Work

Whenever research is being planned and conducted, it is imperative that you consult other work that has been completed in the target area. For example, you may have been asked by your supervisor to conduct a needs assessment for a latchkey program in your community. You are excited about the opportunity to show off some of your newly acquired research skills. However, the next day an ex-classmate calls you from a neighboring city, and you tell her about your assignment. Your friend tells you she has just finished conducting such a study in her community. You are tempted to ignore this piece of information and continue with your own plans because that way you could do your survey alone and collect the credit. Ethically, however, you need to acknowledge your friend's information as useful assistance in the development of your needs assessment; perhaps you may even be forced to recognize that there is no necessity for this type of study in your community at this time.

Citing References Appropriately

Given that you do decide to use information from your friend's study, it is imperative that you give her credit for her work. This applies to a study published locally as a report, as well as to more widely distributed publications. Recognizing the contributions of others can present dilemmas. It would be impossible to credit everyone who has contributed to our intellectual and professional development. However, in the case of specific research endeavors, you must recognize the contributions of others; otherwise, you may be guilty of plagiarism.

Presentation of Results

We need to be as objective as possible in the presentation of our results. Although some guidelines have been suggested in this chapter, it is often difficult to achieve objectivity.

Objectivity is facilitated by distinguishing between the results and the discussion sections in the research report. As we discussed earlier, the results section contains a simple description of the findings. leaving the discussion section to make suggestions, interpretations, and conclusions. This separation is useful in maintaining objectivity. However, we still need to be careful that *all* the relevant results are reported, not just those that we favor—for whatever reason. We also want to ensure that the discussion section completely considers these findings. The results should be reported clearly and concisely, with as little specialized language as possible. As we mentioned previously, the distinction between description and discussion is more difficult with qualitative studies; special attention must be paid to the writing up of these studies.

Confidentiality of Results

Just as confidentiality needs to be ensured during the data collection phase, we also need to preserve confidentiality when writing and disseminating the report. Subjects' identities should not be disclosed without their permission. This may be problematic in qualitative reports with extensive quotes that inadvertently reveal the subject's identity. It is also an issue with single-system studies.

Another related issue is that of **copyright**. This applies not only to published materials but also to in-house reports. Be sure to check on the restrictions that might pertain to distribution and publishing before you disseminate a report more widely.

Human Diversity Issues in Research Writing

Three human diversity issues are involved in research writing. First, we must ensure that bias against certain groups is not contained in the report. Second, we must avoid using exclusive language. Third, we must consider to whom the results are being disseminated.

Bias Against Certain Groups

Part of ensuring objectivity involves excluding biases in the writing that tend to stereotype groups in our society. We are less at risk for this if we have paid careful attention to human diversity issues throughout the research process. Then, we simply ensure that the data are accurately presented and that they are equitably and nonjudgmentally discussed.

Exclusive Language

The issue here is nonsexist writing. Although the predominant use of the male pronoun as a generic pronoun is becoming increasingly less acceptable, we do need to ensure that nonsexist terms are employed consistently. This involves not only the appropriate use of male, female, and plural pronouns, but also the use of terms that are gender neutral, such as *chair* instead of *chairman.*

This language use issue also involves ensuring that terms do not reflect ethnic or cultural biases or a lack of sensitivity to human diversity. Use a descriptor of a cultural group that is recognized by the group itself. For example, using the term *Mexican-American* in New Mexico to refer to Hispanics could be offensive to some individuals who view themselves as Spanish-Americans with minimal connections to Mexico. Sometimes it is best not to lump any group of people together under one label.

Disseminating the Results

The final human diversity issue relating to research writing is the question of who should receive the results. There is a growing argument in favor of giving the findings to the subjects included in the research rather than just to the practitioners and other researchers.

This does not necessarily entail making the entire research report available to the subjects, particularly if it is extensive or excessively technical. Instead, a smaller report can be written specifically for those participating in a needs assessment or program evaluation, in which the results could potentially influence an entire community. One advantage of a single-system study that evaluates individual practice is that the results are routinely shared with the client (usually verbally).

This movement to share the results with the subjects of the study was primarily initiated by proponents of the feminist research methods discussed earlier and some of the other less traditional research approaches discussed in Chapter 1. Advocates of the feminist perspective point out that sharing the results with the subjects is another dimension of how "the researcher and subject can work in different ways to explore a 'truth' that they mutually locate and define" (Davis, 1986). This results in a participatory and consensual style attributed to feminist approaches, not only in research but also in administrative style and social work practice (Norman & Mancuso, 1980).

Giving subjects access to findings is also being increasingly viewed as a minority issue. It is being recognized that research results can be empowering to subjects. Historically, minority subjects have often been used by the researcher and have reaped no benefits. Apart from making the results accessible to the subjects, researchers need to pay more attention to repaying the subjects. It can be argued that this is not a serious problem with social work research because it is applied. The results of needs assessments, program evaluations, and evaluations of individual practice all directly contribute to the development and/or improvement of interventions designed to assist those who were studied. However, sometimes benefits can be extended further—for example, ensuring a proportion of the royalties of book sales are returned to the community or that subjects are paid for the time they have spent being interviewed.

Summary

Four general principles of research writing are know your audience, use appropriate citations and references, correctly structure your research report or proposal, and write the report as clearly and as concisely as possible. The research proposal is a paper proposing the undertaking of a specific type of research. The funding agency may have Requests for Proposals (RFP's) that list the projects they are interested in funding and how the proposals should be submitted. Like the research proposal, the research report should follow an outline structure: statement of the research topic, theoretical framework, research questions and hypotheses, data collection methods, sampling strategy, research design, results, discussion, limitations, recommendations for future research, and implications for practice. Reports may be presented orally, distributed internally (in-house), or published.

In an agency, generalist social workers are involved in writing not only formal reports and proposals but also case reports. The ethical issues involved in research writing include appropriately referencing material, presenting the results objectively, and ensuring confidentiality of the results. Human diversity issues of concern in research writing are eliminating stereotyping of certain groups, avoiding exclusive language, and disseminating the results to the subjects.

Study/Exercise Questions

1 Request sample grant applications from organizations in your city or state that fund research efforts related to social work. Share these in class and discuss their similarities and differences.

2 Select a social work journal article and critique it using the structure of a research report presented in this chapter as a guide.

3　Select research articles from social work journals that contain tables and/or charts.

　　a　Do they clearly illustrate the results of the research?

　　b　What changes would you make to improve them?

Further Reading

Morris, L. L., Fitz-Gibbon, C. T., & Freeman, M. F. (1987). *How to communicate evaluation findings.* Newbury Park, CA: Sage Publications.

　　As part of the Program Evaluation Kit published by Sage, this book includes chapters on identifying your audience, using tables and graphs, and writing reports.

Strunk, W., & White, E. B. (1979). *The elements of style* (3rd ed.). New York: Macmillan.

　　A classic reference on writing; an invaluable guide.

Wolcott, H. (1990). *Writing up qualitative research.* Newbury Park, CA: Sage Publications.

　　A good little book specifically dealing with the task of writing up qualitative results.

References

Bayley, N. (1969). *Bayley scales of infant development.* New York: Psychological Corporation.

Davis, L. V. (1986). A feminist approach to social work research. *Affilia, 1,* 32–47.

Farber, N. (1990). The significance of race and class in marital decisions among unmarried adolescent mothers. *Social Problems, 37,* 51–63.

Fraser, M., & Haapala, D. (1987). Home-based family treatment: A quantitative-qualitative assessment. *The Journal of Applied Social Sciences, 12,* 1–23.

Iannaccone, L. R., & Miles, C. A. (1990). Dealing with social change: The Mormon Church's response to change in women's roles. *Social Forces, 68,* 1231–1250.

Lincoln, Y., & Guba, E. (1985). *Naturalistic inquiry.* Beverly Hills, CA: Sage Publications.

Marlow, C. R. (1990). Management of family and employment responsibilities by Mexican-American and Anglo-American women. *Social Work, 35,* 259–265.

Monthly Labor Review. (1991). Volunteers in the U.S. Washington, DC: Department of Labor, *114* (2).

National Commission on Children. (1991). *Speaking of kids: A national survey of children and parents*. Washington, DC: National Commission on Children.

Norman, E., & Mancuso, A. (1980). *Women's issues and social work practice*. Itasca, IL: Peacock Publishers.

Publication Manual of the American Psychological Association. (1983). (3rd ed.). Washington, DC: APA.

Rauch, J. B., & Tivoli, L. (1989). Social workers' knowledge and utilization of genetic services. *Social Work, 34, 55–56*.

Toomey, B. G., First, R. J., Rife, J. C., & Belcher, J. R. (1989). Evaluating community care for homeless mentally ill people. *Social Work Research and Abstracts* (December), 21–26.

Vera, M. I. (1990). Effects of divorce groups on individual adjustment: A multiple methodology approach. *Social Work Research and Abstracts, 26,* 11–20.

Wasik, B. H., Ramey, C. T., Bryant, D. M., & Sparling, J. J. (1990). A longitudinal study of two early intervention strategies: Project CARE. *Child Development, 61,* 1682–1696.

Whitman, B. Y., Accardo, P., Boyert, M., & Kendagor, R. (1990). Homelessness and cognitive performance in children: A possible link. *Social Work, 35,* 516–519.

13

Using Research Findings in Practice and Evaluating Research

With Patricia Sandau, M.S.W.

One more stage of research needs to be discussed; the use and evaluation of the research findings. This step's equivalent in practice is the implementation and evaluation of the plan. As discussed in Chapter 1, we not only enhance our practice by producing research, but as consumers we also use research findings and results in practice.

Using the results of research in our practice necessitates evaluating the research itself. Conducting research is not a flawless endeavor, as we have seen throughout this text. An important step in the research process is critically assessing research results to identify their strengths and weaknesses.

Our two final tasks—evaluating the research and using the results in practice are linked. By first evaluating the research, we can assess the findings' applicability to our particular practice situation. We will discuss both steps in this chapter:

- ▶ Using research findings in practice
- ▶ Evaluating research
- ▶ The agency in the use and evaluation of research findings
- ▶ Ethical issues in the use and evaluation of research findings
- ▶ Human diversity issues in the use and evaluation of research findings

Using Research Findings in Practice

Although the focus of this chapter is on the use of research findings, remember from Chapter 1 that other sources of explanation and knowledge can be applied in practice: values, intuition, past experience, and authority. Now, however, we return to the use of research findings in practice.

Case Examples

We will consider five cases, each dealing with different client systems: individual, family, group, organization, and community.

▶ *Individual client system*   Sue—an adolescent female who is a substance abuser

▶ *Family client system*   The Kickingbird family—a Native-American family in which an incident of a child's physical abuse has been reported

▶ *Group client system*   Parent support—A number of parents have expressed concerns about their children who have attention deficit disorder

▶ *Organization client system*   The Children's Center—an agency to plan and develop foster care services for children with AIDS

▶ *Community client system*   STOP—a community-wide task force formed to reduce teen suicide (see also Figure 13.1)

For cases such as these, research findings can be used during each of the stages of the problem-solving process. A summary of the stages and the relevance of research findings for each stage follow.

Preliminary Statement of the Problem   The initial step in deciding on a course of action is clarification of the problem. This can be facilitated by consulting existing research.

Statement of Preliminary Assumptions   Consult the research to determine the cause of the problem or at least some of the factors associated with it.

Selection and Collection of Information   Ideas about how to collect information and from whom can be obtained from research.

Analysis of Information Available   Organize the material so that a plan can be developed. Alternatively, the analysis may lead to a reconceptualization of the problem or reveal a need for further information. Again, research findings can be used, perhaps to compare them with the data from the case.

Development and Implementation of a Plan   Before the plan can be developed and implemented, research findings are used to determine if similar plans and interventions have been successful in the past.

Evaluation of the Intervention   Once the intervention has been implemented, we need to consider its effectiveness with each case. Again, existing research can help in evaluating practice.

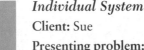

Individual System

Client: Sue

Presenting problem: Dependence on drugs

Referral: Sue, a 15-year-old Hispanic adolescent, was referred to a drug treatment program for substance abuse at her local high school. She was suspended from school and cannot return until she completes treatment. At the treatment intake the worker assessed Sue's drug use pattern and family relationships. A review of her drug use patterns indicated that she has only started using drugs in the past six months. Her use of drugs has increased recently, and she admits that she cannot place limits on her behavior and is preoccupied with drug use.

Preliminary Statement of the Problem

In attempting to clarify the problem with Sue, the worker used research to determine if the patterns of behavior were consistent with a drug dependent individual. The behaviors were found to be similar to those outlined by Jellinek (1960), who developed a model of alcoholism as a disease that progresses according to certain symptoms and behaviors (Acoca & Barr, 1989). The worker also wondered about the relatively short duration of the substance abusing behavior. She found that the average time from the initiation to addiction is significantly shorter for women than men (Ellinwood, Smith, & Vaillant, 1966). Consequently, this research began to provide some basis for understanding the problem.

Statement of Preliminary Assumptions

The worker wondered what problems might be associated with adolescent substance abuse; she found that sexual victimization affects about 75% of women in treatment for substance abuse (Yandow, 1989). In addition, a study of female adolescents who entered drug treatment showed that sexual abuse victims used drugs more frequently than the nonvictims. Sexual abuse victims also appeared to begin drug use at an earlier age than their peers (Harrison, Hoffman, & Edwall, 1989). Research also suggests that addicted women under 30 are more likely than those 30 and over to have histories that include school dropout, unemployment, welfare dependence, and psycho-physiological problems (Harrison & Belille, 1987). Substance abuse in women is also often associated with low self-esteem (Beckman, 1978; Beckman, Day, Bardsley, & Seeman, 1980; Cuskey, Berger, & Densen-Gerber, 1977; McLachlan, Walderman, Birchmore, & Marsden, 1979). This research then helped the worker understand some of the underlying problems associated with teen female drug abuse.

Selection and Collection of Information

The research literature can be consulted to identify assessment tools that can assist in the collection of information on Sue's problem. For example, the tool used by the Chemical Dependency Adolescent Assessment Project in St. Paul, Minnesota (Nakken, 1989) or the Tennessee Self-Concept Scale that has been used for female substance abusers (Wheeler, Biase, & Sullivan, 1986) may be appropriate in this case. Using standardized tools can help us compare clients to other groups of clients experiencing the same or similar issues; this provides a basis for the total assessment of Sue's substance abuse.

Analysis of Information Available

From the worker's assessment, which included standardized assessment tools, it was found that Sue has been sexually abused and had low self-esteem. This supported the research findings cited earlier that found an association between substance abuse and sexual victimization and low self-esteem. The analysis of this information thus laid the foundation for the intervention plan.

Development and Implementation of a Plan

The worker developed a plan to provide an inpatient drug treatment program for Sue, a plan that also addressed the problem of sexual abuse. Research findings can explain the success of inpatient treatment programs of this type. Research indicates that the success rate for the recovery of female substance abusers is only 20% to 30% (Bowman & Jellinek, 1974; Pattison, 1974), suggesting that traditional programs may need to be redesigned to meet the special needs of women (Doshan & Bursh, 1982). Root (1989) discusses how programs are not designed for women who experience posttraumatic stress. The cultural background of the client also needs to be considered. In a discussion of drug abuse treatment for Hispanics, Marin (in press) suggests that many drug treatment programs do not include culturally relevant material. Thus, these evaluations need to be considered when selecting a program for Sue.

Evaluation of the Intervention

This case would be appropriate for a single-system study. Behaviors such as the reduction or abstinence of substance use or improved self-esteem could be monitored. Bloom and Fischer (1982) present a large array of single-system research designs along with a selection of data collection methods that would be appropriate for this case. The research limitations and the problems with obtaining accurate data collection for the substance abuse depend on Sue's ability and that of her parents and peers to be accurate reporters. Also, intervening variables, such as discovering a parental chemical abuse problem, may influence the outcomes of a single-subject design.

Family System

Client: The Kickingbird family

Presenting problem: Report of physical abuse of a child

Referral: The Kickingbird family was referred to a Native-American health and social services agency due to an incident of physical abuse. The family had physically abused their 12-year-old child for leaving the home and not caring for her 3 younger siblings while the parents were away. One sibling had played with matches and had started a fire in the kitchen. The father spanked the 12-year-old until she was black and blue. The incident was reported to the agency by school officials.

Preliminary Statement of the Problem

To identify the problems in the Kickingbird family, the worker must first acknowledge that defining physical abuse of a child is sometimes difficult and can be affected by many factors. One such factor might be cultural variations in its definition; existing research can be consulted to help understand these various definitions. Long (1986) suggests that physical abuse of children within their own families is "a culture-bound issue" (p. 131). Community standards are different for different cultural groups, and the definition of what constitutes abuse is defined within the context of the group. She also suggests that abuse must be assessed and treated within the cultural context.

Statement of Preliminary Assumptions

To determine the factors associated with the abuse in this family, it was useful for the worker to examine the research that has been conducted on child abuse and neglect, particularly among Native Americans. A multitude of contributing factors have been identified. Mannes (1990b) reports that

> *According to the Milwaukee Indian Health Board, Inc. . . . , some of the more general problems that Indian families confront are: (1) perpetuating cycles of violence, (2) social isolation, (3) economic deprivation, (4) poor child-rearing skills, (5) personal frustration, (6) guilt, (7) emotional trauma, (8) marital problems, (9) too many children, (10) rigid sex roles, (11) drug and alcohol abuse and consumption, (12) psychoses, and (13) poor health. (p. 11)*

These factors are, in fact, similar to the patterns of behavior associated with abuse outlined by the National Institute of Mental Health (Gelles, 1987).

Selection and Collection of Information

The worker needed to select a risk assessment tool to help determine the areas of family strength and collect information on the family's service needs; in this way the worker would be able to consistently document the necessary information for the analysis. Risk assessment tools have been developed to assess the risk for a child's entry into foster care: The Washington Risk Assessment (English, 1989) and the Family Risk Scales (Magura & Moses, 1986) are two examples. The Family Risk Scales consist of 26 items that are designed to measure a child's risk for entry into foster care and include measurement of child-related, parent-related, or economic risk factors. Other items covered are living conditions, family residence, social support, parental health, use of physical punishment, use of verbal discipline, sexual abuse of child, child's health, mental health, and school adjustment. The Family Risk scales may need to be used in conjunction with other assessment tools (Fraser, 1990). Many instruments lack information on their reliability and validity; thus, care is recommended when selecting instruments (Rzepnicki, Schuerman, & Littell, 1991).

Analysis of Information Available

Existing research on high-risk Native-American families reviewed by the worker identified a great need for Native-American families to obtain counseling and transportation (English, 1989). Using this information, the worker paid attention to those elements of the risk assessment tool that identified these particular needs. Both of these needs were found to be clearly apparent for the Kickingbird family.

Development and Implementation of a Plan

The worker developed a plan for the delivery of in-home family preservation services that would build on the strengths of the family. This type of program was designed for families whose children are at imminent or high risk for placement. Research carried out on home-based programs indicates an average of 79% effectiveness (Nelson, Landsman, & Deutelbaum, 1990). However, Barth and Berry (1987) and Magura (1981) state that evaluations of family preservation services programs conclude only limited success. Programs designated specifically for Native-American families also vary in their effectiveness (Mannes, 1990a; Tafoya, 1990).

These tentative findings are partly due to the lack of a precise operationalization of *imminent risk* for out-of-home placement (Stein & Rzepnicki, 1983). Workers who determine what imminent risk is may be motivated by a variety of influences, such as cost cuts, program waiting lists, worker relationships with the family preservation services program, or worker caseload size. Another problem with evaluating the findings from family preservation programs is the lack of adequate control groups in many of the studies, making it difficult to conclude that it is the program or some other factor that is responsible for outcomes. Random assignment of cases to different groups and services is the best way of achieving equivalence of the groups and increases the internal and external validity of the findings (Rzepnicki et al., 1991). By recognizing these limitations of the family preservation research findings in developing and implementing a plan, the worker may remain flexible to other service options if this one is unsuccessful.

Understanding the tentative nature of the findings from the evaluation of family preservation services, the worker considered a short-term intensive in-home program to be the least restrictive for this family. The program was developed by Homebuilders in Tacoma, Washington, and provided intervention within 24 hours of referral, around the clock availability of therapists, low caseloads (maximum of 3), and brief services (30 to 45 days) in the home environment (Haapala & Kinney, 1979).

Evaluation of the Intervention

As in the previous case, the use of a single-system design would be appropriate here. Goal attainment scaling to address the father's increased use of appropriate discipline might be used. Some scales from the Multi-Problem Screening Inventory (Hudson, 1990) could be used to demonstrate any changes in parental attitudes. A pretest and posttest using the Child Well-Being Scales (Magura & Moses, 1986) could also be used for evaluating any discipline change in the family. The worker could choose from a variety of single-system designs; Alter and Evens (1990) provide a number of alternatives. Some of the descriptive, least rigorous designs enable the worker and family to monitor progress, while the more rigorous designs—including withdrawal and multiple baselines design—allow the worker to assess which aspects of services or techniques are most beneficial. However, ethical issues may be encountered with withdrawal of services in high-risk child abuse situations (Rzepnicki et al., 1991). Also, generalizability is low from single-system studies.

Group System

Client: Parents in a community

Presenting problem: Concern with children who have attention deficit disorder (ADHD).

Referral: A group of parents from a school district are concerned about the services and support for families of children who have attention deficit disorder (ADHD). They have asked the school social worker to help them develop a plan to meet their children's needs.

Preliminary Statement of the Problem

The first step for the worker is a clarification of the problem and an assessment of its magnitude. Research findings can be an important resource for problem definition. The *Diagnostic and Statistical Manual of Mental Disorders* (DSM) is a reference manual that lists definitions and research findings for psychological disorders (American Psychiatric Association, 1987). Although the DSM can be a useful resource, workers must acknowledge the potentially negative effects on clients by placing diagnostic labels on them. According to the DSM criteria, ADHD refers to a condition in which developmentally inappropriate degrees of inattention, impulsiveness, and hyperactivity are evident. The DSM estimates that 3% of children have ADHD while other estimates have ranged up to 14.3% (Schachar, Rutter, & Smith, 1981). Shapiro and Garfinkel, (1986) screened an elementary school population (315 children) and found that 8.9% of the children qualified for a diagnosis of attention deficit disorder or conduct disorder.

Statement of Preliminary Assumptions

The worker needs to look at the current research to identify the causes of this problem and its associated characteristics. Chess and Thomas (1984) view behavior disorders as a result of difficulty of fit between the capacities of the child and environmental pressures. Others argue for the biological underpinnings of ADHD (Brickman et al., 1985; Dubey, 1976; Rapport & Ferguson, 1981; Tramontana & Sherrets, 1985). In a recent study, Green (1990) noted that the style of interaction and communication in ADHD families is characterized by the following: lack of clear and consistent rules for rewards and punishment; disciplinary responses based on parental moods; attempts to resolve arguments through increased threats and counterthreats; communication characterized by intensity of physical action and sound, such as gestures and yelling instead of words and logic; compliance demanded through the use of force; and finally, disruption of the orderly flow of ideas in communication due to frequent and sudden topic changes. However, the worker should be cautious in accepting this view of ADHD as a family problem because it can reinforce feelings of guilt and inadequacy by the parents and may harm children by stressing a treatment approach that is ineffective unless balanced with other treatments (Johnson, 1988).

Selection and Collection of Information

Several instruments may be appropriate for obtaining information about children with ADHD. Tools for assessing children who show disruptive behavior include interviews with parents; reports from schools and community agencies; medical history and physical examination; neurological examination; psychological testing; allergy evaluation; laboratory studies; interviews with and observation of the child; behavior-rating scales completed by parents, teachers, and significant others in the child's life; and self-report scales (Shekim, 1986). The Connors Scales are often used for assessing hyperactivity and attention deficit disorders (Benton & Sines, 1985). The Self-Report Delinquency Scale (Elliott & Ageton, 1980), the Adolescent Antisocial Behavior Checklist (Curtiss et al., 1983), and the Parent Daily Report (Patterson, Chamberlain, & Reid, 1982) also may be useful in this case.

Analysis of Information Available

The information that the worker gathered for this case can be compared with existing research findings. Between 1960 and 1975, 2,000 articles were published regarding children with hyperactivity or minimal brain dysfunction. When the nomenclature was reviewed and ADHD became identified, 7,000 more articles were published (Weiss, 1985). However, the validity of the psychological testing used in many of these research articles is complicated by the possibility of racial and ethnic bias (Cronbach, 1975). These issues need to be considered when comparing findings from individual cases to the findings in the literature.

Development and Implementation of a Plan

Parent support groups offering child management skills could be considered for this case. In a study in one state, parents requested concrete management skills training from professionals (New Mexico Children's Services Subcommittee, 1991). Parent support groups and advocacy groups have been developed to monitor schools, boards of education, and state agencies to ensure that handicapped children receive services (Johnson, 1988). As a group, parents "can organize and exert political pressure, and they can provide parents with the often desperately needed support that comes through finding out that many have similar problems and that such problems do not always have to be defined in terms of the failure of individual parents and individual children" (Johnson, 1988, p. 354). Parents can provide support, assistance in problem solving, access to useful information, and solutions to social isolation problems (Johnson, 1988).

The effectiveness of these particular groups for parents has not been established through research, but there is extensive literature available on the use of support groups in general (Toseland & Rivas, 1984).

Evaluation of the Intervention

The support group for parents could be evaluated with parent satisfaction inventories. Existing inventories could be modified to meet the needs of this particular group (Toseland & Rivas, 1984). Group designs could be adopted using sources such as Campbell and Stanley (1963). Types of design were discussed in Chapter 7, along with their various threats to internal and external validity.

Organization System

Client: The Children's Center

Presenting problem: Need for foster parents for HIV-infected children

Referral: The Children's Center in a large urban area has had increased demand for foster care services for HIV-infected babies. Large numbers of children have been abandoned in local hospitals and the rate of HIV-infected mothers is increasing. The agency is asking a group of workers to develop strategies for foster care recruitment of these children.

Preliminary Statement of the Problem

According to statistics from the Center for Disease Control (CDC) in Atlanta, the number of children with HIV infection (AIDS) is rapidly increasing. Health officials estimate that 25% to 35% of these children will require substitute care (National Adoption Information Clearinghouse, 1989).

Statement of Preliminary Assumptions

Planning foster programs for HIV-infected babies requires an understanding of why so many of these children are in need of foster care. In New York City, 80% of the infants with AIDS are born of drug-using parents and 42% are African American and Hispanic. Many of these families live in poverty and the family systems are chaotic; support is often unavailable since other family members are not knowledgeable about AIDS (Rowe & Ryan, 1987). The mode of the disease's transmission also contributes to an increasing number of children in need of care: "Ninety percent of children with AIDS acquire the infection in the womb from infected mothers who are intravenous drug users or the sexual partners of intravenous drug users" (Child Welfare League of America, 1988, p. 1). Women who are infected with HIV have a 65% chance of giving birth to an infected baby (Center for Disease Control, 1985).

Selection and Collection of Information

A useful initial strategy in this case would be to assess the knowledge of AIDS by foster parents or potential foster parents; this would assist in the recruitment program. The Child Welfare League of America has a tool that assesses knowledge and attitudes toward HIV and AIDS (Annin, 1990). Beckler (1990) adapted this tool for use by foster parents.

Analysis of Information Available

The survey of foster and potential foster parents carried out by the agency indicated that the number of families willing to provide care for HIV-infected children was low. In addition, their knowledge of the transmission and symptoms of AIDS/HIV was limited. These data corresponded to the research findings cited earlier. The families also indicated the need for increased financial assistance for medical costs, transportation, education on hygiene and safety, respite care, and counseling for the stress resulting from caring for such children. These data also corresponded to the recommendations from the New Jersey Department of Human Services (1989).

Development and Implementation of a Plan

Model programs exist that use intensive care management for biological parents, recruitment of foster-adoptive parents, and training of foster parents (Ford & Kroll, 1990). Consulting these programs and assessing their ability to recruit and train foster parents in the care of HIV-infected babies would be a productive use of the existing research.

In addition, other model programs—such as the New Jersey Special Home Services Provider Program, which supplies financial support, intensive training, counseling, and in-home support—can give ideas for foster parent recruitment (New Jersey Department of Human Services, 1989). Finally, it has been suggested that the recruitment program should include an educational component (Anderson, 1990) in addition to attitude and skills training in caring for HIV-infected babies. This education seems particularly appropriate with the families in this community whose knowledge of AIDS/HIV is limited. Much of the information for the educational component can be drawn from existing research—for example, information on the symptoms of AIDS, such as chronic diarrhea, fatigue, and weight loss (Lockhard & Wodarski, 1989; Oleske, 1987; Rogers, 1985, 1987a, 1987b; Scott, 1987; Shannon & Animann, 1985).

Evaluation of the Intervention

Program evaluation techniques can be used to assist the effectiveness of the training and recruitment program. Measures could include knowledge and attitude inventories for the foster parents and a count of the number of HIV children actually placed.

Community System

Client: S.T.O.P., a community task force

Presenting problem: Teen suicide in community

Referral: A task force has been developed in a rural community after three suicides were committed in three months. Community leaders, school officials, and interested community members have joined together to develop a comprehensive community plan for assisting their youth.

Preliminary Statement of the Problem

An overview of the problem of teen suicide is available in the research findings. According to U.S. Vital Statistics (1978), the third leading cause of death for 15- to 24-year-olds is suicide. In an interview, Garfinkel stated that in the past 30 years the number of childhood suicides has increased by 300% and the number of suicide attempts increased by 350% to 700% (Frymier, 1988). The scope of the problem suggested by Hepworth, Farley, and Griffiths (1986) is that half a million young people attempt suicide each year, and of that number 5,000 succeed.

Statement of Preliminary Assumptions

Much research has investigated the causes of suicide and may provide useful information for this case. An interaction of factors—such as chronic adjustment problems, dislocation, and stress associated with adolescence—and a recent traumatic event seem to contribute to adolescent suicide. Alcohol is a further factor to be considered. Grueling and DeBlassie (1980) found that more than 50% of teenagers who had committed suicide had a history of moderate to severe drinking. Garfinkel (in Frymier, 1988) states that rural youth kill themselves at a higher rate than do urban youth.

Selection and Collection of Information

The community task force to prevent teen suicide would need to gather local statistics on the incidence of suicide in their community. In addition, assessment instruments for individuals, such as the Beck's Depression Inventory, can measure depression and suicidal ideas (Beck et al., 1961; Teri, 1982). The ability of this instrument to accurately measure depression must be assessed for members of diverse cultural groups. Allen-Meares (1987) notes that the items were derived from white and black psychiatric patients between the ages of 15 and 44. More research is needed with diverse cultural groups.

Analysis of Information Available

The survey of community teens indicated high rates of depression. These rates were then compared to the literature. Garfinkel stated that between 6% and 8% of junior and senior high schoolers have been severely or profoundly depressed (Frymier, 1988). The males were found to consider suicide more indirectly and were more likely to use drugs as a coping mechanism. These findings were comparable to those of Harlow, Newcomb, and Bentler (1986).

Development and Implementation of a Plan

The high rates of suicidal thinking and drug abuse indicated in the survey may lead to the community task force choosing educational strategies. One successful program educated teens to monitor their own depression and helped them to identify coping styles and mechanisms (Frymier, 1988). Peer helpers are resources that can be used in this process; 75% of teenagers who are severely depressed or suicidal turn to peers for help, compared to 18% that turn to parents and only 7% that choose to see a mental health professional (Frymier, 1988).

Evaluation of the Intervention

The reduction of teen suicide in this community can be evaluated through a number of methods, including the use of mental health statistics of children at risk for suicide, evaluating the student's level of understanding of the symptoms of stress, and parental and/or school personnel's recognition of the signs of suicide risk.

Limiting Conditions

We may find that the extent and manner in which we use research findings depends on a number of factors, many of which are beyond our control. Mullen (1988) refers to four of these limiting conditions: tradition, philosophy, technological skills, and quality of information.

Traditionally, social workers have not relied on information drawn from research, but rather from theory and experience. Incorporating research into practice still seems alien to many social workers.

Philosophically, research may seem to be dramatically opposed to the practice of social work. Research can be viewed as mechanistic and devoid of a humanitarian perspective. However, as research methods in social work become more sophisticated in their ability to tap the intricacies of human interactions, this perceived gap between social work practice and social work research will narrow.

Technological skills are another limiting condition. Many social workers simply do not understand the complexities of research methods. However, this problem will gradually lessen as graduates of social work programs are required by the Council on Social Work Education (CSWE) to have completed at least one course in social work research methods. The knowledge and skills discussed in this text provide more than enough information for the social worker to use research in practice.

The quality of information limitation refers to the social work research findings themselves. There are both problems with existing research and great gaps in the research literature. Again though, we can optimistically assume that as social workers become more knowledgeable about research through the incorporation of courses and research content in the social work curriculum, so the body of research literature will gradually expand. In the interim, research findings need to be incorporated as much as possible into practice. The limitation of poor quality research is addressed in the next section in which we discuss how to evaluate research information.

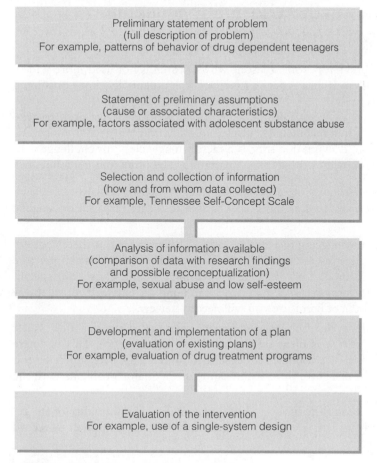

FIGURE 13.1 *Use of research findings in practice*

Evaluating Research

Although we discuss here the evaluation of research as a separate step in the research process (as with steps in the practice process), the step can merge or overlap with other research stages (particularly the evaluation of the intervention step). It is not only the findings per se that are of interest, but also the quality of the research. No research study is completely flawless. One of the researcher's responsibilities in writing up the results of the study is to include a limitations section. This can guide readers in their assessment of this particular piece of research. However, often these sections are incomplete. Being able to identify all the limitations in a research study is critical if research findings are to be used effectively in social work practice.

A number of authors have proposed frameworks for evaluating research (Arkava & Lane, 1983; Fischer, 1981; Nowak, 1981); another is presented in Figure 13.2 (on pages 292–293).

The Agency in the Use and Evaluation of Research Findings

We mentioned previously some reasons why research is not used more widely in practice (Mullen, 1988). A further factor is the potentially time-consuming nature of this activity.

However, to be responsible generalist practitioners, we need to take research seriously and this includes using and evaluating research findings. Although there is no denying that time is a factor in agencies, our challenge is to carry out research within these time constraints. The following guidelines are suggested:

1   Use computer searches as much as possible to locate research on specific topics.

2   Be specific in identifying relevant research. There is a lot out there! For example, if you are researching the second case presented in this chapter (the Kickingbird family), don't look for everything on child abuse, but specifically for physical abuse in Native-American families. This will considerably limit the amount of literature you will need to review.

3   List the findings but only those that are relevant to the practice issues. Be concise. Next, comment on the quality of the evidence. This is where you can refer to the frameworks described above. However, don't be too compulsive in their use; simply note some of the major problems with the research.

4   Keep this record of the findings, limiting conditions, and quality of the research as brief as possible. Enter the information into a computer or record it on file cards.

Ethical Issues in the Use and Evaluation of Research Findings

Although social workers can benefit from applying research findings to their practice, research cannot always provide the answers. Sometimes, the questions we are interested in have not yet been investigated, for any number of reasons. Funding may not have been available, or even if our topic has been researched, maybe this research has been constrained by a particular theoretical framework or a particular type of research method.

Due to these gaps in our knowledge, we cannot always use research. We need to acknowledge this patchiness and not delude ourselves into thinking that we can support every stage of the practice process with information derived from research. An intellectual and personal honesty is required in acknowledging where the gaps in our practice knowledge exist. This honesty also provides a means for developing a personal research agenda—program evaluation, needs assessment, evaluating our own practice, or pure research.

Human Diversity Issues in the Use and Evaluation of Research Findings

When referring to research studies to enhance our practice, we need to ensure that these studies are themselves sensitive to human diversity issues. We may be able to ascertain this when assessing the quality of the research. For example, in the research studies on physical abuse, you note that none of the samples include Hispanic families; consequently, any results from these studies would be limited in their ability to generalize to a wider population. When evaluating research studies, bear in mind the comments made in each chapter relating to human diversity issues for the steps of the research process.

Summary

Using the results of research in practice necessitates evaluating the research itself. The process of using research in practice is explored with five different client systems: individual, family, group, organization, and community. At each stage of the problem-solving process, research findings can assist in our practice. However, there are four limiting conditions that deter the use of research in practice: tradition, philosophy, technological skills, and quality of information. Several frameworks have been suggested to assist in the evaluation of research.

Agency issues include advocating the importance of using research in practice. As generalist practitioners, we are faced with the challenge of conducting research within the agency's time constraints. Ethical issues involve recognizing the gaps in our research knowledge; we cannot support every stage of the practice process with research. Human diversity issues relate to the existing research. We must be sensitive to human diversity when assessing the quality of this research.

Study/Exercise Questions

1 Select an article in a social work journal and apply the framework for the evaluation of research displayed in Figure 13.2.
2 Take a case in which you have been involved either as a volunteer or a practicum student and describe how you would use research findings at each step of the practice process.

A. Statement of the Problem
1. What is the problem under study?
2. Is the problem clearly stated and understandable?
3. Is the research question or hypothesis clearly stated?

B. Literature review
1. Does the literature review include a thorough coverage of the problem?
2. Are the findings and their sources clearly referenced?
3. Does the literature review use current references? If older references are used, are they important links to the history of the problem?

C. Variables
1. Are the dependent and independent variables clearly identified?
2. Are the dependent and independent variables defined and operationalized?

D. Sampling
1. What is the population in the study?
2. What sampling method was used?

E. Data Collection
1. Are the data collection methods clearly specified?
2. Are the data qualitative, quantitative, or both?
3. What procedures were used to ensure reliability and validity of the data?

F. Data Analysis
1. Are tables and graphs understandable?
2. Is there an orderly and clear interpretation of research findings?
3. In the case of quantitative data, were appropriate statistical tests used?
4. Are the generalizations from the findings confined to the population under study?

G. Ethical Issues
1. Are the consequences for human beings considered?
2. Was informed consent obtained from the subjects?
3. Are the subjects protected from harm?
4. Is there assurance that the data is kept confidential?
5. Who is given credit for the research?

H. Human Diversity Issues
1. Is the research question of interest or does it apply to diverse groups?
2. Is the data collection method relevant for the group(s) under study?
3. Is the sample diverse?
4. If there are comparison groups, what is their membership?
5. Is the subject involved in the research project beyond simply being a subject?
6. Does the categorization of data maintain diversity?
7. Is the research report written in an exclusive or stereotypical manner?
8. To whom were the results disseminated?

(*continued on next page*)

FIGURE 13.2 *Guidelines for evaluating journal articles*
Source: From an unpublished outline by Rose Rael

I. Limitations of the Study
   1. Are the limitations of the study clearly stated?
   2. If the limitations are not clearly stated, what limitations can you, the reader, assign to the study?

J. Conclusions and Recommendations
   1. Are the conclusions substantiated by the research findings? Are the conclusions significant and relevant to the problem and population under study?
   2. What are the recommendations for future studies? Does the study identify implications for social work?

FIGURE 13.2 *Continued*

Further Reading

Fischer, J. (1981). A framework for evaluating empirical research reports. In R. M. Grinnell, Jr. (Ed.), *Social work research and evaluation* (2nd ed.). Itasca, IL: Peacock Publishers.

This second edition of this text includes the chapter by Fischer that presents a framework for evaluation of research.

Novak, M. J. (1981). How to read research critically. *Information and Referral: The Journal of the Alliance of Information and Referral Systems, 3,* 67–79.

A useful, short article on how to evaluate research.

References

Acoca, L., & Barr, J. (1989). *Substance abuse: A training manual for working with families.* New York: Edna McConnell Clark Foundation.

Allen-Meares, P. (1987). Depression in childhood and adolescence. *Social Work, 32*(6), 512–516.

Alter, C., & Evens, W. (1990). *Evaluating your own practice: A guide to self-assessment.* New York: Springer.

American Psychiatric Association. (1987). *Diagnostic and statistical manual of mental disorders* (3rd ed.). Washington, DC: American Psychiatric Association.

Anderson, G. R. (1990). Foster parent education: Preparing for informed and compassionate caregiving. In G. R. Anderson (Ed.), *Courage to care: Responding to the crisis of children with AIDS.* Washington, DC: Child Welfare League of America.

Annin, J. B. (1990). Training for HIV infection prevention in child welfare services. In G. R. Anderson (Ed.), *Courage to care: Responding to the crisis of children with AIDS*. Washington, DC: Child Welfare League of America.

Arkava, M. I. & Lane, T. A. (1983). *Beginning social work research*. Boston: Allyn & Bacon.

Barth, R., & Berry, M. (1987). Outcome of child welfare services under permanency planning. *Social Service Review, 61,* 71–90.

Beck, A. T., et al. (1961). An inventory for measuring depression. *Archives of General Psychology, 4,* 561–571.

Beckler, P. (1990). Resources for HIV/AIDS education: Cases. In G. R. Anderson (Ed.), *Courage to care: Responding to the crisis of children with AIDS*. Washington, DC: Child Welfare League of America.

Beckman, L. J. (1978). The psycho-social characteristics of alcoholic women. *Drug Abuse and Alcoholism Review, 1*(5 & 6), 1312.

Beckman, L. J., Day, T., Bardsley, P., & Seeman, A. (1980). The personality characteristics and family background of women alcoholics. *The International Journal of the Addictions, 15*(1), 147–154.

Benton, A. L., & Sines, J. O. (1985). Psychological testing of children. In H. Kaplan & B. Sadock (Eds.), *Comprehensive textbook of psychiatry* (4th ed., pp. 1625–1634). Baltimore: Williams & Wilkins.

Bloom, M., & Fischer, J. (1982). *Evaluating practice: Guidelines for the accountable professional*. Englewood Cliffs, NJ: Prentice-Hall.

Bowman, K. M., & Jellinek, E. M. (1974). Alcohol addiction and treatment. *Journal of Studies on Alcoholism, 35*(2), 98–176.

Brickman, A. S., et al. (1985). Neuropsychological assessment of seriously delinquent adolescents. *Journal of the American Academy of Child Psychiatry, 23,* 453–457.

Campbell, D., & Stanley, J. (1963). *Experimental & quasi-experimental designs for research*. Chicago: Rand McNally.

Center for Disease Control. (1985). Recommendations for assisting in the prevention of perinatal transmission of human T-lymphotropic virus Type III lymphdenophy-associated virus and acquired immunodeficiency syndrome. *Morbidity and Mortality Weekly Report, 34,* 517–521.

Chess, S., & Thomas, A. (1984). *Origins and evolution of behavior disorders*. New York: Brunner/Mazel.

Child Welfare League of America. (1988). Report of the CWLA task force on children and HIV infection: Initial guidelines. Washington, DC: Child Welfare League of America.

Cronbach, L. J. (1975). Five decades of public controversy over mental testing. *American Psychologist, 30,* 1–14.

Curtiss, G., et al. (1983). Measuring delinquent behavior in inpatient treatment settings: Revision and validation of the adolescent antisocial behavior checklist. *Journal of the American Academy of Child Psychiatry, 22,* 459–466.

Cuskey, W., Berger, L., & Densen-Gerber, J. (1977). Issues in the treatment of female addiction: A review and critique of the literature. *Contemporary Drug Problems, 6*(3), 307–371.

Doshan, T., & Bursh, C. (1982). Women and substance abuse: Critical issues in treatment design. *Journal of Drug Education, 12*(3), 229–239.

Dubey, R. (1976). Organic factors in hyperkinesis: A cortical evaluation. *American Journal of Orthopsychiatry, 48,* 353–366.

Ellinwood, E. H., Smith, W. G., & Vaillant, G. E. (1966). Narcotic addiction in males and females: A comparison. *The International Journal of the Addictions, 1,* 33–45.

Elliott, D. S., & Ageton, S. S. (1980). Reconciling race and class differences in self-reported and official estimates of delinquency. *American Sociological Review, 45,* 95–110.

English, D. J. (1989, August). *An analysis of characteristics, problems and services for CPS cases by ethnicity.* Paper presented at the American Public Welfare Association 3rd Roundtable on Risk Assessment. San Francisco.

Fischer, J. (1981). A framework for evaluating empirical research reports. In R. M. Grinnell, Jr. (Ed.), *Social work research and evaluation* (pp. 569–589). Itasca, IL: Peacock Publishers.

Ford, M., & Kroll, J. (1990). *Challenges to child welfare: Countering the call for a return to orphanages.* St. Paul, MN: North American Council on Adoptable Children.

Fraser, M. (1990). Program outcome measures. In Y. Y. Yuan & M. Rivest (Eds.), *Preserving families: Evaluation resources for practitioners and policymakers.* Newbury Park, CA: Sage Publications.

Frymier, J. (1988). Understanding and preventing teen suicide: An interview with Barry Garfinkel, M.D. *Phi Delta Kappan, 70*(4).

Gelles, R. J. (1987). *Family violence* (2nd ed.). Newbury Park: CA: Sage Publications.

Green, R. J. (1990). Family communication and children's learning disabilities: Evidence for Cole's theory of interactivity. *Journal of Learning Disabilities, 23*(3), 146.

Grueling, J., & DeBlassie, R. R. (1980). Adolescent suicide. *Adolescence, 15,* 589–601.

Haapala, D., & Kinney, J. (1979). Homebuilders approach to the training of in-home therapists. In S. Maybanks & M. Boyce (Eds.), *Homebased services for children and families.* Springfield, IL: Charles C. Thomas.

Harlow, L. L., Newcomb, M. D., & Bentler, P. M. (1987). Depression, self-derogation, substance use, and suicide ideation: Lack of purpose in life as a mediational faction. *Journal of Clinical Psychology, 42*(1), 5–21.

Harrison, P. A., & Belille, C. A. (1987). Women in treatment: Beyond the stereotype. *Journal of Studies on Alcohol, 48*(6), 574–578.

Harrison, P. A., Hoffman, N. G., & Edwall, G. D. (1989). Differential drug use patterns among sexually abused adolescent girls in treatment for chemical dependency. *The International Journal of the Addictions, 24*(6), 499–514.

Hepworth, D. H., Farley, O. W., & Griffiths, J. K. (1986). Research capsule. *Social Research Institute Newsletter.* Salt Lake City: Graduate School of Social Work, University of Utah.

Hudson, W. (1990). *The multi-problem screening inventory.* Tempe, AZ: Walmyr Publishing.

Jellinek, E. M. (1960). *The disease concept of alcoholism.* New Brunswick, NJ: Hillhouse Press.

Johnson, H. C. (1988). Drugs, dialogue, or diet: Diagnosing and treating the hyperactive child. *Social Work Journal, 33,* 349–355.

Lockhart, L. L., & Wodarski, J. S. (1989). Facing the unknown: Children and adolescents with AIDS. *Social Work, 34*(3), 215–221.

Long, K. A. (1986). Cultural considerations in the assessment and treatment of intrafamilial abuse. *American Journal of Orthopsychiatry, 56*(1), 131–136.

Macks, J. (1988). Women and AIDS: Countertransference issues. *Social Casework, 69*(6), 340–347.

Magura, S. (1981). Are services to prevent foster care effective? *Children and Youth Services Review, 3,* 193–212.

Magura, S., & Moses, B. S. (1986). *Outcome measures for child welfare services: Theory and applications.* Washington, DC: Child Welfare League of America.

Mannes, M. (1990a). Implementing family preservation services with American Indians and Alaskan natives. In M. Mannes (Ed.), *Family preservation and Indian child welfare.* Albuquerque, NM: American Indian Law Center, Inc.

Mannes, M. (1990b). Linking family preservation and Indian child welfare: A historical perspective and the contemporary context. In M. Mannes (Ed.), *Family preservation and Indian child welfare.* Albuquerque, NM: American Indian Law Center, Inc.

Marin, B. (in press). Drug abuse treatment for Hispanics: A culturally-appropriate, community-oriented approach. In R. R. Watson (Ed.), *Prevention and treatment of drug and alcohol abuse.* Humana Press.

McLachlan, F. C., Walderman, R., Birchmore, B., & Marsden, L. (1979). Self-evaluation, role satisfaction and anxiety in the woman alcoholic. *The International Journal of the Addictions, 14*(6), 809–832.

Mullen, E. J. (1988). Constructing personal practice models. *Social Work Research and Evaluation.* Itasca, IL: Peacock Publishers.

Nakken, J. M. (1989). Issues in adolescent chemical dependency assessment. In P. B. Henry (Ed.), *Practical approaches in treating adolescent chemical dependency: A guide to clinical assessment and intervention.* New York: Haworth Press.

National Adoption Information Clearinghouse. (1989). *Adoption and foster care of children with AIDS: An analysis of existing state policies.* Washington, DC: Administration for Children, Youth, and Families. U.S. Department of Health and Human Services.

Nelson, D. E., Landsman, M. J., & Deutelbaum, W. (1990). Three models of family-centered placement prevention services. *Child Welfare, 69*(1), 3–21.

New Jersey Department of Human Services Division of Youth and Family Services. (1989). *A practice guide to caring for children with AIDS.* New Jersey: Office of Policy, Planning and Support.

New Mexico Children's Services Subcommittee. (1991). *Parents survey results.* Santa Fe: New Mexico Health and Environment Department.

Nowak, M. J. (1981). How to read research critically. *Information and Referral: The Journal of the Alliance of Information and Referral Systems, 3,* 67–79.

Oleske, J. (1987). Natural history of HIV infection II. In K. B. Silverman & A. Waddell (Eds.), *Report of the surgeon general's workshop on children with HIV infection and their families* (pp. 24–25). Washington DC: U.S. Department of Health and Human Services, Public Health Service.

Patterson, G. R., Chamberlain, P., & Reid, J. B. (1982). A comparative evaluation of a parent training program. *Behavior Therapy, 13,* 638–650.

Pattison, E. M. (1974). The rehabilitation of the chronic alcoholic. In B. Kissen & H. Begletter (Eds.), *Biology of alcoholism: Vol. III. Clinical Pathology.* New York: Plenum Press.

Rapport, J. L., & Ferguson, H. B. (1981). Biological validation of the hyperkinetic syndrome. *Developmental Medicine and Child Neurology, 23,* 667–682.

Rogers, M. F. (1985). AIDS in children: A review of the clinical epidemiologic and public health aspects. *Pediatric Infectious Disease, 4,* 230–236.

Rogers, M. F. (1987a). AIDS in children. *The New York Medical Quarterly, 21,* 68–73.

Rogers, M. F. (1987b). Transmission of human immunodeficiency virus infection in the United States. In K. B. Silverman & A. Waddell (Eds.), *Report of the surgeon general's workshop on children with HIV infection and their families* (pp. 17–19). Washington, DC: U.S. Department of Health and Human Services, Public Health Service.

Root, M. (1989). Treatment failure: The role of sexual victimization in women's addictive behavior. *American Journal of Orthopsychiatry, 59*(4), 542–549.

Rowe, M., & Ryan, C. (1987). *A public health challenge: State issues, policies and programs, Vol. I.* Intergovernmental Health Policy Project. Washington, DC: George Washington University.

Rzepnicki, T. L., Schuerman, J. R., & Littell, J. H. (1991). Issues in evaluating intensive family preservation services. In E. M. Tracy, D. A. Haapala, J. Kinney, & P. J. Pecora (Eds.), *Intensive family preservation services: An instructional sourcebook.* Cleveland: Mandel School of Applied Social Sciences, Case Western Reserve University.

Schachar, R., Rutter, M., & Smith, A. (1981). The characteristics of situationally and pervasively hyperactive children: Implications for syndrome definition. *Journal of Child Psychology and Psychiatry, 22* (14), 737–753.

Scott, G. B. (1987). Natural history of HIV infection I. In K. B. Silverman & A. Waddell (Eds.), *Report of the surgeon general's workshop on children with HIV infection and their families* (pp. 22–23). Washington, DC: U.S. Department of Health and Human Services, Public Health Service.

Shannon, K. M., & Animann, A. G. (1985). Acquired immune deficiency syndrome in childhood. *Journal of Pediatrics, 106,* 332–342.

Shapiro, S. K., & Garfinkel, B. D. (1986). The occurrence of behavior disorder in children: The interdependence of attention deficit disorder and conduct disorder. *Journal of the American Academy of Child Psychiatry, 25,* 809–819.

Shekim, W. O. (1986). Dimensional and categorical approaches to the diagnosis of attention deficit disorder in children. *Journal of the American Academy of Child Psychiatry, 25,* 653–658.

Stein, T. J., & Rzepnicki, T. E. (1983). Decision making at child welfare intake: A handlbook for practitioners. New York: Child Welfare League of America.

Tafoya, N. (1990). Home-based family therapy: A model for Native American communities. In M. Mannes (Ed.), *Family preservation and Indian child welfare.* Albuquerque, NM: American Indian Law Center, Inc.

Teri, L. (1982). The use of the Beck inventory with adolescents. *Journal of Abnormal Child Psychology, 10,* 227–284.

Toseland, R. W., & Rivas, R. F. (1984). *An introduction to group work practice.* New York: Macmillan.

Tramontana, M. G., & Sherrets, S. D. (1985). Brain impairment in child psychiatric disorders: Correspondences between neuropsychological and C.T. scan results. *Journal of the American Academy of Child Psychiatry, 24,* 590–596.

U.S. Vital Statistics, 1974 & 1975, Volume II—Mortality. (1978). Washington, DC: National Center for Health Statistics.

Weiss, G. (1985). Hyperactivity: Overview and new directions. *Psychiatric Clinics of North America, 8,* 737–753.

Wheeler, B. L., Biase, D. V., & Sullivan, A. P. (1986). Changes in self-concept during therapeutic community treatment: A comparison of male and female drug abusers. *Journal of Drug Education, 16*(2), 191–196.

Yandow, U. (1989). Alcoholism in women. *Psychiatric Annals, 19,* 243–247.

Library Resources

Compiled by Donnelyn Curtis,
Reference Librarian, New Mexico State University

Included in this appendix are listings of:

▶ Encyclopedias and dictionaries
▶ Journals
▶ Indexes and abstracts
▶ Bibliographies
▶ Government documents
▶ Statistical sources

Encyclopedias and Dictionaries

Barker, R. L. (1987). *The social work dictionary.* Silver Spring, MD: National Association of Social Workers.

This volume provides social work definitions and identifies and describes organizations, trends, philosophies, and legislation relevant to social work. It gives concise definitions of over 3,000 terms as they are used by social work practitioners and offers a chronology of important events in the history of social work and the NASW Code of Ethics.

Corsini, R. J. (Ed.). (1987). *Concise encyclopedia of psychology.* New York: Wiley.

Over 2,100 entries—about 1,500 on subjects and 650 on people. Cross-references and further reading given for many entries and includes a bibliography of approximately 2,500 references in an appendix.

Encyclopedia of social work. (18th ed., 3 vols.) (1987). Silver Spring, MD: National Association of Social Workers.

> This is the only encyclopedia devoted entirely to social work. It contains 225 articles, all with reference lists. In addition, it provides a good overview of issues and activities in social work and social welfare, serving as an excellent starting point for background information or a literature search. Also includes a separate biographical section and an index.

Evans, G., & Farberow, N. L. (1988). *The encyclopedia of suicide.* New York: Facts on File.

> Provides an overall view of suicide in its cultural contexts. Entries for terms, concepts, individuals, and organizations that have some connection with suicide. It also offers a 20-page history of suicide and appendices of statistics, associations, and sources of information, including a bibliography.

Harris, D. K. (1988). *Dictionary of gerontology.* New York: Greenwood Press.

> Contains short definitions of gerontological terminology. For each term there are references to books and articles.

International encyclopedia of the social sciences (18 vols.). (1968). New York: Macmillan and Free Press.

> Articles cover concepts, principles, theories, and methods in all the social sciences. Emphasis is on the analytical and comparative aspects of topics rather than the historical or descriptive. Arranged alphabetically, but includes a comprehensive index as well as cross-references.

Kadish, S. H. (Ed.). (1983). *Encyclopedia of crime and justice* (4 vols.). New York: Free Press.

> This contains lengthy articles exploring aspects of crime from a multidisciplinary perspective. Touches on causes and effects of crime, the social and behavioral aspects of rape and domestic violence, the relationship of alcohol to crime, and treatment of offenders. Indexed.

Maddox, G. L. et al. (Eds.). (1987). *The encyclopedia of aging.* New York: Springer.

> Brief, authoritative, signed overviews of key topics and issues in gerontology. A 128-page bibliography of publications on the subject of aging and a comprehensive index.

O'Brien, R., & Chafetz, M. (1982). *The encyclopedia of alcoholism.* New York: Facts on File.

> One of a series of Facts on File. In addition to the statistical appendix, graphs and tables are integrated into the entries.

O'Brien, R., & Cohen, S. (1984). *The encyclopedia of drug abuse.* New York: Facts on File.

Similar in scope and format to *The Encyclopedia of Suicide,* but with additional appendices for street language and slang synonyms for drugs.

Reich, W. T. (Ed.). (1978). *Encyclopedia of bioethics* (4 vols.). New York: Free Press.

A collection of articles discussing issues and concepts of medical ethics; extends medical questions to address the social impacts of biological activity, such as death and dying, abortion, aging, drug use and abuse, and mental illness. Each issue is presented in a historical and legal context, with various opinions on controversial topics. A bibliography and cross-references follow each article. Indexed.

Timms, N., & Timms, R. (1982). *Dictionary of social welfare.* London: Routledge & Kegan Paul.

This volume defines both specialized welfare terminology and interdisciplinary terms that relate to social welfare. Short entries are followed by references to related sources. The focus is British.

Selected Social Work Journals and Journals in Related Areas

Affilia
American Journal of Family Therapy
American Journal of Orthopsychiatry
American Journal of Psychology
British Journal of Social Work
Child and Youth Services
Child Development
Child Welfare
Clinical Social Work Journal
Computers in Human Services
Counseling and Values
Crime and Delinquency
Cultural Survival Quarterly
Day Care and Early Education
Death Studies
Exceptional Children
Families in Society (previously *Social Casework*)
Family Planning Perspectives
Family Process
Family Relations
Gender and Society
Gerontologist
Group and Organization Studies
Health and Social Work

Hispanic Journal of Behavioral Sciences
Human Organization
Human Services in the Rural Environment
Information and Referral
International Journal of Aging and Human Development
International Social Work
Journal of Aging and Social Policy
Journal of Applied Psychology
Journal of Applied Social Psychology
Journal of Divorce & Remarriage
Journal of Gerontological Social Work
Journal of Health and Social Policy
Journal of Homosexuality
Journal of Marriage and the Family
Journal of Multicultural Social Work
Journal of Social Policy
Journal of Social Work Education
Journal of Social Work Practice
Journal of Sociology and Social Work
Journal of Women and Aging
Marriage and Family Review

*National Women's Studies
   Association Journal* (NWSA
   Journal)
Omega: Journal of Death and Dying
   (Amityville)
Public Administration Review
Public Welfare
Research on Social Work Practice
School Social Work Journal
*Signs: Journal of Women in Culture
   and Society*
Social Forces
Social Policy
Social Problems

Social Psychology Quarterly
Social Service Review
Social Work
Social Work in Education
Social Work Research and Abstracts
Social Work with Groups
Sociology and Social Research
*Suicide and Life-Threatening
   Behavior*
Urban Affairs Quarterly
Urban Studies
Women and Criminal Justice
Youth and Society

Indexes and Abstracts

Many of these indexes and abstracts are available in computerized form (known as CD-ROM, or compact disk-read only memory).

ABI/INFORM. Ann Arbor: University Microfilms, Inc. (from 1987).

> Gives citations and abstracts for articles in business journals. Many of these articles relate to social welfare and social policy, often from a business point of view. Among the appropriate subjects for this data base would be business and the community, corporate philanthropy, and demographics.

AGRICOLA. Wellesley Hills, MA: Silver Platter Information, Inc. (from 1970).

> Primarily a source for agricultural references, AGRICOLA also indexes articles, reports, books, and government documents in the areas of home economics, nutrition, and rural sociology. For example, there are citations to articles on the prevention of teenage pregnancy, the WIC (women, infants, and children) program, and prenatal nutrition.

Child development abstracts and bibliography. Society for Research in Child Development. Chicago: University of Chicago Press. (from 1928).

> Issued three times a year with annually cumulated author and subject indexes. Contains abstracts of articles from American and international periodicals. It also contains a section of book notices.

CIJE (*current index to journals in education*). Phoenix: Oryx Press. (from 1969).

> An ERIC publication consisting of two parts: a main entry section that contains abstracts of articles in journals organized only by general category, and an index section. The subject index provides basic bibliographical information about journal articles as well as an ERIC journal number that refers to the abstract in the main entry section. An author index follows the subject index.

Cumulative index to nursing and allied health literature. Glendale, CA: Glendale Adventist Medical Center. (from 1977, vol. 22).

Indexes all major nursing periodicals published in English and selected periodicals for allied health professionals such as laboratory technology and physical therapy. This index continues the *Cumulative Index to Nursing Literature,* which ends with volume 21.

Current contents: Social and behavioral sciences. Philadelphia: Institute for Scientific Information. (from 1974).

Weekly. Reproduces the contents pages of approximately 1,300 international journals grouped within broad categories as well as articles from multiauthored books. Indexed by title keyword and author.

ERIC. Wellesley Hills, MA: Silver Platter Information, Inc. (from 1966).

This is the electronic version of the *CIJE* (*Current Index to Journals in Education*) and *RIE* (Research in Education) indexes, giving bibliographic citations and abstracts for the ERIC document collection on microfiche and for journal articles in the fields of education and other social sciences. ERIC is a good source for information about children and their welfare, especially concerning group programs, in and out of schools. There is an on-line tutorial available.

Human resources abstracts. Beverly Hills, CA: Sage Publications. (from 1956).

Quarterly. Indexes and annotates journal articles covering human, social, and personnel problems.

INFOTRAC ACADEMIC INDEX. Foster City, CA: Information Access. (from 1988).

Provides easy access to articles in periodicals of a popular nature (*Time, Newsweek,* and so on) as well as some scholarly journals such as *Child Welfare* and *Social Work.* Allows access to news stories through references to *The New York Times.*

Psychological abstracts. Lancaster, PA: American Psychological Association. (from 1927).

The abstracts volumes give bibliographical information as well as a summary of articles in psychology journals. An abstract is identified by a number that is obtained by using the subject index volume.

Public affairs information service bulletin (***PAIS***). New York: Public Affairs Information Service. (from 1915).

Semimonthly. Public policy is the emphasis of this index. Includes journal articles, books, pamphlets, and documents. Quarterly cumulations and an annual cumulation with author indexes.

Social sciences index. New York: H. W. Wilson. (from 1929).

Indexes periodicals in the fields of the social sciences. This index is very good for multidisciplinary or interdisciplinary topics. Author and subject entries are arranged in one alphabet. Book reviews are listed separately.

Social work research and abstracts. Silver Spring, MD: National Association of Social Workers. (from 1977).

> Lengthy abstracts organized in broad categories, with author and subject indexes. Each quarterly issue begins with a research section, comprised of articles and "Research Notes." There is a cumulative index at the end of the year.

Sociological abstracts. San Diego: Sociological Abstracts. (from 1952).

> A classified abstract journal covering sociology. Includes abstracts to articles, papers presented at sociological meetings, abstracts of books, book review bibliography, and document delivery information.

Women studies abstracts. Rush, NY: Rush Publishing. (from 1972).

> Quarterly. Subject index to articles from a wide range of periodicals. Includes additional listings of articles not abstracted and a listing of book reviews.

Selected Bibliographies

AIDS and ethics: A bibliography. (1990). Silver Spring, MD: National Center for Social Policy & Practice, Information Services.

Benson, H. B. (1988). *The dying child: An annotated bibliography.* New York: Greenwood Press.

DeYoung, M. (1987). *Child molestation: An annotated bibliography.* Jefferson, NC: McFarland and Co.

DeYoung, M. (1987). *Incest: An annotated bibliography.* Jefferson, NC: McFarland and Co.

Edwards, D. L. (1986). *Breaking the cycle: Assessment and treatment of child abuse and neglect.* Los Angeles: The Association for Advanced Training in the Behavioral Sciences.

Elliot, M. W. (1984). *Ethical issues in social work: An annotated bibliography.* New York: The Council on Social Work Education.

Maggiore, D. J. (1988). *Lesbianism: An annotated bibliography and guide to the literature, 1976–1986.* Metuchen, NJ: Scarecrow Press.

Malinowsky, R., & Perry, G. L. (Eds.). (1988). *AIDS information sourcebook.* Phoenix: Oryx Press.

Meling, L. R. (1987). *Adoption: An annotated guide.* New York: Garland.

Nofsinger, M. M. (1990). *Children and adjustment to divorce:* An annotated bibliography. New York: Garland.

Zollar, A. C. (1990). *Adolescent pregnancy and parenthood: An annotated guide.* New York: Garland.

Government Documents

Adolescent drug abuse: Analysis of treatment research. (1988). Washington, DC: U.S. Department of Health and Human Services, Public Health Service.

Catalog of federal domestic assistance. Washington, DC: Office of Management and Budget. (from 1971).

Annual directory of over 1,000 assistance programs administered by 52 federal agencies in the areas of child abuse, education, community planning, law enforcement, mental health, and more. The three major sections are the program descriptions, indexes to the programs, and appendices. The programs are indexed by agency, applicant, function, and subject. There is a supplemental volume that lists new programs, deletions, and changes.

Child sexual abuse victims and their treatment. (1988). Washington, DC: U.S. Justice Department, National Institute for Juvenile Justice and Delinquency Prevention.

CIS/Annual. Washington, DC: Congressional Information Service. (from 1970).

Monthly. Covers hearings, committee prints, documents, House and Senate reports, special publications, executive reports, and treaty documents. Published in two parts: an index (every third monthly index is a quarterly cumulation) and an abstract. The paperbound parts are kept in separate binders. The cumulated indexes and abstracts are also separate parts of the *CIS/Annual.* The *Index of Subjects and Names* (of those testifying in hearings) uses access numbers for reference to abstracts of committee publications in the abstract volumes. Supplementary indexes provide access to the abstracts through the title of a publication; the number of a bill, report, or document; or the name of a committee or subcommittee chair.

The homeless mentally ill: Services of the population. (1988). Washington, DC: U.S. Department of Health and Human Services, National Institutes of Mental Health.

Income of the population aged 55 or older. (1986). Washington, DC: U.S. Department of Health and Human Services, Social Security Administration.

Index to government periodicals. Chicago: Infordata International Incorporated. (from 1970).

Issued quarterly, cumulated annually. Author and subject entries for articles in periodicals published by the U.S. government. The journal abbreviation list in the front of each index volume gives the SuDoc classification number for the periodical.

The national Hispanic council on aging. (1986). Washington, DC: U.S. Department of Health and Human Services, Aging Administration.

U.S. Superintendent of Documents. Monthly catalog of United States government publications. Washington, DC: Government Printing Office. (from 1895).

> Title varies. A bibliography of publications issued by all branches of the U.S. government. The catalog consists of a text and four indexes: author, title, subject, and series/report number. Includes *Cumulative Subject Index* (1900–1971) and *Cumulative Title Index* (1789–1976).

Young unwed fathers: Research, review, policy dilemmas and options. Summary Report. (1988). Washington, DC: U.S. Department of Health and Human Services, National Institute of Mental Health.

Youth indicators 1988. Trends in the well-being of American youth. (1988). Washington, DC: U.S. Department of Education, Educational Research and Improvement Office.

Statistical Sources

American statistics index. Washington, DC: Congressional Information Service. (from 1973).

> Annual (monthly supplement). An index to all federal government publications that contain significant statistical data. Indexed by subject and name, title, agency report number, and categories (geographic, economic, standard classification systems, and so forth).

County and city data book. (1988). Washington, DC: U.S. Department of Commerce, Bureau of the Census.

> Extracts statistics from private sources and several different census series. Access is by county, Standard Metropolitan Statistical Area (SMSA), and cities with a population of over 25,000. A copy is also available in government documents.

Rosen, S. N., Fanshel, D., & Lutz, M. E. (Eds.). (1987). *Face of the nation 1987: Statistical supplement to the 18th edition of the encyclopedia of social work.* Silver Spring, MD: National Association of Social Workers.

> A digest of statistics of interest to social work students and practitioners. Most of the statistics are generated in the United States, with a few tables giving international data. Subjects quantified are the economy, employment, health, government revenues, child welfare, mental health, and so on. Government document sources are often listed and can be used as references to more detailed statistical information.

State and metropolitan area data book. (1986). Washington, DC: U.S. Department of Commerce, Bureau of the Census.

> Arranged in three parts: state, metropolitan areas arranged alphabetically, and metropolitan areas ranked by population.

U.S. Bureau of the Census. *Statistical abstract of the United States.* Washington, DC: Government Printing Office. (from 1878).

> A single volume giving quantitative summary statistics on the political, social, and economic organization of the United States. References are given for the sources of all tables. Statistics cover a period of several years, usually 15 or 20.

Computer-Related Content

B

- ▶ The use of computers in searching the literature (Chapters 2 and 13).
- ▶ Computerized measurement packages (Chapter 4).
- ▶ Computer-assisted sampling (Chapter 5).
- ▶ Analysis of qualitative data using computer software (Chapter 11).
- ▶ Analysis of quantitative data using computer software (Chapters 8, 9, and 10).
- ▶ Using computer word processing software in writing reports (Chapter 12).

Content on Human Diversity

NASW Code of Ethics and Content on Research

- ▶ The social worker engaged in research should consider carefully its possible consequences for human beings. (Chapter 4)

- ▶ The social worker engaged in research should ascertain that the consent of participants in the research is voluntary and inferred, without any implied deprivation or penalty for refusal to participate, and with due regard for participants' privacy and dignity. (Chapters 5 and 6)

- ▶ The social worker engaged in research should protect participants from unwarranted physical or mental discomfort, distress, harm, danger or deprivation. (Chapters 6 and 7)

- ▶ The social worker who engages in the evaluation of services or cases should discuss them only for professional purposes and only with persons directly and professionally concerned with them. (Chapters 4 and 12)

- ▶ Information obtained about participants in research should be treated as confidential. (Chapter 4)

- ▶ The social worker should take credit only for work actually done in connection with scholarly and research endeavors and credit contributions by others. (Chapters 2 and 12)

Other topics include:

- ▶ Applicability of question to social work (Chapter 2)
- ▶ Including relevant variables (Chapter 3)
- ▶ Maintaining integrity of the data (Chapter 8)
- ▶ Displaying results accurately (Chapter 9)
- ▶ Selection of most appropriate test (Chapter 10)
- ▶ Recognizing gaps in the research (Chapter 13)

Glossary

AB design   A single-system design in which there is a comparison between the baseline (A) and an intervention period (B).

ABAB design   A single-system design that is also known as a withdrawal or reversal design where the AB design is duplicated in order to increase the validity of the results.

ABC (successive intervention) design   A single-system design in which the baseline (A) is followed by one intervention period (B) and a second intervention period (C).

Alternate form   A method of testing an instrument's reliability where different but equivalent forms of the same test are administered to the same group of individuals, usually close in time, and then compared.

Anonymity   A condition in which the researcher cannot identify a given response with a given respondent.

Applied social work research   Research that produces practical outcomes and is directed at solving problems encountered in social work practice.

Autocorrelation   The relationship between the outcome or dependent variable scores in single-system studies.

Availability sampling   A nonprobability sampling method where available or convenient elements are included in the sample.

Bar graph   A visual means of displaying data at the nominal level of measurement.

Baseline   Repeated measurement before the introduction of the intervention that allows the comparison of target behavior rates before and after the intervention.

Baseline comparison   A strategy for comparing the equivalency between experimental and comparison groups where the comparison group is composed of cases handled prior to the introduction to the program.

Bivariate measure   A method of measuring the relationship between two variables.

Case studies   Descriptive qualitative accounts of cases.

Causal flowcharts   A visual means of representing causal connections of qualitative data.

Causality   A scientific principle that involves meeting certain conditions: first, two factors are empirically related to one another; second, the cause precedes the effect in time; and third, the relationship between the factors cannot be explained by other factors.

Celeration line   A means of predicting the dependent variable in single-system studies.

Changing criterion design   A single-system design that involves setting goals for the client that change over time.

Clinical significance (practical significance)   Significance level that is achieved when the specified goal of the intervention has been reached.

Close-ended questions   Questions that provide respondents with a fixed set of alternatives from which they choose.

Cluster sampling   A form of probability sampling that involves randomly sampling a larger unit containing the elements of interest and then sampling from these larger units the elements to be included in the final sample.

Coding   A means of organizing and collecting information so that it can be entered into a computer.

Cohort groups   A strategy for increasing the equivalency between experimental and comparison groups where the comparison group is composed of groups that move through an organization at the same time as those in the program being evaluated, but they do not receive the services of the program.

Community forum   A public meeting or series of meetings where the individuals are briefed on the issues and then asked for input; a form of purposive sampling.

Comparison groups   Subjects who receive another type of intervention or who receive no type of bona fide intervention and who have not been randomly assigned. Comparison groups can be used to increase the internal and external validity of group designs.

Confidentiality   A state in which the researcher knows the identity of the respondents and their associated responses but guarantees not to disclose this information.

Construct validity   A means of testing an instrument's validity; involves examining the extent to which an instrument measures a theoretical construct.

Contamination   The difficulty of distinguishing between the experimental and comparison groups, either due to contact between the subjects of each group or due to no clear distinction between the program experiences of the clients in each group.

Content analysis   A method of coding written communication to a systematic quantifiable form.

Content validity   A method of testing an instrument's validity that involves ensuring the content of the instrument to the concepts being measured.

Contingency table   A measure of association, also known as cross-tabulation.

Control group   Subjects who do not receive the intervention being evaluated and who have been randomly assigned.

Correlation   A measure of association used with interval or ratio level data.

Correlation coefficient   A statistic that measures the extent to which the comparisons are similar or not similar, related or not related.

Cost-benefit analysis   Program costs compared with the dollar value of the program results; a ratio of costs to benefits is computed.

Cost-effectiveness study   Program costs compared to some measure of program output; a cost per unit is calculated.

Cross-classification   A method of qualitative data analysis that creates categories by crossing one dimension or typology with another.

Cross-sectional design   A method of measuring behavior as it occurs at one point in time or over a relatively short period of time.

Cross-tabulation   A measure of association, also known as contingency tables.

Data   Information that is collected for research.

Deductive reasoning   A process of drawing conclusions from the general to the particular; opposite of the process of induction.

Dependent variable   The outcome variable that has been presumably affected by the independent variable.

Descriptive research   A process of recording and reporting phenomena as objectively as possible; not primarily concerned with causes.

Descriptive statistics   A means of summarizing the characteristics of a sample or the relationship among the variables.

Discontinuity   A difference in data levels between the baseline and intervention periods.

Discourse analysis   A way of understanding how the researcher's social context can influence how data are understood and analyzed.

Drifts   Trends that occur across the intervention and baseline periods.

Ecological fallacy   The danger of reaching conclusions in your study using a unit of analysis other than that used by the study.

Element   The item under study in the population and sample; in social work, a client system.

Emic   A system of organizing and developing categories of qualitative data that are derived from those being studied rather than constructed by the researcher.

Empiricism   Observation through the use of our senses.

Ethnography   A method of describing a culture or society.

Etic   A system of organizing and developing categories of qualitative data that are developed by the researcher rather than derived from those being studied.

Expected frequencies   Cross-tabulations that are what one might expect to observe according to probability.

Experience   A form of knowledge that includes firsthand, personal participation in events.

Experimental designs   Group research designs that randomly assign to the control group and experimental group.

Experimental group   In a program evaluation, the group that receives the intervention being evaluated.

Explanatory research   Studies directed at providing explanations of events to identify causes.

Exploratory/descriptive single-system designs   A design focusing on describing the process of an intervention more than the outcome.

Exploratory research   A form of research that generates initial insights into the nature of an issue and develops questions to be investigated by more extensive studies.

Exploratory single-system design   A design focusing on assessing the impact of an intervention on a target behavior.

External validity   The extent to which the research results are generalizable to the wider population.

Fixed format   In computer programming a format in which each code has its specific column assignment in each row of data.

Focus group   A group formed to help develop the research question.

Formative program evaluation   An examination of the planning, development, and implementation of a program.

Frame elicitation   A means of framing questions to elicit from subjects what they include in a particular topic or category.

Frequency distribution   A description of the number of times the values of a variable occur in a sample.

Generalist social work practice   A form of social work practice taught in B.S.W. programs that involves practice with different-size client systems and uses a number of different interventions and practice roles.

Generalization   The application of research findings to other situations.

Generalize   The ability to apply the findings from studying the sample to the population.

Goal attainment scales (GAS)   Scales used in single-system studies that reflect the achievement of outcomes; they both set client goals and assess whether the goals have been met.

Group design   The effect of a variable or variables on another variable or variables for a number of different client systems or elements.

History   A threat to the internal validity; those events that occur, other than the intervention, to affect the outcome.

History–treatment interaction   A threat to the external validity.

Human diversity   The whole spectrum of differences among people, including but not limited to gender, ethnicity, age, and sexual orientation.

Hypothesis   A probability statement about the relationships among certain factors.

Independent variable   The presumed causal variable in a relationship.

Inductive reasoning   The use of observation to examine the particular and then develop a generalization to explain the relationship among many of the particulars; the opposite of deduction.

Inferential statistics   A means to determine if an observed relationship is due to chance or in fact reflects a relationship among factors; allows us to generalize the findings to the wider population.

Instrumentation   A threat to internal validity; the way in which the variables are measured may change when measures are taken more than once.

Internal validity   The extent to which the changes in the dependent variable(s) are a result of the introduction of the independent variable(s) rather than other factor(s).

Interval measures   Measures that classify observations into mutually exclusive categories in an inherent order and with equal space between the categories.

Key informant   Someone in the community who is identified as an expert in the field of interest; a form of purposive sampling.

Level of measurement   The extent to which a variable can be quantified and subsequently subjected to mathematical or statistical procedures.

Likert scale   A common measurement scale consisting of a series of statements with five response alternatives.

Line graph   A graph that uses a line to connect the data points.

Literature review   A resource for consulting with the written material relevant to the research problem.

Logical analysis   In qualitative data analysis, the process of looking at the relationships between the variables and concepts.

Longitudinal design   A study that tracks behavior over a significant period of time.

Mainframe   A large nonpersonal computer usually found in an instructional setting.

Matching   A strategy for increasing the equivalency of experimental and comparison groups; certain characteristics that are thought to be important in impacting outcomes are selected and these characteristics are equally represented in each group.

Maturation   A threat to internal validity; a change that is not a result of the intervention but of the subject's becoming more mature with the passage of time.

Mean   A measure of central tendency; the result of summing all values of the observations and then dividing by the total number of observations.

Measuring instrument   The method or means by which data are collected.

Median   A measure of central tendency; a value where 50% of the cases lie above the value and 50% of the cases lie below the value.

Missing values   Incomplete data.

Mode   A measure of central tendency; the value possessed by the greatest number of observations.

Mortality   A threat to internal validity; subjects dropping out from the groups resulting in a lack of equivalency between the groups.

Multiple baseline design   A replication of the AB design by applying the same intervention to two or more target problems, to two or more clients, or in two or more settings at different points in time.

Multivariate measure   A method of measuring the relationship of two or more variables.

Needs assessment   Questions concerned with discovering the nature and extent of a particular social problem to determine the most appropriate type of response.

Negative cases   A means of validating findings from qualitative research.

Negative correlation   A relationship between two variables; as the values of one variable increase the values of the other variable decrease.

Nominal measures   Measures that clarify observations into mutually exclusive categories with no ordering to the categories.

Nonprobability sampling   The process of selecting a sample where each element in the population has an unknown chance of being included in the sample.

Normal distribution   A bell-shaped curve that is symmetrical; the mean, median, and mode are the same, and most of the scores cluster around the mean, median, and mode.

Null hypothesis   A hypothesis that there is no association between the variables.

Objectivity   A characteristic of the scientific method; the condition in which to the greatest extent possible the researcher's values and biases do not interfere with the study of the problem.

Obscure variable   A third variable that has hidden the real degree of association between the independent and dependent variables.

Observation Each case or unit of analysis included in the sample.

Observed frequencies Frequencies in a cross-tabulation derived from the sample.

Observer reliability The comparison of different administrations of the same instrument by different observers or interviewers.

One-group posttest only design A type of quasi-experimental group design.

One-group pretest/posttest design A type of quasi-experimental group design.

One-tailed hypothesis (directional hypothesis) A hypothesis that specifies not only that there is an association between variables but also predicts whether the relationship is negative or positive.

Open-ended questions Questions that do not provide respondents with responses, leaving them free to formulate their own responses.

Operationalize A means of specifying the manner by which the variable is to be measured.

Ordinal measures Measures that classify observations into mutually exclusive categories with an inherent order.

Output The final product obtained from submitting a computer program to the computer; this can be displayed on the screen or as hard copy (printout).

Overflow comparison groups A strategy for increasing the equivalency of comparison and experimental groups where the comparison groups are those who are referred to a program but who cannot be served at that time.

Participant observation An observation method involving the observer fully submerging himself or herself to become one of the observed group.

Perfect correlation A relationship between two variables where the values of each variable increase or decrease at the same rate as each other.

Pie charts A visual representation of data used to show the relative contributions of each of the values to the whole variable.

Population All possible cases that are of interest to the researcher.

Positive correlation A relationship between two variables where as the values of one variable increase the values of the other variable also increase.

Posttest-only comparison group A type of preexperimental group design.

Power The probability of correctly rejecting a null hypothesis.

Preexperimental designs (quasi-experimental designs) Designs that use comparison groups rather than control groups or no type of comparison group or control group and have limited internal and external validity.

Pretest–posttest comparison group A type of experimental group design.

Probability sampling The process of selecting a sample where each element in the population has a known chance of being included in the sample.

Problem-solving process Specific steps in generalist social work practice.

Process recording A written record of what transpired with a client system.

Program evaluations   A research question concerned with the assessment of a program's overall functioning.

Provisionality   A scientific principle involving realization that all scientific findings are tentative and that no ultimate truths can be established.

Pure social work research   Research centered on answering questions about human behavior to satisfy intellectual curiosity with little concern for the practical benefits that might result.

Purposive sampling   A nonprobability sampling method that includes purposively including in the sample elements of interest.

Qualitative methods   The nonnumerical examination of phenomena focusing on the underlying meanings and patterns of relationships.

Quantitative methods   The creation of categories of phenomena under study prior to investigation and the assignment of numbers to these categories.

Quasi-experimental designs (preexperimental designs)   Designs that use comparison groups rather than control groups or no type of comparison group or control group and have limited external validity.

Quota sampling   A nonprobability sampling method that includes a certain proportion of elements with specific characteristics in the sample.

Random assignment   The process by which every subject has an equal chance of being assigned to a control group or the experimental group.

Range   A measure of variability; the distance between the largest and the smallest value.

Rapid assessment instruments (RAI's)   A standardized series of questions or statements to connect data in single-system studies.

Rates-under-treatment   A type of secondary data that uses existing data from agencies to determine the needs of the community.

Ratio measures   Measures that classify observations into mutually exclusive categories with an inherent order and equal spacing between the categories; the ratio measure reflects the absolute magnitude of the value (and has an absolute zero point).

Reactive effect   The degree to which the presence of the researcher affects the behavior being observed.

Reactivity   The problem of the observer's behavior inhibiting or affecting the subject's behavior.

Record   A line of data.

Record length   The number of columns in each line of data.

Reductionism   The extreme limitation of the kinds and numbers of variables to be considered when explaining or accounting for broad types of behavior.

Regression   A statistical analysis that allows an estimate of how much change in the dependent variable is produced by a given change in the independent variable or variables.

Regression to the mean   A threat to external validity; the tendency of test scores to regress to the mean.

Reliability   The extent to which a measure reveals actual differences in what is being measured, rather than differences that are inherent in the measuring instrument itself.

Replicate   The repetition of a study.

Representative sample   A sample that accurately represents the distribution of relevant variables in the population.

Research log   Informal but systematic records of ideas and progress relating to a research study.

Research methods   Means of systematically organizing empirical observations.

Research proposal   A paper proposing the undertaking of a specific type of research.

Response rate   The proportion of the sample that responds to a questionnaire or interview.

Reversal design   A design that is the same as ABAB single-system design.

Rival hypothesis   A means of validating findings from qualitative research.

Sample   A group of subjects chosen from the population.

Sampling   A means of determining the subjects of the study.

Sampling error   The extent to which the values of a sample differ from those of the population.

Sampling frame   A list of all the elements in the population from which the sample is selected.

Scales   A measurement technique that combines a number of items into a composite score.

Scattergram   A means of plotting the relationships between two interval or ratio level data.

Secondary data   Existing forms of information that have been previously collected.

Selection   A threat to internal validity; the possibility that the group of people selected for one group will differ from those selected for the other group.

Selection–treatment interaction   A threat to external validity.

Self-monitoring   A process in which a client collects data on his/her own behavior.

Semistructured interview   An interviewing situation in which the interviewer is freer to pursue hunches and improvise in asking questions.

Shareware   Inexpensive software packages that can still perform most of the statistical procedures of commercial packages.

Simple random sampling   A form of probability sampling in which the population is related as a whole unit and each element has an equal chance of being included in the sample.

Single-system design/study   An evaluation of a single subject or system.

Skewed distribution   A distribution in which most of the scores are concentrated at one end of the distribution rather than in the middle.

Slopes   Trends that occur in the data within the baseline or within the intervention period.

Snowball sampling   A form of nonprobability sampling that identifies some members of the population and then has those individuals contact others in the population.

Social indicators   A form of secondary data that involves selecting demographic data from existing records to predict a community's needs.

Social work ethics   Values and ethical standards recognized by the profession of social work and codified by the National Association of Social Workers.

Solomon four-group design   A type of experimental group design.

Standard deviation   A measure of variability that averages the distance of each value from the mean.

Standardized observation   An observation technique in which behaviors are categorized prior to the observation according to their characteristics, including their frequency, duration, or magnitude. These categories can then be quantified.

Static group comparison   A type of quasi-experimental group design.

Statistical Analysis Systems (SAS)   One of the main statistical software packages used for data analysis in the social sciences.

Statistical Package for the Social Sciences (SPSS)   One of the primary statistical software packages used for data analysis in the social sciences. SPSS/PC+ is a personal computer version.

Statistically significant   A state when the null hypothesis is **rejected** and the probability of it occurring due to chance falls at or below a certain cutoff point, usually 5% or the .05 significance level.

Stratified random sampling   A form of probability sampling in which the population is divided into strata and subsamples are randomly selected from each stratum.

Structured interview   An interviewing situation in which the interviewer knows ahead of time the questions to be asked and in many cases is simply verbally administering a questionnaire.

Successive intervention design   A design that is the same as ABC single-system design.

Summative program evaluation   An assessment that determines whether goals and objectives have been met and the extent to which program efforts are generalizable to other settings and populations.

Survey research   Studies focusing on describing the characteristics of a group.

Systematic random sampling   A form of probability sampling in which every *N*th element of the sampling frame is selected for the sample.

Target problem scales   Scales used in single-system studies to track the changes in a client system's target behavior.

Testing   A threat to internal validity; the effect the testing itself may have on the subject.

Test-retest   The repeated administration of the instrument to the same set of people on separate occasions.

Theories   Scientific descriptions and/or explanations of logical relationships among phenomena.

Time series design   A type of quasi-experimental design in which a number of measurements are made both before and after the intervention.

Transcribe   The act of writing down verbatim a recording of the interview.

Treatment diffusion   The act of ensuring that there are no interferences during the course of the evaluation that may affect either the equivalence of the groups or the representativeness of the sample.

Triangulation   A means of validating findings from qualitative research.

Two-tailed hypothesis   A hypothesis that states that there is association between two or more variables, but does not predict if the association is negative or positive.

Type I error   A rejection of the null hypothesis; the conclusion that a relationship exists between the variables when no relationship in fact exists.

Type II error   A failure to reject the null hypothesis; failing to identify a relationship between variables.

Unit of analysis   The situation or person who is the object of the study.

Unstructured interviews   Interviews that are similar to conversations except that the interviewer and interviewee know that an interview is being conducted and the interviewee is privy to information of interest to the interviewer.

Unstructured observation   Observation that is used when little is known about the behaviors being observed and no categorization of the behaviors has been done before the interview.

Validity of a measuring instrument   The extent to which we are measuring what we think we are measuring.

Values   Different qualities of variables.

Variable   Characteristic of a phenomenon; something that varies and subsequently has different values.

Visual significance   A state that occurs when the visual presentation of results from a single-system study looks significant.

Withdrawal design   A design that is the same as an ABAB single-system design.

Index